JOTTINGS OF A GERIATRIC JUDGE

Russell Callander

Belvedere Publishers
Auckland

Jottings of a Geriatric Judge/ Russell Callander. -- 1st ed.
ISBN 978-0-473-51431-0

Belvedere Publishers
87A Long Drive
St. Heliers Bay
Auckland 1071
Phone: 64 9 575 0427
Mobile 64 214 70741
judex@xtra.co.nz
www.belvederepublishers.com

Cover: Copy of an original wood engraving of geriatric Lady Justice published in "Punch" Magazine, London, 28 July 1866.

Printed in Auckland, New Zealand by Benefitz DMA Ltd.

Also by the author:
Judge JR Callander, Court in the Act, the lighter side of law and order in New Zealand, Auckland, Reed Books, 1996.

Pre-publication Book Reviews

Lifer-Time Magazine: Written with conviction and highly recommended for all who enjoy real courtroom drama about human greed and stupidity. ****

The Oklahoma Daily Harbinger: A sad and comprehensive Kiwi compendium of human folly, recklessness and idiocy; instructive and revealing. *****

Journal of Gerontological Studies: Presenting clear personal symptoms of frontotemporal dementia and bad syntax, the judge has accurately chronicled significant aspects of human cognitive instability. This revealing work should be studied by all who don't yet dribble. ***

Hollywood Enquirer: Move over, Judge Judy. ***

N.Z. National Sentinel: More than the mere jottings of a geriatric judge, this record of New Zealand courtroom absurdity shows us as we are: a drunken, dishonest, disorderly and destructive society. Our politicians need to take note. ****

Australian Bar Daily: The myth of Kiwi innocence has now been exp0osed. Those sheep-loving Hobbits across the Tasman now have their own incomparable convict heritage. It makes our lot look like slow learners. He may be no eminent jurist or renowned legal scholar, but we give His Honour full marks for his humour and potpourri of courtroom anecdotes. A compulsory read for all to whom the lighter side of law appeals. ****

Newsletter of the Severe Sentencing Society:

This disturbing book exposes the wimpish inability of a long-serving judge to impose the robust punitive sanctions that we, the people, demand. We recommend this book only as positive proof that lily-livered sentencing losers like Callander are a primary source of our unacceptable crime rate, democratic decline, and societal sickness. *

Kazakhstanskaya Pravda:

жақсы жаңа зеландиялық жазу

*****

N.Z. Prison Inmates Dark-web blog:

Why did he disguise our names? It would have been our second brief flare of fame. Most of us knew the judge. Occasionally, he got it right, but mostly he was a dumb old fart who turned a blind eye to innocence. Still, a good cell read for those with time on their hands. **

Dedication:

To my wonderful wife, Suzanne, with love, and for often telling me to get on with it; reminding me that a book can't be read until it is written.

Acknowledgments:

- My parents, George and Thyra, for not adopting me out at birth, and for finally accepting I was all their fault.
- Dr Marozane Spamers LLD, M.Phil. for pointing out the incompetence of my spelling, grammar and punctuation.
- My son Richard, for finding even more incompetent spelling, grammar and punctuation, and proving that fathers can learn from sons.
- My daughter Tessa, for encouragement, advice and love.
- Chris Else, and Peter Mitchell, for expert advice on shrinking the original manuscript and warning me of inappropriate jottings about misogyny, race, gender, culture, sexual orientation, political incorrectness, controversy, and other reader human conditions that I had earlier thought made life worthwhile, thought-provoking and jot-worthy.
- My judicial superiors, inferiors, ulteriors, and peers, both geriatric and fledgling, for keeping me on the straight and narrow, and often making me grimace at my stupidity.
- The denizens of my courtrooms – staff, police, prison officers, probation officers, social workers, offenders, witnesses, and vocal members of the public gallery – without whom these jottings would not have been jotted.
- My close friends, who were astonished at the time I wasted on my computer when I could have wasted even more time with them playing golf, bowls or poker.
- My grandchildren for never seeing me as a prehistoric, antiquated, old fossil with ill-considered, unfashionable beliefs.
- The late Sir David Beattie, GCMG, GCVO, QSO, KStJ, QC, perfect role model, and for urging me to become a judge.
- The late John S. (Jack) Huyler, M.A., teacher, writer, diarist, horse whisperer and friend, at the Thacher School, Ojai, California, for recommending me to jot.
- Garrick Tremain, of the incisive wit and deft hand, for generously providing several pertinent and mischievous cartoons.
- Kevin Gordon Greer QSM, lifetime friend, for smiling and keeping me solvent.

Pre-Jot

In 1991, I aspired to be a diarist. Like most of my aspirations (and New Year resolutions) it was short lived. It only lasted for that one year before sloth, indolence and inertia won the day. Rather than writing (and thinking) an extra hour a day, it was easier to sleep in and let my thoughts recede silently into the night and fog. It is true, of course, that spending an hour a day writing a journal never killed anyone, but, as Ronald Reagan said in another context, why take the chance?

It was not just laziness, but an inability to see that keeping records of what life was like as a front-line judicial trench-dweller in rural NZ in 1991 could be of some latter-day interest, not just to the diarist but to family members and even, perhaps, to others. But diarist I really was not. Therefore, I was realistic and only kept a detailed journal for that one year. Since then I jotted down anything that struck me as of interest. Jottings are much more fun than diary entries. They give permanence to happenings and thoughts I believed to be noteworthy or curious at the time. They also avoid some characteristics of a lousy memory.

I was then aged 50 and had been on the bench for 13 years. I am now rising 80. I retired from the bench in May 2013 after 35 years.

Dramatic cases of rape, fraud or drug dealing are exceptional. Most cases are humdrum and ordinary. The District Court is the largest and busiest court in the land, the court of first instance, a sort of busy central railway station where all lawbreakers begin their journey, and where most citizens will have their only courtroom experience. Most likely that experience will be in a traffic court, appearing as a witness, or while doing jury service. These jottings reflect the day-to-day hurly burly of a people's court where conflicts are sorted, offenders are punished, and justice is administered in a common-sense and speedy way.

They also show how a judge's day is spent. Always busy. Often stressful. Sometimes distressing. But somehow always fascinating, because each day is about people – with their myriad problems, personalities and pretensions.

I believe the American journalist, satirist and critic H.L Mencken wasn't too far off the target when he wrote:

> *My own favourite object of mirth is one of the most austere and venerable figures in our society, to wit, the judge. If I frequent courtrooms little, it is only because I have a high theoretical respect for his office, and so do not want to be tempted to laugh at him. That temptation, in his presence, is almost irresistible. There he sits for hour after hour listening to brawling shysters, murkily dosing his way through obvious perjury, contemplating a room full of smelly loafers, and sadly scratching himself as he wonders what his wife is going to have for dinner, all the while longing horribly for a drink. If he is not a comic figure, then there is none in the world.*

Except for cases of notoriety or those that attracted significant public media attention, I have changed the names and identifying details of those appearing before me. Parodying the caution always opening the 1950's -70's TV police drama *Dragnet* – "Ladies and Gentlemen, only the names have been changed to protect the guilty!"

These jottings may not be the "sensational read on the train" that Oscar Wilde said of his own diary, but they may perhaps have their own particular attraction.

Courts

Judges, just like H.J. Heinz' pickles, come in 57 varieties. Some judge cats and dogs; others judge talent. My focus is on the judicial variety, those who decide cases of many different sorts. By far the most deal with offending in its diverse forms: from minor traffic breaches to murder, summary hearings and jury trials. Other judges decide civil disputes: breaches of contract or disputes between individuals, companies and public institutions, where compensation is sought for wrongdoing. Family Court judges resolve issues relating to the welfare of children, marriage, property and mental health. Specialist judges resolve issues of employment, environment, tax, land use, Maori issues, youth offending, coronial inquests, and landlord-tenant disputes.

Appellate judges correct mistakes made by these judges. They deal with troublesome legal issues, interpreting legislation, and applying precedents from earlier landmark cases. Big brain stuff. Not so much about people, but Law. Sometimes appellate judges get it wrong and the case jumps up to even bigger brained judges on higher appeal courts. If in turn, they are seen to be out of touch, politicians change the law by statute.

The largest court in Australasia is our New Zealand District Court. In 58 courthouses throughout the country, of all architectural styles and sizes, 175 judges deal with over 200,000 cases each year. It is the busiest court in the land, a sort of busy central railway station where all lawbreakers begin their journey, and where most citizens will have their only courtroom experience, as accused, witness, juror or observer.

Stupidity Aggression & Greed

These jottings highlight three universal human characteristics: stupidity, aggression and greed.

Stupidity needs no elaboration. We all do dumb things, and sometimes that leads us to break the law.

Aggression, innate and often unthinking - particularly extreme forms of violence, - puts many offenders in prison, often for a long time. Aggression manifests many forms, from bullying, sport, domestic violence, road rage, terrorism, racism, and warfare.

Greed is the common denominator of most offences. Greed, in the broad sense of the word, harvests most human failings. Most religions see it as such. Phyllis Tickle in her book Greed – the Seven Deadly Sins[1] writes:

> *But whether a religious system conflates or separates vice and sin, the truth remains that every system from Hinduism to Christianity has agreed over the centuries that of our seven demons, greed is the mistress.*

In Exodus 20:17, written about six hundred years before Christ, it was clearer for them then than it is for us. The Biblical injunction was:

> *You shall not covet your neighbour's house; you shall not covet your neighbour's wife, or male or female slaves, or ox, or donkey, or anything that belongs to your neighbour.*

Theft, in the broad sense of that word, happens because of greed – wanting more than someone is entitled to. Usually, it is wanting things that belong to others. Murder is the theft of a life; violence is the theft of the victim's personal security; rape is the theft of a person's bodily integrity. We humans seem to have an almost insatiable appetite for more – for money, status, power (political, managerial, matrimonial, or relational), sex, fame, thrills, food, mind-altering substances, or government hand-outs.

Greedy offenders – especially white collar or corporate fraudsters – are mainly motivated to steal because they have a sense of entitlement. Trusted business managers steal from employers because they believe they are underpaid and entitled to more. Trusted accountants steal because they see it is unfair that their wealthy client has so much more than them. Sales assistants steal because they feel undervalued and want a better standard of living. Factory workers thieve from the warehouse because "everyone does it". They are just like the vast number of otherwise good citizens who cheat on their tax payments or lie about their entitlement to government welfare payments.

Greed is universal. Some say greed is in our genes and that without the motivation it provides the human race would not have evolved

My Own Crime and Punishment

The Greek poet Callimachus[2] said "being a thief myself I recognized the tracks of a thief". It takes a thief to catch a thief. A similar epigram says "an old poacher makes the best gamekeeper." Perhaps my later career as lawyer and judge rested on a similar premise, and that my budding criminal propensities as a 12-year-old signposted a later modest talent in understanding the criminal mind. It takes one to judge one!

---

[1] Oxford, England, Oxford University Press, 2004

[2] writing in the second half of the 3rd century BC.

For decades Kiwis bought tickets in an Australian lottery – Tattersalls. Today we have Lotto.[1] The purpose is the same: to make a pauper a prince, or at least have a few happy minutes dreaming about it. A "Tatts" ticket was the reason, as a skinny little 12-year-fraudster and forger, I ended up caught, convicted and sentenced to custody at Gibb House, Scots College, Wellington, under the watchful military scrutiny of Colonel Keith Glasgow.

A few months earlier, I had decided two things about my parents: firstly, that they never had much joy in life, and secondly, that they never really appreciated my sense of humour. I decided to resolve both these problems with one major scam.

My parents bought Tatts tickets every week. While they were never paupers, they still fantasized about what they would do if Lady Luck smiled in their direction: replace the Vauxhall Velox with a new Vauxhall Wyvern, have a week's holiday at Raumati Beach, lay new floral Axminister in the living room, and replace the copper with an agitator washing machine.

I decided I could give them some fleeting happiness. I decided that they would win second prize in Tatts – normally about £5,000 which is just under $1,150,000 today (2019). I thought a little harmless fraud and forgery would achieve that goal.

In 1952, there were no photocopiers or computers. So, I had to resort to methods that were more primitive. My task was to fabricate a fictional letter from the NZ Manager of Tattersalls to fool my parents into thinking they had won the second prize. Some cunning preparation was required.

First, I waited until Dad got a business letter addressed to him so I could re-use the franked envelope.

Second, I went to the clipboard in the kitchen where my parents kept their old Tatts tickets for several months. I found one of the expired tickets with the sort of background colour I could match. I then removed it to my bedroom.

Thirdly, I biked up to Bennett's bookshop in Broadway and bought a few pieces of blank paper of the same light brown colour as the Tatts ticket.

Fourthly, I went to the Palmerston North Public library and borrowed a book entitled *Everyman's Guide to Form and Style for Business Correspondence.*

Fifthly, I then biked home and with my mother's nail scissors I carefully cut out the ornate scrollwork on the Tatts ticket.

Sixthly, I carefully glued the cut-out onto the blank paper so it looked like a letterhead.

Finally, I typed the letter on an old Imperial typewriter Dad had in his home office. It read:

---

[1] "Lotto" replaced "Golden Kiwi" in1987.

Tattersall's Lotteries *16 August 1953*
47 Ghuznee Street,
Wellington

Dear Sir or Madam,
Re our lottery Number 1792, drawn 18 October 1952
We record that we have received no reply to our telegram to you of 23rd ultimo wherein we advised that you were the lucky second prize-winner of the above-mentioned sweepstake in the sum of £5,000.
Please send us your ticket by registered post to the above address and we will arrange for a bank draft to be dispatched to you forthwith.
Our warmest congratulations,
Yours faithfully,
Peter G Mathias
NZ Manager

I sealed the letter in the used envelope and put it in our letter box. The Postman always arrived at our place about 4.00 p.m. I was home from school by then to watch the fun! My bedroom overlooked the driveway by the letter box. I watched my unsuspecting mother stroll down to collect the mail. She might have strolled down but she didn't stroll back. She opened my letter and she sprinted back! (I had never seen her run before!) She darted inside to the phone in the front hall. My bedroom was within earshot. She feverishly phoned my father. She told him the electrifying news. She read the letter to him, her voice choking with excitement and jubilation!

"Yes! Of course, it's true. I've just opened it. Yes. £5,000," I heard her say.

"You go to Syme & Co and buy the liquor. Yes, champagne would be marvellous. And gin. Money no object! Fine. I'll phone Fred and Ada, Cliff and Morva, Neville & Olive and the others. And start preparing food. And George, darling" – I had never heard her call him darling before – "isn't it marvellous?"

Dad came home about an hour later. He unloaded a huge amount of booze out of the Vauxhall Velox. He hugged Mum (I had never seen him do that before either). He read the letter. He obviously took it hook line and sinker. They laughed a lot (I hadn't seen them do much of that either).

At about 6.30 p.m., the family friends arrived. They gushed into the house with crocodile smiles. They hypocritically said how ecstatic they were at my parents' good luck. To celebrate, they started pouring vast quantities of gin and ginger ale down their insincere throats.

I joined the party after about an hour. One of the matrons puffed her De Reszke[1] all over me and said, "Russell, how absolutely fabulous that your parents have won Tatts!"

"Not all that fabulous", I laughed, brazenly, cockily, "they haven't read the letter properly."

An immediate and ominous silence fell on the room. Champagne glasses were frozen in mid-air. My dad retrieved the letter off the clip board. His face turned a kind of volcanic ash colour. I thought I heard him say the word "bastard."

"Fake, Fraud, Forgery."

And then the laughter. I had never seen such uncontrolled happiness. My parent's friends laughed as I had never heard before. I thought I saw my father crying but I may have been wrong.

After everyone left, we had a family meeting (I had never been to one before). It was a conversation that people now call "meaningful". The main topics meaningfully discussed were my parentage and my psychiatric condition. My father started the discussion off.

"Son", he said (I had never heard him call me that before). "Son, wipe that smirk off your face. Son, your mother and I think you are a budding criminal, and need discipline.

"Your mother and I have made a decision. We have had enough. Your unacceptable behaviour has broken the camel's back. We have decided to send you to boarding school starting in form two next year. Not only will that get you out of our hair – but it will also enable us to rent out your room![2]"

He then told me to go to my room while he wrote to the only six New Zealand boarding schools that took boarders before third form. I remember three of them were the Friends School in Wanganui, Hereworth School in Hawke's Bay, and Dilworth School in Auckland. For my angry father the religious affiliation was irrelevant. If there had been a Zoroastrian Boarding School in Eketahuna that would have done just as well. He told me I would go to the first school that replied. The following week an acceptance letter arrived from a man signing himself Col. Keith Glasgow D.S.O., E.D., M.A. He was the Headmaster of Scots College, Wellington. A vacancy existed. Like a sentenced prisoner, off I went for three years.

This admission or confession of my early life of crime highlights that we are all sinners of one sort or another. Perhaps it takes one to judge one!

---

[1] De Reszke cigarettes stopped production in the late 1950's. They were named after Jean de Reszke a Polish opera singer who and were advertised as 'the Aristocrat of Cigarettes'.

[2] This was a cruel attempt at humour. They never rented out my room. It became a sewing room for my sister.

Burglars, Thieves & Robbers

Witless Winston

Winston was an unemployed 20-year-old thug, built like a bear but with very little brain[1]. He appeared on a charge of stealing garage tools, dangerous driving causing injury, and refusing to provide a specimen of his blood. His case is typical of the aggressive bullying and irresponsibility frequently exhibited by young people.

He stopped at a service station and asked for $6.00 worth of petrol. While the attendant was attending to the petrol, Winnie went to the tyre bay and took tyre levers and a tyre hammer worth $200. The attendant protested that he was not permitted to loan tools to anyone. Winnie became nasty and accused the forecourt boy of being racist. I could see nothing at all racist in the attendant's attempt to prevent his employer's tools being stolen.

At that point, another car full of the Winnie's friends arrived in the forecourt. The attendant prudently decided to take the matter no further. Winnie then slid into the driver's seat and a mate got in the passenger's seat next to him. The car then skidded out of the service station with the stolen property. The police were phoned from the

[1] As A.A. Milne's Winnie the Pooh said. "For I am a bear of very little brain, and long words bother me."

service station. But it wasn't the police that stopped the car. It was Fate. Winnie lost control of his car at a nearby intersection. The car slewed across the road for some distance before literally flying off the road into a reserve area, hitting a Norfolk pine-tree and splitting it in two with the force of the impact.

The passenger received head injuries of a surprisingly minor nature. More surprisingly, Winnie must have someone in Hades who loves him (there would be few up here who did) because he was uninjured. He became aggressive with the ambulance officers trying to help him. He was arrested, handcuffed, and taken to the police station. He refused to breathe in the breath test bag or to provide blood. The nurse inserted the syringe into his arm but he kept backing around the room and the nurse couldn't properly obtain a sample. I remanded him for pre-sentence report and later gave him two months' imprisonment to reflect on his behaviour.

Stealing from the Magistrate

It was in 1977, the year before I started on the bench, that my later colleague Hector Gilliand, also a native of Palmerston North, suffered a scholarly misfortune. The Auckland Magistrates Court was located in a 1912 building in Kitchener Street overlooking the Domain. In the 1950's an ugly, characterless five-story building had been added to the rear of the original Edwardian Baroque construction[1]. On the top floor was a courtroom with a public toilet. In the early seventies, the toilet was converted into a Magistrates' Chamber and Hector "the Protector" (as he was nicknamed) became its occupant. I followed him as tenant. I wondered what the five plumbing nuts were – protruding obviously and equidistantly from the window wall. I was told that was where the urinals had been!

The chamber was unlucky for Hector. A well-known villain appeared one Friday morning in the main police court on the first floor. Suddenly, he jumped from the dock and made his bid for freedom. The elderly police orderlies (affectionately known as "Dad's Army") were caught off guard and the athletic young criminal had a good head start. The police rushed after him, into the foyer, and down the steps outside to Kitchener Street to raise the hue and cry[2]. But he had completely vanished.

He was a cunning devil (unfortunately no one can remember his name!). Instead of doing the normal and charging out the court door into the park, he ran up the stairs instead. He reached the fifth floor. No one was present. Hector's door was ajar. The

---

[1] The Baroque part is now the entry foyer to the 39 floor Metropolis apartment complex.

[2] "hue and cry" has mediaeval origins as a community response to crime. All able bodied citizens were legally bound to shout and yell and run after the alleged criminal in the hope of catching him and bringing him to justice.,

criminal entered, locked the door, and scaled up a wardrobe to an inspection hatch in the ceiling. There, it seems, he remained until Saturday morning.

The problem was that Hector Gilliand had spent many months writing a learned legal treatise on Domestic Proceedings. It was shortly to go to Butterworths for printing and publication. He kept the hand-written manuscript in a disused old briefcase next to his desk.

On the Monday morning, Hector was dismayed to find that his room had been entered. His chocolate cake had been eaten, his peppermints consumed. Worst of all, his briefcase was missing. It did not take long for the detectives to discover what had happened. On the Saturday morning, the wily criminal had phoned the airport booking office from the Magistrates Court giving his name as H.Y. Gilliand S.M. and requesting a ticket to Australia be charged to the Justice Department. As bona fides he gave his Visa card reference number.

The police were much too late. The criminal had long since disembarked in Sydney where, for all I know, he is still using the briefcase and basking on the Manly Beach reading up on domestic proceedings. More likely, the carefully written book manuscript ended up in a trash can at the airport.

Panty Pinchers

A professional burglar was arrested after he burgled our local lingerie shop and stole $15,000 worth of undies. He was a panty pincher on a grand scale, but in fact the man in question did not have an underwear fetish. He was just a good old-fashioned burglar who was stealing the goods for profit not for sexual arousal.

Over the years, I have dealt with several panty or pantyhose fetishists. I have only dealt with one person who had a foot fetish. He stole women's shoes from porches, open houses, gymnasiums, etc. The real excitement for him (as with Prince Charming vis-à-vis Cinderella) was to acquire high heels.

Although it can be a serious psychological problem corrected only by in-depth cognitive behavioural therapy or psychoanalysis, as with most human behaviour it is always a question of degree. Most people fantasize about something. It only becomes a problem to the rest of us – for society – if the fetish affects a person's ability to function properly or hurts someone else. Such behaviour is not considered to be a psychiatric disorder "unless it causes distress to the individual or harm to others". From a legal standpoint, the issue is not the eroticism but the theft or sometimes the offensive nature of the behaviour. The fetishist steals underwear off clotheslines or from laundromats. Some men are found with thousands of items.

Welcome to the Annexe

A young gang member spent all afternoon drinking in a local hotel. He became angry at the behaviour of his partner. He left the hotel, and took a utility vehicle from a local car yard. Unwisely, the car firm had left the keys in the ignition. Off he drove, lost control, and ended up in a paddock. He persuaded a local farmer to use his tractor to pull him back onto the road. Undaunted, he then drove to a nearby hotel where he added further liquid fuel to his already overcharged system. Off he drove again. He repeated the farm paddock excursion. This time he smashed a fence and hit a concrete water trough. That was the end of the stolen utility. It disintegrated. The car firm wanted $14,000.

He was still fuming at his partner. He stood at his neighbour's gate yelling and raving, while he cut up her underwear with a knife. When the police arrived, he was sitting in a rocking chair on the porch with a hookah pipe at his feet and enough cannabis for 30 cigarettes. The police went inside and saw a large framed painting on the wall. He was asked where it came from. He smiled the knowing smile only cannabis users can smile and proudly announced that he had painted it himself. He was, however, unable to explain how the words Welcome to the Annexe were inscribed on the frame. Enquiries rapidly revealed that the painting was stolen from the local Hospital Maternity Annexe a week earlier. He then admitted taking it off the wall while at the annexe with his pregnant partner. The sergeant put him in a cell to calm down and "cool off".

He took the sergeant literally. Two hours later police noticed the rear car park of the police station was flooded. So was the cellblock. In his anger, he had wrenched the stainless-steel sink off the wall with the obvious result.

The defendant was, and always had been, unemployed. He had no assets apart from three seriously disadvantaged children. His explanation to the police was that he was just taking the ute for a test drive. I remanded him for a reparation report – but it looked hopeless. He was also driving while disqualified and very drunk. He had previous convictions for both. I gave him six months imprisonment. He had no means to pay for the ute.

Stretched Cadillac

Many hard-working horticulturalists from the Te Puke area are wealthy from kiwifruit growing. Two couples with lots of cash, and a very new and very long and large Cadillac, stopped in Opotiki (which is not a wealthy community) to buy liquor before heading up the East Cape on holiday. They parked their shining symbol of affluence immediately outside the Masonic Hotel. The middle-aged driver went into the liquor store next to the hotel to buy the wine, whiskey and other alcoholic necessities.

The presence of the car and its affluent occupants for some disturbing psycho-social reason intensely ignited some suppressed anger and envy among a group of intoxicated unemployed men drinking in the public bar. With a roar, they ran outside and bashed and kicked the Cadillac. One youth jumped on the car bonnet and roof of the car screaming racist expletives. To save the car and themselves, the driver's wife slid over and quickly drove the car away, with nary a thought for poor hubby in the liquor store. A minute later he was out on the street with two heavy cases of wine, whiskey and other alcoholic necessities. These were mana from heaven for the thirsty, angry and envious denizens of the public bar. They pummeled hubby to the ground and relieved him of his liquor.

But thieves seldom prosper. Diagonally across Elliot Street, adjacent to the courthouse, was the police sergeant's house. The sergeant's wife, paused her ironing of several blue shirts to witness the whole saga outside the hotel. She called out to the sergeant to do his duty. He did just that. His lack of blue shirt and sturdy boots did not deflect him from his duty. He charged across the road to apprehend the drunken robbers. But they fled to all points of the compass.

He could only chase one of them, an 18-year-old youth who ran east through the historic church of St Stephen the Martyr where the unfortunate Rev. Carl Völkner had been ritually hanged and decapitated in 1865 by members of his own disgruntled congregation. The sergeant arrested the youth and he appeared before me in the Opotiki Court two months later charged with assault and theft. He defended the charges. The boy looked nothing like his ugly mug shot. He was well-dressed, tidy and intelligent. He said he had been drinking with the others and ran outside to see what the ruckus was about. He did not touch the car, assault the complainant, or steal any liquor. He had run away to avoid arrest for something he had not done. He told me he had no criminal record and the prosecutor confirmed that was true. I found him not guilty.

Stolen Guitar

I had seldom seen a jury look so bored. They had probably never seen a judge look so bored! The court attendant looked bored. The prison guards looked bored. Sandra, my associate, looked bored.

The accused was charged with four counts of theft as a servant. He had been employed by a local music store as a relieving manager during the August school holidays the previous year. He was alleged to have stolen a guitar, a guitar bag and $265 cash.

The testimony droned on all day about accounting procedures, analysis of till tapes, invoice books, receipt books, staff instruction information and so on ad infinitum.

Both prosecutor and defence counsel were very young, very earnest, very inexperienced, and very inclined to ask 14 questions when one would do. As Mr Justice Barry O'Regan used to say to such counsel: "Counsel, you have been flying round and round the airfield all afternoon. When, oh when, are you going to land?"

Or, as Joe Watts[1] would say, "Oh! For Goodness sake get to the point!"

The only thing to relieve the day's tedium was the testimony of a pleasant, bespectacled young woman who had purchased the guitar in question. She said it was her husband's birthday the following week and she decided to buy the guitar for him as a gift. He then suggested she also buy a guitar amplifier. She said that as it was their wedding anniversary two days after the birthday, she agreed to also buy him the amplifier. The accused then asked if she wanted a case for the guitar. She then smiled at the jury and said that as it was Father's Day two days after the wedding anniversary and two days after the birthday, she agreed to buy the case for her husband as well. She then added, "Expensive time of the year!"

The jury convicted the accused and I sentenced him to community service and to pay reparation.

Condominium

An elderly Londoner appeared in court charged with stealing 15 packets of contraceptives from a supermarket. They were not for his own use over the ensuing week, thank heavens. He said he used them to waterproof pot plants. Either the pot plants are very small or the London males of today are genital giants.

Dick Kearney[2] gave me a copy of an information laid in the Henderson Court on the 17th April, 1991. Believe it or not, the defendant aged 71, retired, of New Lynn, was charged as follows:

> *I, John Victor Maxwell of Henderson Constable say on oath that I have just cause to suspect and do suspect that [Name] on the 6th day of April 1991 at West Auckland did commit an offence against the Crimes Act 1961 Section 227(D) in that he did steal Trojan condoms and Holdfast glue to a total value of $17.27 the property of Woolworths Ltd New Lynn being an offence punishable summarily.*

---

[1] See p. 39.

[2] My delightful, funny and erudite colleague for many years, Richard Ronald (Dick)Kearney was appointed to the bench in 1980 and retired in 1995. He joined the Waitangi Tribunal shortly afterwards in 1996, serving on it for eight years. He died in 2005, aged 74, greatly missed by everyone.

Understandably, his name and identifying details were suppressed from publication to avoid him being idolised by the aged widows of West Auckland. With these two products in combination, and with the high libido and stickability seldom seen in septuagenarians, he deserves community commendation. A French judge would discharge him (if that is the word) and recommend him for the Croix de Bare! He pleaded not guilty and was given a firm fixture.

A Little Tipple

A 30-year-old woman was charged with receiving. She obviously likes a wee dram: she was caught with 56 bottles of whisky and 23 bottles of bourbon to a value of $2,795.00!

Money Bag

A chubby or tubby and certainly grubby 20-year-old appeared with large whanau support. His blind grandmother asked me to be merciful. He was charged with a street robbery. It was spur of the moment, but very frightening for the service station manager victim. The youth saw the manager leave the service station with a bank bag. He rushed up, shoulder-butted the manager and grabbed the bag. The manager was then pushed onto the footpath but clung like grim death to his $10,000. The youth finally ran off without the money, but was pursued by other staff from the service station. Rugby skills are not quickly forgotten: they tackled him with great skill. He had quite a few previous convictions, and one was for burglary. I pointed out that robbery was a serious crime and that the six-month jail term I was imposing was shorter than he probably deserved because I was giving credit for his guilty plea, his remorse, and the fact that he now had whanau support.

Hard Times

A married couple from Mount Maunganui had fallen on hard times, and yet their natural ebullience and positivity had enabled them to survive six children, a very recent bankruptcy for $20,000, the collapse of their coffee shop business, and a burglary of their home with all their possessions stolen. They were before me for giving their landlord's bacon slicer and refrigerator to two creditors. I gave them a suspended sentence as they had recovered both chattels and returned them to the premises. They really deserved full marks for not letting the world sink them into utter despair.

Lazy Neighbour

Neighbourliness was not one of Steve's finer attributes. Angered by his elderly widowed neighbour constantly urging him to "do some work for once in his life", he broke into her locked garage, siphoned the petrol from her car, and stole her lawnmower. There was an argument about the value of the lawnmower.

The old lady said it is only a year old and worth $690. The defendant said it was 20 years old with a rusted skirt, worth $50.

I loved the way Mr Christensen, a perceptive probation officer, put things in his pre-sentence report:

> *The victim, a neighbour, had often cast aspersions on his lack of industry, and Sam, having tired of this, decided to commit the offence.*

I gave him five months' periodic detention. He had previous convictions for dishonesty.

Imperialist Aggression

The only defended case one day took an hour and a half. It was a charge of burglary; the defendant allegedly stealing the complainants leather jacket, leather pants and motorbike boots. The prosecution witnesses all looked as though cannabis had addled their senses and as there was only one eyewitness on the issue of identification – and he was as addled as an egg – I found the evidence too dubious to convict. The defendant was a fairly tough cookie. He was apparently some sort of radical Māori as it was mentioned that he had planned to go off and fight for the honest Iraqi legions of Saddam Hussein against the white imperialist invaders. The charge did not, however, relate to stealing the leather clothing of a white imperialist aggressor but of a skinny, passive, Māori youth. We didn't get into the pros and cons of the Gulf War as it was irrelevant to the case, but I wondered whether this patently ill-educated thug (he had many convictions) realised that many of the coalition forces and supporting United Nations countries were far from being "white imperialist". Does he know what this word means? I am not sure even I do in the modern context!

Urined off

A snatch thief in Johannesburg, South Africa, must have been surprised when he examined the medical bag he snatched off a doctor's assistant in the street. All it contained was 10 bottles of urine. He was, I am sure, highly urined off! And then there were the English lorry hijackers who must have been somewhat loose-bowelled when, after considerable planning, they hijacked a huge articulated truck only to find a full load of toilet paper. Wiped the smile off their faces?

Enormous Omelette

A pleasant, chubby, middle-aged woman with a cheery smile was charged with stealing 20 dozen eggs off her employer (an egg producer). She was a first offender. She said she stole them for her own consumption. She said no one else in her whanau likes eggs. I warned her about cholesterol. Her boss had not sacked her. Her obvious zeal for the product was excellent publicity. If eggs last two weeks in the refrigerator, her daily consumption would have to be 17 a day before they started to go off! I fined her three times the retail price of the eggs.

Railway Alarm Bell

Among 80 defendants one busy court day was a young share-milker charged with stealing the flashing lights, cross arms, and alarm bell at a railway crossing. Value: $800. At first face this might seem funny but in reality, it was a very dangerous act. He might have derailed a train and killed people. I remanded him without plea and never heard what happened to his case. Did he want to decorate his living room? Or to direct his cows into the Herringbone? Or was he simply frustrated by the delay caused by the train and decided to speed things up?

The Prison Gate

Many offenders do not consider the consequences of their stupidity. It is sad that so many people fail to think sensibly about the consequences of their actions before they rush out and do some stupid criminal act that they will later very much regret. There was a disturbing case reported in the media. Some thieves stole a gate off a paddock at the Rangipo prison farm. A cow and her calf walked out onto the main highway and an unfortunate motorist was killed as he collided with them. A stupid thing to do.

Shoplifters

50 people appeared before me one day: a potpourri of cases, a ragbag of people and a hodgepodge of stories. One man stole five dozen eggs – to make a soufflé? Another stole $130 from his grandmother.

A pleasant young woman has been issued with a trespass notice after having been caught stealing dog-worming tablets from the shopping mall. Her lawyer submitted that it is illegal to ban people from a shopping centre. It was, he thought, a serious encroachment upon their civil rights. I was told it is now the practice at most shopping centres to issue trespass notices, and it seems to be eminently sensible when one remembers that multi-millions are lost each year to shoplifters.

Cattle Rustlers

I sentenced four Ruatoki men – three teenagers and an older man – on charges of shooting and barbecuing a $540 steer. Reminiscent of the Wild West! The police arrived just as the last juicy T-bone was being scoffed. I thought this was a one-off offence, but the Registrar told me that the three remaining European farmers in the area have recently lost 12 cattle between them. The beasts were all shot with .22 rifles with silencers.

Local elders had been very worried about the group who had been doing the killing. They wanted no part of it and told the Police and the farmers of their concern. They wanted the offenders brought to justice. They apparently hoped I would imprison them all as they didn't want it to be thought that all the meat eaten at tribal gatherings was stolen from the few European farmers surviving in the area.

But for shooting and stealing just one cattle beast I could not imprison them. Bearing in mind that the Criminal Justice Act says they should remain in the community unless all other options are inadequate, I could not have imprisoned them anyway. There was no proof that the four men today were those who shot the other eleven animals. Very strong suspicion, sure. But suspicion and innuendo are not enough. The law requires proper and compelling proof.

Ruatoki[1] is a place with problems. 95% unemployment! The 5% in work are a handful of schoolteachers and three council employees. The Mongrel Mob gang rules the area. The local bailiff told me that until recent Government action there were people living in shacks with rammed earth floors and even pigs dossing down with them in the room at night. Now they had new state housing of modest size and quality. The bailiff tells me the new houses were already looking terrible. Not a plant growing nearby. Not more than very essential maintenance completed. Broken windows. Holes in walls. What a sad indictment of a dysfunctional rural community.

Some blame it all on the trauma of 19th century colonisation still adversely affecting today's generations. That seems to me to be an easy distraction. Human history has always been overlaid with one group dominating another, seizing land, stealing wealth, and enslaving or killing the weak. That has been the norm, not the exception. It is not for me to attempt to explain and judge such obvious human events.

---

[1] Ruatoki is a small Maori settlement at the bottom of the Urewera Valley about 20 km south of Whakatane

Putting aside all the weighty geo-political, social or philosophical issues consequent upon poverty and lack of education, why is it that some dysfunctional individuals cannot seem to maintain a decent home environment, one that has been provided to them by the State. Damaging good housing, refusing to repair structural defects, and disfiguring housing with graffiti and filth, is hard to explain, let alone comprehend.

Rosie the Road Racer

Platinum blonde, 20-year-old Rosie was a sight to behold. Māori women like Rosie stand out on a marae. She preferred her clothes on the tight side, and she was under an observably false impression that the gold ring in her nose did something to improve her beauty. She was formidable, surly, crude, and a danger to the rest of us.

I had dealt with her in the past in the Youth Court. She had now graduated *summa cum laude* into the adult court. Never leave the keys in your car when you pop into the shop to buy your newspaper. Rosie might be watching from the shadows.

One unfortunate man did just that. Within seconds, Rosie was in and off in his Ford Laser. A little later she was spotted by the police and was pursued by a patrol car, siren on, red lights flashing. A second patrol car, similarly illuminated, joined in the chase. It pulled in front of Rosie, so she rammed the rear of the patrol car and overtook it. Soon thereafter she was checked at 120 kilometres per hour. At the next intersection, she clipped another car at the roundabout and squealed off up State Highway 2.

At times her speed reached 150 kilometres per hour. She deliberately drove on the wrong side of the road and oncoming traffic was forced to take evasive action by driving off the road to avoid her. The pursuing police became so worried at the way she was cutting corners and endangering other motorists, that they pulled back in the hope that she would then slow down. They used radio telephone to call ahead to the police at Te Puke. They should have called for an Apache helicopter with a heat-seeking missile.

Jellicoe Street is the pleasant, tree-lined main street of Te Puke. The kiwifruit growers of that pleasant town had never seen such a thing. It was like a Clint Eastwood movie. There is a grassed and treed median along the middle of the road. Rosie decided to really prove her metal by driving up the opposite side of the median for 100 metres against the traffic at 100 kilometres per hour in the 50 kmph area. How there wasn't a disaster, I could not comprehend. And then off she went towards Rotorua at 150 kmph, cutting corners, and endangering other motorists by veering across their path.

Outside Rotorua Airport, the police set up a roadblock with a box formation of police vehicles.[1] She rammed one of them. But this was not a movie. She tried to escape but was captured. The Ford Laser was extensively damaged. Two police vehicles were

[1] These days they use spikes that lacerate vehicle tyres.

damaged. A police sergeant suffered a whiplash injury. Rosie, built like a sumo wrestler, was uninjured. She was affected by alcohol but not drunk. I sentenced her, on a clutch of charges, to 15 months imprisonment.

For Heifer & Heifer

Despite a probation recommendation for a community care report, I sent one young fellow to jail for six months. He was sentenced on a theft and a burglary. The theft was of a young heifer he had shot and butchered. The burglary was of a padlocked shed in Opotiki. The defendant broke in and stole some electric appliances and petrol. Both offences took place early in the new year. This was only two weeks before the defendant had been sentenced to 3 months' periodic detention for shooting protected native wood pigeons.[1] The probation officer and counsel both urged a Community Care programme with physical fitness programmes, outdoor programmes, sport and recreation, and casual work programmes for 12 months.

But I took a dim view of his offending, especially since he had 18 previous burglary convictions at age 22, and I doubted that he had "now taken a more positive outlook" and had "reached a turning point" in his life. I was sure his sudden remorse and change of attitude had a lot to do with his keen awareness of the likelihood of being imprisoned. I decided to compromise and instead of giving him 12 months' imprisonment, I made it 6 months on condition that he be subject to a community rehabilitation programme on his release from prison. He denied ever telling the police that "Us Māori are all people of the land – beef and stuff belongs to us."

I doubted that the hard-working farmer would agree, just as I am sure his kaumatua[2] would not have agreed with him last year when he claimed he had the right to shoot protected wood pigeons.

He did not remain in custody for long! The Registrar told me he was placed in the cell exercise yard by an out of town police officer who was unaware that there was a hole in the netting on top of the high fence. Another prisoner helped him up and over, and he hasn't been seen since. Sergeant Pennefather[3] came into my chambers and told me it was all the fault of the resident sergeant (for whom he was standing in) in not having the netting fixed. He said this with a smile on his face. Kieran Hickey, the Registrar, warned me not to pick up any hitchhikers on the way to my lodgings at Ohope.

---

[1] Kererū – One of the world's biggest pigeons, endangered, and totally protected.

[2] Maori tribal elders.

[3] A curious English name originally meaning "Penny Miser" or "Penny Pincher".

Bestial Burglar

I had a young bestial burglar for sentence. I say bestial advisedly and with singular accuracy. Justice Robert Fisher[1] in the Hamilton High Court sentenced the same lad last month to 2 years probationary supervision for bestiality. He is further proof that cannabis and alcohol do not happily mix – unless, of course true happiness lies in having sex with a heifer.

The lad (17) had been smoking and drinking and on the way past the cowshed saw the heifer. The heifer had long eyelashes over her wide brown eyes and clearly appealed to the youth. He was suddenly smitten. The heifer did nothing to reject his advances, so the lad had his way with his bovine beauty. The farmer, eternally protective of his herd, happened upon the scene at the crucial moment and caught his heifer in flagrante delicto with his farmhand. Like Queen Victoria, he was not amused although the heifer did not seem to mind. I ended up feeling sorry for the lad and his family.

Is bestiality a personality disorder? Or a lack of proper sex education? Or an uncontrolled sexual promiscuity or unbridled libido? I ended up being very gentle with him on the burglary charge. I gave him four months' periodic detention. He had, after all, broken into the tent and caravan of a holidaymaker and had stolen her camera, cash and other valuables. He should really have gone to prison.

Mornin' Fred

There is an English anecdote, that resonates here. An illiterate young English farmhand was standing trial for bestiality with a heifer. The key prosecution witness was an elderly neighbouring cowherd. Early one morning, the cowherd was walking along a lane when he looked across a field and testified that he saw the accused standing on a box having sex with a heifer. He was cross-examined by defence counsel.

"You were at least 100 yards away from my client, were you not?"

"That I were," replied the cowherd.

"Then you surely could not see my client well from that distance?"

"I saw very well."

"Well why did you not cry out, or say something to the lad?"

"I did, sir"

"Well what did you say?"

"I said, 'Mornin Fred'."

---

[1] We were contemporaries at University. He excelled. He holds a Doctorate of Law, and for 15 years was a High Court Judge. He is greatly admired for his legal acumen, writing skills, and ability to cut to the quick. He is still working as a leading arbitrator.

Saddle Sore

A gritty sandblaster named Geordie was caught after two burglaries and an attempted burglary. He must have been interested in setting up a riding school because the burglaries were both of saddleries. He and a mate stole the entire contents of the Stampede Saddlery in Military Road. The lot! Saddles, bridles, halters, spurs, stirrups, boots, and other leather goods. When the distraught owner arrived, his shop consisted of four walls, a ceiling and a floor. Fortunately, the defendant, who is a known burglar, was caught with two mates later in the week at 1.45 a.m. wearing balaclavas, with a large bunch of keys and armed with screwdrivers. One was caught hiding the registration plates on their car with insulation tape. Given his extensive history of crime, I sentenced him to 15 months' imprisonment.

Car Infatuation

Cars infatuate some young men more than girls. Oscar was an intense 26-year-old with a surfeit of adipose tissue who has been enthralled by motorcars since he was 15. His passion still persists. He has 56 criminal convictions, 21 of which are for unlawfully taking motor vehicles. He also has 15 previous convictions for driving while disqualified and five for driving with excess alcohol content.

As a 15-year-old, Oscar was sent to residential periodic detention and then advanced to Borstal training at age 16. In the last ten years, he had been to prison ten times for a total of four years nine months – and all because of his obsessive inability to stop stealing cars. Nothing would stop him. He moved from Wellington to Waimana, where he was living with whanau members in the hope that he would keep out of further trouble. He impressed the probation officer that he was genuine in wanting to keep out of prison.

The day he appeared before me, he faced three more excess breath/blood alcohol charges and 1 more of driving while disqualified. A community care programme was proposed. It included counselling, treatment for his alcoholism, life planning, seeking employment and budgeting help. I decided it was pointless sending him back to prison once more and I put him on the programme for six months. If he was serious about making changes in his life, it might just work. I told him what I thought and said that if he came back again before me, I would give him a prison sentence "such as he had never had before". That could, of course, mean anything! But hopefully he put the worst interpretation on it. Some years later I checked. He had not been arrested since.

A Magnum of Chardon

A young woman was charged with stealing a magnum of Chardon[1] from a local hotel. It is hard to hide such a large bottle under a jacket, even with adequate padding (both fabric and natural). It is also difficult to conceal a large salami sausage. Reuters reported an arrested shoplifter was caught with such an item in her knickers. She said she was missing her Italian boyfriend.

The Chardon thief was quickly apprehended as she came out of the chiller room into the bottle store. The police were called. According to them, she admitted her attempt to steal the bottle and said her friend Bunny had put her up to it.

I could write a book about Bunny. I knew her well. She was thoroughly dishonest and seldom uttered a truthful word to the police or to the judge. An inveterate liar, [2] she had a long list of both convictions and children. It is not surprising because she and her siblings were dragged up by an exceptionally useless and equally dishonest and drunken father. Her many children suffered because of her abysmal motherhood and I am told most of them are by different fathers.

Putting it kindly, she lacked even a teaspoon of parenting skills and at least one of her daughters had been removed from her house by social workers. The child had been sexually abused at parties by various male relatives and other drunk revellers. So, when police said the defendant was told by Bunny to steal the bottle it didn't cause even one hair in my eyebrow to elevate. Not surprisingly, Bunny also persuaded the defendant to plead guilty.

The defendant told me a totally different story. She denied taking the bottle, denied making admissions to the police, and denied saying Bunny had put her up to it. She also sought an adjournment when the case was called at 4.30 p.m. I asked for her reason. She said her baby had been in the car all day and she wanted to get home. I promised her that the case would not take long and suggested she go out and bring the baby into the court. She did so, and when she stood up to cross-examine the bottle store attendant, she handed over the baby to Bunny, who was seated next to her acting as McKenzie friend.

A McKenzie friend is a lay person who may help a defendant in court but has no right of audience – that is, may not address the court the way legal counsel may.

Bunny took the baby, looked at me with a challenge in her eye, exposed one breast and immediately started to nurse baby. I let her go right ahead. I was well aware that I would have been labelled a prudish pakeha lacking sensitivity for both Māoridom and

---

[1] Not to be confused with *Chandon*, this is a cheap pink, bubbly wine that is priced at under $10.00 a bottle because no self-respecting wine-drinker would otherwise ever buy it. But I suppose it does make the world seem rosier – especially after a magnum.

[2] Not an "invertebrate" liar as a police report once had it.

motherhood had I suggested that a courtroom was an inappropriate place to allow baby to suckle.

I was intrigued that she was nursing her friend's baby in this way but said nothing. I found the defendant guilty of attempted theft and found, to my considerable surprise, that she was a first offender. And then I had a swipe at Bunny. I fined the defendant $75.00 and costs $65.00 and warned her that she was keeping very poor company in choosing Bunny as a friend. I told her that Bunny and some of her family have kept the local court in gainful employment for years. I said that she might be wiser to choose as a friend someone who was not a liar, a thief, and a cheat. This caused great merriment from the Māori gallery, all of whom knew Bunny and her notorious family.

Bunny gave me the evil eye but then scuttled from the court across the road to the Majestic Hotel.

Interestingly, the bailiff told me after court that the baby was Bunny's and not the defendant's. Bunny had handed the baby to her friend to use as an excuse for the adjournment. The bailiff said it was common among the female criminal element in the area to use babies as a buffer against arrest or an excuse to avoid jail.

Witnesses

Unreliable

We human beings are a strange species. We are capable of believing the most incredible, unbelievable preposterous nonsense. We have terrible memories, our perceptions are often greatly distorted, and our worldview is circumscribed by the lessons we were taught as children, whether culturally, socially, or in terms of our family's religious credo.

I have found many witnesses to be extremely unreliable. Some are outright liars. Many sincerely believe what they say is true, when, on any rational analysis of overwhelmingly credible evidence, it is obvious that they are wrong and what they have told the court is patently incorrect.

Memories can be falsely implanted. Eyewitnesses are notoriously wrong. The law requires judges these days to very carefully instruct a jury about the dangers of accepting identification evidence. DNA analysis has established that many men in the USA convicted of murder, rape and other grave crimes were not in fact guilty of those crimes. They had been misidentified by well meaning, honest, but unreliable witnesses. People will adhere to their beliefs even in the face of overwhelmingly contrary evidence. Peer pressure is a major influence. Most people will go with the flow of the commonly held beliefs of their social or religious group.

Mumble, Mutter & Murmur

Witnesses who don't open their mouths when speaking are insufferable. Whether this infirmity is caused by the desire to keep chewing gum intact in the mouth rather than have it spill out onto the floor of the witness box, or whether it is just a genetic inability to part the lips, drop the jaw, and enunciate words, I never know. But if such people inaudibly mumble, mutter and murmur I can't assess their testimony and a court hearing may run on the rocks as a result. Just like at the English maritime enquiry into a cargo ship that had run aground on a sandy East Anglia Beach. The witness mumbled, and the court reporter misheard the question and typed it up as:

"Where were you when the shit hit the fan?"

Mr Matilda

Charles Matilda was a transparent liar. I remanded him in custody for sentencing. He lied about just about everything. He was a male "Matilda".

Matilda told such dreadful Lies,
It made one Gasp and
Stretch one's Eyes;
Her Aunt, who, from her Earliest Youth,
Had kept a Strict Regard for Truth,
Attempted to Believe Matilda:
The effort very nearly killed her.[1]

Charles Matilda was travelling home to Fairfield at 12.30 am, when he drunkenly lost control of his car at an intersection of two suburban streets and straddled a crash barrier. Two neighbours heard the crash and independently rushed outdoors to the accident scene.[2] His defence was that the real driver of the car had scarpered immediately after the accident.

"Well, how come you were the only person the two neighbours saw at the scene?"
"The driver had already gone by then?"
"But the neighbours were there within a minute or so."
"Oh, he had already run off down Elliot Street."
"But the police dog found no tracks of such a person."
"The dog must have missed the scent."

A police dog handler was called to testify. Constable Hohaia told me his dog Jade followed various short tracks leading to a nearby address but nothing was found in the direction the defendant indicated. There was no scent of any person running away.

Mr Matilda testified that he had been at Fairfield with a friend drinking and watching football – a Test Match New Zealand vs Australia. Someone asked to borrow his car, but he refused. He smoked a joint. He said he would go with them. A man called "Tony" drove his car to the Dinsdale Hotel. Strangely, improbably, but rather typically, he could not remember Tony's surname. It is strange how criminals are so incompetent at

---

[1] Hilaire Belloc (Joseph Hilaire Pierre René Belloc) French-born British writer 1870–1953. *Cautionary Tales* (1907) 'Matilda'.

[2] Eye witnesses are often at the scene within minutes of the event occurring!

remembering the names of their drinking buddies and associates! On the way back to Fairfield, Tony crashed the car.

> *"What did he look like, this Tony?"*
> *"He is a dark white person."*
> *"A what?"*
> *"A dark white person." (A Māori Caucasian?)*
> *"How come you still had the car keys?'*
> *(pauses) "Tony must have given them to me before he ran off."*

Mr Matilda had an ugly criminal history. For this conviction, I sentenced him to six months imprisonment and disqualified him for 18 months. The trick with telling lies in court is that you have to do it well. You must think it through with great care so it all stacks up in a logical and sensible way. If not, deceit will be obvious to everyone, including, one hopes, the judge! Crims forget to practice. Practice makes perfect. Several practice sessions in front of critical and sober family or friends would quickly show that the lie won't work and will only make things worse.

It was Abraham Lincoln who said, "No man has a good enough memory to be a successful liar." For the most part I think that is true. But I have also been conned by witnesses with excellent memories.

Liar, Liar.

Fortunately, incorrigible liars are relatively rare. But over the years I have seen many witnesses, of both genders, lie through their chompers to escape conviction. They are probably not "inveterate" but are just "giving it a go". The rewards of a good lie make it profitable. Like President Donald Trump, true pathological liars just never stop.[1] They have an ingrained focus on deception. They will lie even when there is nothing to be gained from the lie. They lie to protect their self-image, ego or perceived status. They lie to hide their insecurity. They clothe themselves with lies to present a better appearance. There is no known treatment. I suppose long-term psychotherapy or one on one counselling might help, but I doubt it. Understandably we all can lie. Mostly white lies, and often for self-preservation.

Are judges better able to detect liars? The clear answer is "No!" What about police officers or trained investigators? Again, a negative. How about polygraph lie detectors? Similarly, they are virtually useless. Experts who have scientifically studied lie detectors say they are no better than a Ouija board at a séance! What the polygraph does is to

---

[1] *The Washington Post* has tallied all the "falsehoods" As of Oct. 9 2019, his 993rd day in office, he had made 13,435 false or misleading claims, according to the Fact Checker's database that analyses and records everything the President has said in public or on Twitter.

detect physiological responses such as heart rate, respiration and skin conductivity. These responses are often just fear responses, totally unrelated to deception. New Zealand Courts have never permitted evidence from such devices. Some USA jurisdictions did so, but no longer. The best research shows that lie detector results are wrong between 25 to 75% of the time. A nervous person telling the truth may show up as a liar. A pathological criminal liar, cool as an Arctic wind, will score on the polygraph as being as honest as your bathroom mirror.

Loathsome Spotted Reptile

Peter Cook in his deliciously demented performance as a judge in the 1979 TV movie *The Secret Policeman's Ball*[1] has the judge sum up witnesses to the jury:

> *"Ladies and gentlemen of the jury, it is now my duty to advise you on how you should vote when you retire from this court.*
> *... We have heard, for example, from Mr Bex Bissell - a man who by his own admission is a liar, a humbug, a hypocrite, a vagabond, a loathsome spotted reptile and a self-confessed chicken strangler. You may choose, if you wish, to believe the transparent tissue of odious lies which streamed on and on from his disgusting, greedy, slavering lips. That is entirely a matter for you.*
> *Then we have been forced to listen to the pitiful whining of Mr. Norman St. John Scott - a scrounger, parasite, pervert, a worm, a self-confessed player of the pink oboe; a man, or woman who by his, or her, own admission chews pillows! It would be hard to imagine, ladies and gentlemen of the jury, a more discredited and embittered man, a more unreliable witness upon whose testimony to convict a man who you may rightly think should have become Prime Minister of his country or President of the world.*
> *You may on the other hand choose to believe the evidence of Mrs. Scott - in which case I can only say that you need psychiatric help of the type provided by the excellent Dr. Gleadle.*
> *On the evidence of the so-called "hit man", Mr Olivia Newton-John, I would prefer to draw a discreet veil. He is, as we know, a man with a criminal past, but I like to think - ho, ho, ho - no criminal future. He is a piece of slimy refuse, unable to carry out the simplest murder plot without cocking it up, to the distress of many.*
> *On the other hand, you may think Mr Newton-John is one of the most intelligent, profound, sensitive and saintly personalities of our time. That is entirely a matter for you.*
> *I now turn to the evidence about the money and Mr Jack Haywire and Mr Nadir Rickshaw, neither of whom, as far as I can make out, are complete and utter crooks, though the latter is incontestably foreign and, you may well think, the very type to boil up foul-smelling biryanis at all hours of the night and keep you awake with his pagan limbo dancing. ...."*

---

[1] 1979 Amnesty International fund raiser

Put a Sock in it

Some witnesses won't listen to the question or won't shut up. Sometimes the lawyer does the same. When a witness swears to tell the whole truth, this does not mean that witnesses must tell me their entire life history. In this litigious society, court time is precious and costly, and such windbag chinwags often do irreparable harm to the case by not focusing on the real issues, rather jabbering on interminably about totally irrelevant issues. Once, at a jury trial, I had complete sympathy with a lawyer who, in exasperation, told a witness to: "Just shut up, and put a sock in it!"

The opposing lawyer objected and asked me to intervene and require an apology. I declined to do so. The witness had been raving on about nothing for twenty minutes and had not responded to my several polite requests that he be more concise and precise. He had relentlessly droned on. I remembered the American judge who in similar circumstances had directed the use of duct tape, but I simply suggested: "Perhaps two socks?" The young foreperson of the jury grinned and gave me the "thumbs up!"

Breath of Life

In 1992, I presided over the Rotorua trial of a young man who had viciously attacked another young man in a public bar in Tokoroa. The victim was struck several times with a billiard cue and fell to the floor, unconscious, and stopped breathing. The jury and I formed the clear opinion that had it not been for a young nurse who rushed to help him, the charge would have been murder, not aggravated assault. an unsophisticated timber worker was an eyewitness. he described the unprovoked, drunken assault and then went on to describe the quick actions of the young nurse.

"He looked like he was dying until she gave him artificial insemination."

Yes or No

Prosecutor: "Is it easy for you to lie in the witness box?"

Accused: "No it's not."

Which I thought was a remake of the old "Have you stopped beating your wife?"

A simple answer is seen as incriminating whichever way the answer is given:

"Yes" (I have stopped beating my wife, having done so earlier)

or

"No" (I am still beating my wife).

The way around that, or any similar question, is not to answer the question with a simple "yes" or "no", but to challenge the assumption behind the question. Although lawyers try to pretend to the contrary, a witness is not bound to just answer "yes" or "no".

A good response to the question "Have you stopped beating your wife?" would be "I have *never* beaten my wife".

"I neither did, nor do I now" is better. Sometimes lawyers say: "Just answer the question with a yes or no". But that is not a requirement in any cross-examination. Witnesses may always give a considered extended answer to any question.

Earthly Justice

Some years back a defendant witness dropped dead before me in court. He was an old alcoholic vagrant charged with stealing cash from a fellow resident in a Grafton doss-house.

He was being properly and mildly cross-examined by the prosecutor Sergeant Dennehy when, his denial still on his lips, he closed his eyes and crashed heavily onto the floor of the witness box. A doctor giving evidence in the adjacent court was rushed in to assist the sergeant, who was giving mouth-to-mouth resuscitation. Anxiously, we all looked on, hoping for his recovery. After a few minutes, the doctor looked up at me and told me that the old man had died before he hit the floor. Traumatic for all of us in the courtroom. Death is the only certain way to defeat earthly justice.

Identification

Exotica

Counsel said his client's defence was based on misidentification. He submitted that the police witness had confused the defendant with another passenger in the car. The defendant was tall, heavily and very exotically tattooed, and of very solid and unusual construction – not easily confused with his passenger who was short, not tattooed, and of slim and conventional construction! Guilty.

My Brother's Keeper

In another case the defendant said that Traffic Officer Simpson, the Katikati,[1] cop for 17 years, had got it wrong when he said he saw him driving towards him in the township in a dark white Ford Falcon. The defendant said he had been at Waihi Beach all day and had not visited Katikati that day. His wife testified to the same effect. His brother Abel threw his weight behind his sibling by saying that *he* was actually the driver observed by Officer Simpson. Unfortunately, despite the notes he said he wrote down at the time, the brother got the date wrong. It was accepted that the Ford Falcon car belonged to the defendant, but the defence was that Abel had been the only driver for the entire previous week. When questioned about the timeframe Abel told me:

"I don't know about time, man! I just let time go past!"

This cannabinoid nonchalance was replicated in the defendant, who presented as a Rastafarian with dreadlocks nearly waist long. The problem for him was that Abel looked nothing like him: he had a short Afro hairstyle and was of a much sturdier build. And to make matters worse for Rasta, Officer Simpson had known him for years as he had been born and bred in Katikati. The Officer knew of no one else in the district who looked and smoked ganja like a Jamaican Rastafarian and who drove a beat-up dark white Ford Falcon. The fact that one brother looked like Bob Marley, and the other like a young Michael Jackson, made it less likely that the officer was mistaken in his identification.

I found him guilty. He had several previous convictions for driving while disqualified. This meant that the penalty was much greater, and I advised him that he was entitled to have the case heard again before a jury.

"Whaddaya mean?"

---

[1] A pleasant town 40 km west of Tauranga, noted for its murals and horticulture.

"Well, because you have previous convictions, the penalty now jumps to five years' imprisonment. You can run the case before a jury in the hope that it will believe the traffic officer was mistaken, and that your evidence and that of your wife and brother will be believed by them."

He grinned a broad somewhat cannabinoid grin.

"Nah! Judge! Too busy for that stuff, man! I'll just flow with the tide!"

He was silly enough to repeat a little perjury: he had received a six months sentence of imprisonment the year before on a charge of attempting to defeat the course of justice. The traffic sergeant said he had tried a similar dodge by lying in court then. Slow learner? A month later I sentenced him to 18 months' imprisonment.

Identifying Chico

In 1990, a Disputes Tribunal Referee, District Court Judge, and High Court Judge all decided the fate of Chico, a sulphur-crested cockatoo. The main issue became one of identification: was the bird really Chico or an imposter?

It all started when "Mrs. West" first met Chico, thought to be male, in a pet shop in Greerton, Tauranga. She immediately saw him as a potential partner for her own sulphur-crested cockatoo, thought to be female. Mrs. West admired his handsome looks, arrogant stance, loud voice, and affable personality. She spoke to Chico's owner, "Mrs. East" and a deal was struck. Chico would accompany Mrs. West to her home in "the Gorge" and spend the next year "mating" with Mrs. West's own "female". There was always a question mark as to the gender of the two birds.

Judge David Bracken Wilson[1], in the District Court, heard expert testimony from a veterinary surgeon who said it is very difficult to tell the gender of cockatoos. It requires examination of the bird's "vent", a daunting and dangerous task, because cockatoos have beaks like bolt cutters and, quite understandably, do not relish their vents being examined by homo sapiens. Both owners were, however, intuitively satisfied that the birds were male and female and hopefully would produce chicks that would add considerably to their respective bank balances.

Mrs. East kept telephoning Mrs. West to see whether "love was in the air" and for 12 months received glowing reports. Sadly, the reports might have been glowing, but the birds were not. Not an egg was laid. Mrs. East finally asked for Chico's return, but here the contract ran into difficulties. Mrs. West refused to give Chico back. She said that the deal was for a permanent life in "the Gorge" and that it would be emotionally harmful for Chico to return to urban life.

[1] For many years, David was the sole judge in the Bay of Plenty. Greatly respected by his peers, the legal profession & the public, he died in 2015 aged 83. I spoke at his funeral. He was a judge for 27 years.

A complaint of theft was laid with the police, but the wily old police sergeant could smell trouble a mile off. He pointed out that the matter was one of contract, and suggested that Mrs. East would be much wiser to forgo a police complaint and sue in the civil court for Chico's return.

After a difficult and heated hearing, the Dispute's Referee ordered Mrs. West to return Chico "forthwith". Mrs. West refused, and the bailiff was sent in. The bailiff arrived at the Gorge unannounced. He was met by a startled Mrs. West, who asked him to wait at the door. The bailiff later observed her to be crawling through the undergrowth towards the aviary. A little later the bailiff was handed a cockatoo wrapped in a towel. He took the bird back to Greerton and handed it to Mrs. East.

Things went from bad to awful. Mrs. East took one look at the bird and cried "foul!" Several other people who knew Chico also cried "foul." "This feathered fake", they all cried, "is not Chico. It is a much inferior imposter, a fraud, a phoney!"

Questions of identification have always been of grave concern to the law and a source of serious consequences when mistakes are made.

Judge Wilson, who heard the prosecution for theft, and Justice Noel Anderson[1] who heard the appeal, were aware that all questions of identity require a special need for caution before convicting in reliance upon the correctness of the identification, especially when the subject is a sulphur-crested cockatoo.

As we say to juries about human identification, the reason for this is that it is quite possible for an honest witness to make a mistaken identification and notorious miscarriages of justice have occurred as a result. A mistaken witness can be a convincing one and even several apparently convincing witnesses can all be mistaken. It is to be remembered that sometimes people make mistakes in the recognition of others, even of relatives or close friends, so an even higher standard may well be expected when identifying a combination of feathers, claws, pedal warts, beaks and vents.

The judge must carefully examine the circumstances in which each witness made the identification. Only then should the court be satisfied that identity has been proved beyond reasonable doubt.

Judge Wilson, sensing the enormity of his task, and the inevitability of an appeal, gave the most careful attention to the identification evidence. He decided the bird returned by the bailiff was not Chico. Justice Anderson summed up Judge Wilson's findings at the appeal:

> *"This parrot did not impress the people who had known it. The Chico of their memory was not apparent to them as they observed the bird that had been delivered. No longer did the bird strut with handsome arrogance about its cage. The pedal wart which had previously*

---

[1] See p 53.

distinguished it had disappeared. Its vocabulary had become limited in range and the assertiveness of its speech was less than might be desired. Whereas Chico had displayed a marked antipathy to the wife of a former owner, this bird showed something almost in the nature of affection. Plainly, if this bird were Chico, the exigencies of matrimony had both reduced it in stature and cowed its temperament. But it was so unlike Chico that none who previously knew Chico could accept that the bird before them was the bird they had known."

Judge Wilson had convicted Mrs. West of theft. On appeal, Justice Anderson agreed that she had "deliberately and fraudulently detained" Chico "in a manner amounting to fraudulent conversion and ultimately theft".

Tequila

Some years after our local "Chico" litigation, there was a similar dispute in Florida. In 1996, a woman bought an African Grey parrot she named 'Tequila'. Ten years[1] later Tequila flew away. Another woman found the parrot, adopted him, and named him 'Lucky'. Three years later, quite by chance, the two women met up at a Dunkin' Donuts coffee house, and their fondness for parrots was discussed. Remarkably, they discovered they were talking about the same parrot. It seems they had a detailed conversation about "feathers, claws, pedal warts, beaks and vents" and discovered it was the same bird. What had begun in a friendly way, ended in most unfriendly litigation with Tequila's owner suing to recover "her parrot".

Tequila/Lucky was produced in court as evidence, but identification was not an issue. Ownership was. The judge ordered the bird be returned to the original 'owner 'as it was 'lost property' just like any other chattel. The second 'owner' sought several years compensation for the cost of caring for Tequila/Lucky, but failed. It is unclear what Tequila said about the whole saga.

---

[1] In human care African Grey Parrots can live up to 60 years

Judges

Swearing In

These days, when new judges are sworn in and take the oath of office, there is a special court hearing to welcome them. Other judges and members of the law society are present. The judge invites members of his family and friends. A senior judge, usually the chief judge, makes a welcoming speech and gives a brief résumé of the new judge's background and alleged attributes. The judge is then sworn in, and gives a speech in reply. The President of the local Law Society also makes a speech extolling the virtues of the new appointee. It is all quite formal and grand.

When I took the judicial oath, and was appointed to the magistracy on Saturday 10th December 1977, no such niceties happened. My swearing-in ceremony was so casual that, for some time, I was quite disheartened by how it all went. On that Saturday morning, I was mowing my lawns, which is what men did in Palmerston North on Saturday mornings. My wife called me in to answer the telephone. It was the local magistrate Joseph Walter Poultney Watts, S.M.[1] I was surprised by his phone call. He

---

[1] In 1968 he was appointed to the bench at Nelson as a magistrate. He became our local magistrate in 1975. He retired in 1982, and died in 1986, aged 71.

asked what I was doing. I told him. He said he had received some papers from Wellington to swear me in as a magistrate. I was delighted to hear they had arrived. I thought he was going to schedule a time for my swearing-in ceremony later in the week. I asked what day would suit. He guffawed.

"We don't go to any fuss. We don't have a ceremony. What are you doing now?"

I reiterated that I was mowing my lawns.

He said, "Forget that, hop in the car and come up to the court and I'll swear you in right away." I was astonished. "But I'm not dressed for the occasion."

"Never mind", he retorted "Neither am I. I'm just about to take my rubbish to the garbage tip."

"Can I bring my family?"

"Goodness me, no," he replied. "That's not what we do. We haven't got time for that. Come up now."

I quickly changed out of my grubby gardening clothes, washed the grass stains off my hands, splashed on some cologne and drove the short distance to the courthouse. Mr. Watts met me at the court door. He was wearing stained trousers and a very tired old tartan shirt. He took me to his chambers. He swore me in, using the ancient words of the judicial oath and oath of allegiance to the Queen.

> *"I swear that I will well and truly serve Her Majesty Queen Elizabeth the Second, her heirs and successors, according to law, in the office of Stipendiary Magistrate; and I will do right to all manner of people after the laws and usages of New Zealand without fear or favour, affection or ill will."*

With that, he shook my hand with considered disinterest. He thought that at age 36[1] I was much too young to be joining the august ranks of the judiciary. He excused himself to drive his rubbish trailer to the dump. He said that I could go back and finish my lawns. I did just that. No tea and sausage rolls. No back-slapping by friends and family. No reporter from the Manawatu Evening Standard. No photographs. Not even a fly-past of jets from Ohakea air base!

---

[1] My formal warrant of appointment was signed by the Governor-General Sir Keith Holyoake on 12 December 1977. I turned 37 the following day.

Curriculum Vitae

Before my appointment, I was asked to provide a resume of my education and career. I have now lost it. But I know it was brief and accurate.[1] Unlike this one I presented years later in a failed application for judicial advancement!

> *"Born Palmerston North, Black Friday, December 1940. Bad luck for all concerned.*
> *Education: not much.*
> *Scots College, Wellington: Robbie Burns junior prize for bawdy poetry, 1954. Expelled 1954.*
> *Victoria University of Wellington, BA 1962 in psychology: Bedlam scholar. LLB 1963, unexpectedly.*
> *1963: the NZ Liquor Industry Due Diligence Award.*
> *First employment, 1958: lifeguard in car wash.*
> *Second employment, 1959: loafer, bread bakery."*

Sir David Beattie

Sir David Beattie[2] was instrumental in me going on the bench. He was a good friend of my senior partner Graham Crossley. Whenever he presided in Palmerston North, he visited the Crossley home and enjoyed the generous hospitality always provided by Graham and his wonderful wife, Ruth. Sometimes I was invited to act as bar steward and sober driver!

In 1977-78 he chaired the Royal Commission on the Courts, which made widespread and positive changes to the court structure in New Zealand. In early 1977, during a lull in my bar steward duties, he told me that the Commission was to recommend to the Government the creation of a District Court the judges of which would have jurisdiction over all family disputes, summary criminal cases, most criminal jury trials, youth offending and lower-end civil disputes.

He gave me a wink and a nod. He recommended that I go on the Magistrate's Bench as soon as possible as all magistrates would become District Court judges if Parliament adopted his Commission's recommendations.

I was a bit young – at 36 – but I took his advice and let it be known that I was interested in going on the bench.

---

[1] Many people lie on c.v's. A recent British Higher Education Degree Datacheck survey found 33% of graduates or job applicants make false claims in their c.v. 40% of graduates exaggerated their academic qualifications, while 11% claimed a degree they had never earned.

[2] Sir David, gentleman, sportsman, and special human being, served as a Supreme Court judge from 1969 until he was appointed Governor-General in 1980. He was articulate, personable, charitable and a very capable lawyer nd judge He retired in 1985, and died in 2001, age 76.

Not long after his appointment as Governor, our judges' common room in Auckland invited him to a cocktail party in his honour. There were about fifty judges and retired judges present – from all over the upper North Island. We were astonished that he went around the room, shook hands with everyone, knew every name, and made a personal comment to each individual. The only other person I have known with this wonderful ability to remember people and names, is Sir Anand Satyanand, Governor-General from 2006 to 2011.

District Judge to Governor-General

Two of my close colleagues on the District Court rose to great heights. Both became Governor-General of New Zealand.

Dame Silvia Cartwright[1] joined me on the District Court in 1981.She was a Family Court Judge. She became well known in 1987 when she very competently chaired *the Commission of Inquiry into the Treatment of Cervical Cancer at National Women's Hospital* (the Cartwright Inquiry). She became my boss in 1989 when she became the first female Chief District Court Judge. In 1993, she was elevated to the High Court as the first female High Court Judge. Silvia became our 18th Governor-General in 2001. Thereafter she was appointed a United Nations trial judge in Cambodia to investigate the war crimes committed there during the Khmer Rouge regime in the late 1970s. She is sensible, intelligent and caring.

Sir Anand Satyanand[2] came to our bench in 1982 and initially presided in my home town of Palmerston North where he was greatly admired for his many skills both legal and personal. In 1995, he became Ombudsman for 10 years. He then followed Dame Silvia as Governor-General until his term expired in August 2011. Truly a man for all seasons.

Qualities of Judges

What qualities are expected of judges? In listing these attributes, it made me reflect on my many inadequacies. But for the perfect judge the qualities are:[3]

> *Sound knowledge of the law and experience of its application.*
> *Requisite applied experience and/or application of legal knowledge in other branches of legal practice.*
> *Capacity to discern general principles of law and in doing so to weigh competing policies and values.*

---

1 Dame Silvia Rose Cartwright, PCNZM, DBE, QSO, DStJ

2 Sir Anand Satyanand, GNZM, QSO, KStJ

3 http://www.justice.govt.nz/publications/global-publications/j/judicial-appointment-processes/judicial-appointments-office-of-district-court-judge.

Overall excellence demonstrated in a relevant legal occupation.
Personal honesty and integrity.
Open-mindedness and impartiality.
Courtesy, patience and social sensitivity.
Good judgement and common sense.
Ability to work hard, to listen and concentrate.
Collegiality, breadth of vision, independence, and acceptance of public scrutiny
Effective oral and written communication.
Ability to absorb and analyse and explain in a concise and lucid manner complex and competing factual and legal material.
Mental agility, administrative and organisational skills.
Capacity to be forceful when necessary and to maintain charge and control of a court.
Ability to inspire respect and confidence.
Impartiality and collegiality.

Or to use a shorter version discussed at a conference by my friend and Chief Judge Sir David Carruthers[1]

> *"Be kind. Be patient. Be dignified. Don't take yourself too seriously. Use commonsense. And remember that all cases are important."*

Sir David personifies all these qualities. As Hamlet said of Yorick:
"…a fellow of infinite jest, of most excellent fancy"
He was a leader whose wit, character, intellect, people skills, and gifted communication talent, commanded our genuine respect.

My Other Chiefs

Sir David was an admirable Chief Judge. During my career, I had the good fortune to have other Chiefs with similar skills, each unique and exceptional.

The first was Sir Desmond Sullivan, the foundational Chief District Court Judge. Des had been in law practice in Palmerston North. He supported my appointment to the magistracy in 1978. He was greatly respected, industrious and caring. He was a Magistrate from 1966 to 1981, and Chief District Court Judge from then until he retired in 1985 with a knighthood. He died in 1996, aged 76.

Sir Desmond was succeeded by Sir Peter Trapski, who had been Principal Family Court Judge. He retired in 1989. An amiable man who disliked conflict, he had practiced law in Tauranga until he became a Magistrate in 1972. He received a Papal Knighthood in 1995.

---

[1] A schoolmate of mine at Scots College, Sir David twice became my boss: as Chief Judge 2001-2005, and as Chair of the Parole Board until 2012.

Dame Silvia Cartwright, with her many skills, became my boss in 1989 until she was elevated to become the first woman High Court judge in 1993.

That year, Sir Ronald Young became Chief until 2001 when he was also appointed to the High Court. He retired in 2015, but, bored in retirement, is currently Chair of the Parole Board. He was an efficient organiser, hard-working and sensible.

After Sir David Carruthers left office in 2005 he was succeeded by my colleague Russell Johnson who tragically died of cancer in 2011. Russell was a supportive and friendly leader, greatly missed. He was not just a leader on land but on the sea. He was a Commander in the Royal New Zealand Naval Volunteer Reserve until 1992.

Judge Jan Doogue succeeded him in 2011 and presided over my retirement function on 3 May 2013. Compassionate, talented and an excellent administrator she is well respected by us all.

Lousy Bastard

Gerry Monaghan was a Wellington magistrate around the time the indomitable Ben Scully[1] was about to retire from the bench. Scully was the senior "beak" who was noted for expressly adding an extra pound (before 1964) or dollar to his fines for every minute after five which lawyers took to make pleas in mitigation. Whether this is apocryphal or not, I don't know, but the story has been around so long there might be some substance to it. Despite being a fairly tough nut, he also had much humanity and a wealth of worldly wisdom. But he scared young (and not so young) lawyers half to death when he stormed into court each day and impatiently savaged anyone who transgressed. Gerry said a disgruntled prisoner once called Ben a "lousy bastard". Ben instantly responded:

"Better to be called one, than to be one!"

He was a magistrate in Wellington from 1949 to 1976 when he went to Samoa as Chief Justice for 2 years. The Samoans greatly admired him.

Far from being a 'lousy bastard', he was regarded as a sensible, capable and kindly judge. In Samoa, I inherited the pineapple patch he had grown in the grounds of the residence I occupied. As with him, the pineapples were few and far between. Midnight raids by Samoan children saw to that.

A Teenage Perspective

Occasionally, I spoke to senior high school students about law, order, and justice. At the end of my talk I would invite questions. The most common was: "How much do judges get paid?" followed by: "How soon can I be a judge?" Punishing the wicked,

---

[1] Michael Bernard Scully S.M., died in 1985 aged 79.

while being reasonably well paid for so doing, seems to hold a particular appeal for teenagers!

Eminently Forgettable

Some judges are very ambitious. While some have an understanding of Latin (which was once a compulsory subject for law students), they tend to forget the maxim *Sic transit gloria mundi*, which literally translates to "Thus passes the glory of the world" or figuratively "worldly fame does not last". As my friend, John Cadenhead[1], often said of retired judges: "We are yesterday's men."

Most people want to forget the name of the judge. Ask a University history class to name three former Chief Justices, or even the names of three current judges, and you will invariably draw a blank. We are eminently forgettable. But not so His Honour Judge Allan Lawson, my one-time colleague on the Auckland District Court. In 1993, a photo appeared in a newspaper showing Sam Hunt, a renowned New Zealand poet. He was sitting outside his boat shed home. A large and handsome Muscovy duck stood nearby. The duck's name: "Judge Lawson." Named, said Sam, after the judge who disqualified him for six months on a drink/drive charge. Every time the duck quacks, or does certain other things, it reminds the poet of his day in court.

English Judges

Henry Cecil in his book, *The English Judge*[2], mentions the English High Court judge who, at the end of last century, was found in a brothel. "But," said Judge Leon (Henry Cecil), "at least he had the grace or forethought to be found dead."

On a different tack, Henry Cecil's book is worth a read, as it humanises the judiciary and explains to the layman many of the myths of the bench. He starts the book with the observation of a mischievous schoolboy who wrote in answer to the question 'What is your image of the English Judge?'

> *The English judge is usually short and fat or tall and thin and he is generally sarcastic and always wears National health glasses or a monocle. He is generally biased towards youngsters and lenient towards young women showing plenty of leg. The judges are always old and carry pictures of Judge Jeffreys round in their pockets, so that they can do a spot of hero worship during the recess.*

---

[1] John was my colleague from 1985 until he retired in 2004. He qualified PhD, the first sitting judge to do so. He was a wise, sensible and helpful judge, highly regarded by us all. He died in 2017 while on holiday in Hawaii.

[2] London, Stevens & Sons Ltd, 1972

I wonder what a Kiwi sixth former would say of us? At least the English schoolboy had not heard of the demand by Wat Tyler, leader of the Peasants' Revolt in 1381, that "old Justices should be hung".

It is interesting to note that the infamous "hanging judge", Jeffreys, was not "old" in our sense of the word. He was appointed Chief Justice in 1683 at the age of 35. By 1688, he was Lord Chancellor. With the abdication of James II in that year, Jeffreys went into hiding, was captured in a tavern by a former dissatisfied customer, and was imprisoned in the Tower of London where this "ruffian in ermine" died (not of a sharp blade, but of kidney disease) the following year at age 40.

Pale and Pained

Sir John Mortimer[1] describes another English Judge in *Rumpole a la Carte:*[2]

> *He is a pale, long faced, unsmiling fellow who probably lives on a diet of organic bran and carrot juice. He heard Ballard open the proceedings against La Maison with a pained expression, and looked at me over his half-glasses as though I were a saucepan that hadn't been washed up properly.*

Make it Snappy!

Some judges, while wise in their law and learning, are poor communicators. Some mumble, drone on incessantly, and completely lose contact with jurors, witnesses, lawyers and the public. My friend Judge Ron Gilbert[3] sagely advised me against talking too long to a jury. "Talk for more than 20 minutes and half the jurors will be cross-eyed with boredom," he said. As a barrister in Dunedin he was renowned for his remarkable success before juries. He said juries tuned out after 20 minutes, and for a lawyer to bore a jury with long examinations or addresses, was counter-productive. Lawyers should not waste words with excessive questioning or long speeches to the jury.

Judge John Cadenhead worked with him as a junior barrister in several trials. John said he tallied the number of questions Ron asked witnesses in cross-examination during two manslaughter trials that ran consecutively.

---

[1] Sir John Clifford Mortimer CBE QC FRSL. I had a fascinating chat with this intriguing man at a New Zealand Law Conference in Christchurch. My favourite quote from him is: *I refuse to spend my life worrying about what I eat or drink. There is no pleasure worth forgoing just for an extra three years in the geriatric ward.* Despite considerable over-consumption of both, he survived to age 85, in 2009.

[2] London, Blackstone Publishing, 1990.

[3] Ronald James Gilbert, sensible and wise, died in 2010 aged 84.

"They totalled 37 questions. He addressed each jury for about seven minutes and obtained verdicts of not guilty in each case."

A summing up should be brief, orderly and clear. Young jurors, raised in the digital age, want a straightforward and brisk summary of the evidence, and a clear description of the law, preferably in written form. Yet I have known some judges to take many hours, or even a day, to instruct a jury. Such a situation seems to have prompted a juror listening to a summing up by Lord Russell of Killowen[1] to call out "make it snappy, old cock!" The judge's reaction, according to an observer[2] "evoked a tornado of wrath which would have flattened a forest."

The Two Generals

After World War II, two former Major-Generals became judicial officers on the NZ Bench. One became a magistrate, the other the Chief Justice. Before the war both were successful lawyers.

The Chief Justice was Sir Harold Barrowclough,[3] who commanded the 2nd NZ Division in the Pacific. The returned veterans much preferred to appear before Mr L.M. Inglis.[4] From 1945 to 1950, he had served as president of a military government court in the British zone of occupied Germany, presiding over criminal cases brought by Germans involving the Allied occupying powers, and cases dealing with Allied nationals. He was later appointed Chief Judge of the Allied Control Commission's Supreme Court, with the nominal military rank of Major General, and was the highest civilian judicial officer in the British-occupied zone of Germany.

His wartime nickname, "Whisky Bill", indicates the admiration of his soldiers for certain undoubted tastes he then and later exhibited. He was the local Magistrate in Palmerston North next-door to us in Victoria Avenue.

Pat Cunneen, retired Courts Manager for the Northern Region, knew Mr Inglis well, and considered him the best judicial officer at any level, he observed or assisted over the 43 years he worked in the Courts.

While he was the "Beak" in Palmerston North, he heard a case against one of his "old soldiers", a former infantry sergeant, who had consented to him hearing the case (he only presided in such cases if the soldier agreed). The police claimed the defendant had drunkenly punched another man outside a dance hall. He vigorously denied the charge.

---

[1] Both his father and grandfather were also Law Lords, the grandfather Chief Justice of England.

[2] Hon. George William Lyttelton, who taught at Eton School for his entire career.

[3] Major General Sir Harold Eric Barrowclough KCMG, CB, DSO & Bar, MC, ED, PC died 1972. He attended my own secondary school Palmerston North Boys' High School.

[4] Major General Lindsay Merritt Inglis, CB, CBE, DSO & Bar, MC, ED, died 1986.

After hearing the witnesses, the "Brigadier" was about to give his decision. It looked grim for the defendant. The defendant then tied a large white handkerchief to the end of his umbrella and hoisted it towards the roof of the courtroom.

"Whisky Bill" smiled when he saw the flag, entered a guilty plea, and confirmed in his decision that the defendant had only surrendered when faced with overwhelming odds. He fined the defendant a sum commensurate with his crime, adjourned the court, and asked to see his former sergeant in his chambers. A clerk then heard him say, "I knew you were guilty the moment I saw it was you! Come into my chambers and have a whisky!"

Finicky

The accounts of Justice Alec Haslam's[1] eccentricity became legend. Once, while he was sitting in Napier, he spoke at breakfast to Trevor de Cleene[2] who, as counsel in the trial, was staying at the same hotel. The judge had learned that Trevor was staying in the room next to him. He apologized to Trevor and hoped he had not kept Trevor awake at night. Trevor replied that he had heard nothing and was untroubled. The judge was relieved at that. He said that he slept poorly and tended to indulge in nocturnal furniture re-arrangement!

Ken Seebeck, the capable and tenacious Registrar of the Palmerston North courts while I was in practice there, told how on more than one occasion he had to get telephone technicians to re-wire the telephone in the Supreme Court judge's chambers because Sir Alec, for unknown reasons, had ripped it out of the wall.

Sir Alec admitted my friend Michael Behrens to the bar.[3] Later that same week, Mike and I went to lunch during the adjournment. As we were returning to the court, I noticed Justice Haslam walking towards us on the footpath. Out of court, without his wig, he looked very different. He was a handsome man, with a full head of hair. I acknowledged the judge by wishing him "Good afternoon, Sir." Mike and I then walked on back to the court.

That afternoon, Michael was singled out by the judge who berated him for not acknowledging him in the street. It was, he said, a grave discourtesy to one of Her Majesty's judges to not recognise and acknowledge him. Michael apologised and said that he had not recognised the judge out of court. The judge remonstrated that it was

---

[1] Died in 1997, aged 93; was a judge of the Supreme Court from 1957 - 1976. A Rhodes Scholar to Oxford University in 1927, he gained a DPhil.

[2] See p 261

[3] Michael was a very capable and wise lawyer and judge. For some years, disenchanted with legal life, he abandoned legal practice to work as a journalist in Palmerston North. Later he returned to practice, was appointed Queens Counsel, and became a District Court Judge in 2004. In 2002, he was lead counsel in the controversial Mark Lundy murder trial.

the duty of all barristers to recognise the visiting Supreme Court justice. Michael apologised, but was very distressed by the whole reprimand. The rest of us were aghast at the insensitivity, self-important and obsessional reaction of the judge.

Seen on TV

Sir Richard Wild[1], Chief Justice, was the eminent son of the foundational headmaster of Feilding Agricultural High School. Sir Richard had lived in Feilding as a youth and attended the school. In 1966, the law practitioners of Feilding decided to hold a small cocktail party honouring his appointment as Chief Justice. The occasion was held at the local Gentlemen's Club. I attended. Most of the lawyers had their spouses with them. The Chief Justice spoke to one of the wives, an attractive, naive young thing who obviously did not share her husband's knowledge of matters legal or judicial. The conversation between the judge and the lawyer's wife went something like this:

Lawyer's wife: "I recognise you from television, but I can't think where."

Chief Justice: "Oh! That may well be so."

Lawyer's wife: (staring hard): "I've seen you more than once."

Chief Justice: "Yes."

Lawyer's wife: "You're from Wellington, aren't you?"

Chief Justice: "True!"

Lawyer's wife (A few minutes later, her face lighting up with sudden, but mistaken, insight): "I've got it!" (touching his arm) "You're the presenter of 'The Inventors!' (a then current TV Show portraying innovative New Zealand inventions).

Fortunately, her husband, a delightful conveyancer, never aspired to courtroom advocacy or judicial office!

Impatience

An issue of *Capital Letter* (Vol 14 No 18),[2] included a note of the case of the Impatient Judge. I have complete sympathy for whoever that may have been. Justice

---

[1] Sir Herbert Richard Churton Wild GBE KCMG QC, was appointed chief justice in January 1966. He died in May 1978, aged 65. Four months earlier he sent me a fulsome note congratulating me on my appointment as a magistrate. I did not know then that he was only days from retiring after diagnosis of an inoperable brain tumour. He was noted for his incisive and logical mind, administrative skills, and dedication to hard work.

[2] The Capital Letter: A weekly review of administration, legislation and law published by NZ Financial Press, edited by Ms Penny Pepperell.

Noel Anderson[1] declined to grant an appeal based on the fact that the judge had grown so irritated by the direction of the cross-examination that he or she said:

> *"I am now losing my patience in this matter and will adjourn.*

Justice Anderson commented that it

> *"...is inevitable in the course of judicial experience that one's patience is less durable on occasion than generally."*

and that the judge had been prudent in retiring.

Judicial Giants: Lords Denning & Cooke

Two celebrated and influential judges, one English and the other a New Zealander, stood head and shoulders above their contemporaries. Both became peers. The English judge by convention and seniority, the New Zealand judge by stint of judicial gigantism. The two men were not only oceans apart in geography, but also in their style, personality and performance.

Lord Denning[2], a judge in Britain for 38 years became an almost household name, renowned for his colourful use of simple English. As law students and young lawyers, we were all delighted with his simple, colourful, and clear judgments. He often side-stepped the strict legal precedents to decide a case on broad-based principles of fairness and justice.

The opening paragraph of one his judgments in *Lloyds Bank v. Bundy* [1973] 3 All ER 757 is a good illustration:

> *"Broadchalke is one of the most pleasing villages in England. Old Herbert Bundy, the defendant, was a farmer there. His home was at Yew Tree Farm. It went back for 300 years. His family had been there for generations. It was his only asset. But he did a very foolish thing. He mortgaged it to the bank."*

On Lord Denning's death at age 100 former UK Prime Minister Tony Blair wrote:

> *"He was always the soul of courtesy, helping out young barristers or someone with a hopeless case and for some time I was both...His judgments were a model of lucidity. He was prepared to use the law for its true purpose in the interests of fairness and justice. He had a tremendous feel for ordinary people."*

---

[1] A courteous and competent High Court judge based in Hamilton. A first-rate jurist, he went on to greater things. He was elevated to the Court of Appeal in 2001 (where he later became President) and to the Supreme Court in 2006.

[2] Alfred Thompson "Tom" Denning, Baron Denning, OM, PC, DL (23 January 1899 – 5 March 1999)

He was the last British judge appointed for life. Perhaps unwisely he chose to continue on the bench too long. He retired at 83 having written a controversial book *What Next in the Law?*[1] that disclosed racist views and caused a public outcry.

> *"The underlying assumption is that all citizens are sufficiently qualified to serve on a jury, I do not agree. The English are no longer a homogeneous race. They are white and black, coloured and brown. They no longer share the same standards of conduct. Some of them come from countries where bribery and graft are accepted as an integral part of life and where stealing is a virtue so long as you are not found out... They will never accept the word of a policeman against one of their own."*

Elsewhere he wrote how donning his black cap to pass a death sentence had never troubled him.

Robin Brunskill Cooke[2] was our only judge to become a Law Lord. He had legal and judicial DNA. His grandfather was the Crown Solicitor in my home town of Palmerston North. His father Justice Phillip Cooke K.C., M.C. was a much-admired Supreme Court judge. The DNA continues with the 2018 appointment of Lord Cooke's son Francis as a High Court judge.

As lawyers and young judges, we were in awe of his monumental intellect. He was undoubtedly our greatest jurist. He shaped our own New Zealand perspective of the law, rather than slavishly following British precedents that were sometimes inappropriate in our unique South Pacific environment. He was realistic, sensible and perceptive.

Contrasting Lord Denning, Lord Cooke was careful, seldom controversial and never yodelled from the mountaintop.

When I was Chief Justice in Samoa my wife and I invited him to dinner. He was unassuming, pleasant and good company. He had a huge brain. His encyclopaedic knowledge of the law was staggering. I felt like a kitten at the paw of the Lion King.

I remember only disagreeing with him once, and that was not on a point of law. (How could it be!) It was on how to assess the credibility of witnesses. I was seated next to Sir Robin (then President of the Court of Appeal) at a legal dinner. Justice Robert Smellie of the High Court and Justice Mervyn Finlay a judge of the New South Wales Supreme Court were at the same table. As the only inferior judge at the table, I felt somewhat like a minnow in the whale harbour, but a few good wines dispelled any feelings of inadequacy.

I happened to express my view that one of the hardest tasks of any front-line judge was to decide which of two differing and opposing witnesses was telling the truth. I said I found it difficult to assess the credibility of two such witnesses, both of whom

---

[1] London, Lexis Law Publishing, 1982.

[2] Lord Cooke of Thorndon ONZ, KBE, PC, QC (1926 – 2006)

appeared to be honest, believable, sincere, logical, and accurate in their recollection of events. I told my august company that in such a situation I fell back on the onus of proof. I would simply say in my decision (in a criminal case) that I was required to decide the case beyond reasonable doubt and that because I could not decide which of the witnesses to believe, I would dismiss the case

Sir Robin was aghast. He said I must never do that. It was quite wrong. He said it was the vital task of every judge to make a decision as to the credibility of each witness, not to just dodge the issue as too difficult. Every witness must be assessed and a decision made as to their credibility. Justice Smellie instantly agreed with Sir Robin.

I felt as if I was a junior barrister being reprimanded by the Court of Appeal. I think I just had another wine, but did not agree with either of them. And then, Mervyn Finlay, our Australian guest, came to my rescue. He said he agreed with me, and that over his career on the bench, he had experienced the same quandary about having to decide between two seemingly compelling witnesses. In such cases, he said he did exactly as I did.

Justice Mervyn Finlay

Mervyn and I became friends. Perhaps it was because we both had the same inability to decide which witness was telling the truth. More likely because I enjoyed his delightful personality and sense of humour. Suzanne and I enjoyed a delightful dinner at his beautiful Sydney home with his gracious and lovely wife Prue. While the ladies talked in the lounge, he showed me the sporting and legal memorabilia in his study. His collection was fascinating. One photo showed him at the end of WWII as a young RAAF officer. He was an Olympic rower, a member of the bronze medal winning crew at the 1952 Helsinki Olympics. Earlier he had been New South Wales state 880 yards running champion. A Queen's Counsel, he was a Supreme Court Judge from 1984 until his retirement a decade later. He died in his 90th year – 2014. A true scholar and gentleman.

We had a lively and joyful correspondence by email, revelling in the humour and eccentricity that life on the bench reveals.

He light-heartedly asked whether I knew the real evidence about the "Three Wise Men". I thought he was talking about the three incumbents of the Court of Appeal. He wasn't. He was putting me right about the magi visiting Bethlehem after the birth of Jesus. Mervyn knew my interest in the falsehoods and fabrications of Judeo-Christian writings. He reminded me of the need to carefully examine evidence.

He pointed out that the only mention of the celebrated camel trek that centuries later became part of the Christmas story is in Matthew 2:1-12. No other Gospel or Epistle writer mentions it. There is no mention of them being kings. They were "wise men – magi", from the East, probably well versed in astronomy. No record of their number (there were three gifts[1]). No mention of a stable. No mention of Joseph, shepherds, or animals. And the three were sent by King Herod as investigators. The verses read:

> *In the time of King Herod, after Jesus was born in Bethlehem of Judea, wise men from the East came to Jerusalem, asking, "Where is the child who has been born king of the Jews? For we observed his star at its rising, and have come to pay him homage."*
> *When King Herod heard this, he was frightened and all Jerusalem with him; and calling together all the chief priests and scribes of the people, he inquired of them where the Messiah was to be born. They told him, "In Bethlehem of Judea; for so it has been written by the prophet: 'And you, Bethlehem, in the land of Judah, are by no means least among the rulers of Judah; for from you shall come a ruler who is to shepherd my people Israel.'"*
> *Then Herod secretly called for the wise men and learned from them the exact time when the star had appeared. Then he sent them to Bethlehem, saying, "Go and search diligently for the child; and when you have found him, bring me word so that I may also go and pay him homage."*
> *When they had heard the king, they set out; and there, ahead of them, went the star that they had seen at its rising, until it stopped over the place where the child was. When they saw that the star had stopped, they were overwhelmed with joy. On entering the house, they saw the child with Mary his mother; and they knelt down and paid him homage. Then, opening their treasure chests, they offered him gifts of gold, frankincense, and myrrh. And having been warned in a dream not to return to Herod, they left for their own country by another path* [2]

Mervyn left me with warm memories of a wise, rational and compassionate judge and friend.

Appeals

A judge at my inferior level must make a decision and get on with the next case. Worrying about having made a wrong finding is unproductive and can even cause ill-health. If a judge can't move on without stress, he should move to another career. Unlike nearly all other professions we have the benefit of an appeal process to correct us if we are wrong. Mistakes can be corrected without too much trauma to the litigant. Surgeons and other medical practitioners do not have that back-stop. Neither do engineers and architects. My architect father said if he made a mistake he would spend the rest of his life shutting his eyes as he drove past it.

I have been lucky with appeal courts. The only significant area in which I have been overturned is with sentencing – usually when I have imposed a prison sentence considered to be too long.

---

[1] The Eastern Christian Churches have 12 wise men, not three.

[2] USA, New Revised Standard Version, 1989,

Sometimes I have disagreed with the appeal court and believed my decision was the correct one. Appellate courts also get it wrong. Justice Robert Jackson of the US Supreme Court commendably said "We are not final because we are infallible, but we are infallible only because we are final."[1]

Deep End

Before becoming a judge in 1953, Mr Justice, Sir George McGregor[2] had been Crown Solicitor in my home town of Palmerston North. He spoke to us at the Manawatu Law Society after his retirement in 1970. He told us that in 1952 he was sworn in as a judge on a Friday afternoon in Wellington and then directed to preside over a week of jury trials in Westport commencing the following Monday. He travelled by ferry and train over the weekend and on the Monday commenced a murder trial. Unlike many newly appointed Supreme Court judges (who had only practiced in civil or commercial law), criminal law held no fears for Sir George.

The accused had shot dead the ticket office clerk at the Reefton station. He then ran out onto the railway tracks but a slow train entering the station managed to stop in time.

The trial was short and simple. On the Wednesday, the jury speedily found the accused guilty of murder, and for his first ever sentence the new judge had to don the black cap and pronounce the death sentence. He said it shook him to the core – which I found intriguing for a steely, competent, and experienced lawyer who had prosecuted for the Crown in Palmerston North for many years. As a postscript, he added that the accused did not lodge any appeal and was duly hanged a few weeks later.

Much later, during my time in Samoa 1982-3, I also had the grim duty, on three separate occasions, to sentence three men to death by hanging. Even though I knew the death sentence would not be carried out, in favour of a commutation to life imprisonment, it was distressing to wear the black cap[3], look at a man in the eye, and impose such an awful sentence. Samoa abolished the death penalty in 2004. We had done so in New Zealand, in 1961.

---

[1] The USA Supreme Court Database (2018) reports that since 2000 only 36% of decisions have been unanimous. In New Zealand between 2004-2013, 56% of our Supreme Court decisions were unanimous.

[2] Senior puisne judge, died 1976, aged 76. In 1972 he completed a controversial report into the conviction of Arthur Allan Thomas for the murders of Harvey and Jeannette Crewe in June 1970.

[3] Not really a cap but a square of black fabric placed on top of the wig with one corner facing forward.

'Gussie' Wallace

The first female judge in New Zealand was my friend and colleague, Georgina Catriona Pamela Augusta Wallace[1], affectionately and more concisely known as 'Gussie'. She helped me many times. Created a Dame in 1993, Dame Augusta served in various judicial capacities, including on the Waitangi Tribunal (three years from 1996), and chairing the Abortion Supervisory Committee (1977-79).

Dame Augusta was a District Court judge for over 18 years. She died in 2008. In 1990, she survived a grievous machete attack by a 16-year-old youth in the Otahuhu Youth Court that led to a review of court security. Her husband, Neville, was a career army officer. He retired from the army after serving as an infantry Lieutenant-Colonel in Vietnam. He then studied law and practiced in South Auckland. A delightful man, much admired by us all.

[1] As the first woman judge she pretended to be tough. It was really an act. "I've spent a lot of time fostering, especially among young practitioners, a grim image, even a dragon image. In this profession it can be helpful to look forbidding."

Drunk or Disorderly

One Puff Enough

Joe was a tall, wild-eyed man with mental health issues. He was overcome by emotion (or something) in the Post Bank a few days before Christmas. He was waiting in a line to be served when he saw an attractive young woman with long blonde hair. He moved up behind and blew on her neck and back, which were exposed by her halter neck top. She told him to stop. He did so but repeated the performance a minute later. The young woman was intimidated and frightened. She ran to a teller for help.

Joe was charged with disorderly behaviour. He didn't seem to think he had done much wrong and grinned when I suggested others might have been thought him a pervert or a weirdo.

The large public gallery in Court thought that was a great joke. I doubted that anyone thought he was a pervert. But from the young woman's perspective what he did was frightening, disturbing, and offensive. I fined him $400 with the usual $65 court costs to make him realise that most young women don't want a creep like him anywhere near them let alone blowing on their neck in the middle of the banking chamber.

Party Time

The case was typical of its type. The defendant, a young, greasy-headed man with a wispy excuse for a beard, was charged with resisting two police officers acting in the course of their duty, and intentionally damaging a police shirt and a singlet.

Two police officers, one built like Sylvester Stallone's weightlifter brother, were directed to a party at which between 200 and 300 teenagers were all behaving themselves in the impeccable manner exhibited by modern youth. One teenager, however, made a complaint about the defendant to the police and Stallone located O'Finnegan the defendant awake in a bedroom.

"Have you got a knife, sir?" inquired Stallone's brother in the polite manner exhibited by all police officers.

"Na! Fuck off, Mate! I've got nothing", said O'Finnegan, with corresponding courtesy. He lifted his arms.

"Go, on search me!"

Accepting this unexpected invitation, the constable rapidly located a pig-sticker knife in a pouch, and 4 capsules of Class B cannabis oil in a pocket.

"You are under arrest!" came the unwelcome words, and O'Finnegan was ushered out the door.

In the wink of an Morepork's[1] eye, both constable and knife-owner were on the floor of the lounge. It wasn't a fight. Only a drunk would intentionally fight a huge man like Stallone. The officer simply sat his huge muscular rumps on O'Finnegan and listened to the last of the air escaping from the young man's flattened lungs as he applied the handcuffs to his wrists.

The constable told me the defendant had deliberately shouldered him against the wall as they left the bedroom. The youngster said he had accidentally tripped, bringing down the full weight of the law on top of him. He said he was not resisting.

O'Finnegan, wrists now welded together in front of him, was frogmarched outside to the patrol car. His fiancée and two other supportive young revellers followed. The fiancée, a young woman with apparently as much Celtic DNA as her man, became very hostile. She vehemently told the constables what she understood to be their dubious parentage. She also expressed her understanding that their entire on-duty lives were spent indulging in various sexual gymnastics of a dubious sexual nature. A young woman police officer, who had prudently remained outside by the patrol car, warned the young harridan to stop using such ancient Indo-European expletives. But she persisted with her foul language. She was, as male gang members coarsely say, "bitch deaf". The policewoman indicated that she would arrest the young woman. At this stage, the defendant allegedly shoulder-charged another young officer and threw him off balance.

This officer immediately reacted by shoving O'Finnegan headfirst into the back seat of the patrol car. Perhaps he should have first opened the car-door wider because all witnesses agreed that O'Finnegan's head may have dented the doorframe of the patrol car. It made a noise like an Exocet missile penetrating an Iraqi tank. The constable fell into the back seat of the car on top of the head-strong defendant. The defendant said his back was hurting on the transmission pipe. He allegedly said, "Help me up, quickly, or I'll rip your fucking shirt!"

He was not helped up quickly enough. I examined the officer's blue shirt. It had no buttons - only little jagged holes. The singlet was also torn.

Two other partygoers testified that the defendant had not shoulder-butted the second policeman and that the defendant had been deliberately shoved into the door frame.

Everyone denied consumption of drink or drugs. Very strange, and most unlikely, that.

---

[1] The morepork (*Ninox novaeseelandiae*), an owl native to New Zealand & Tasmania, in Maori called the ruru.

One witness, a stroppy little 15-year-old with purple hair and nose rings, was very vocal about what she saw. I asked if she had been drinking. She said she had not. I then said: "What about smoking dope?"

The question seemed to take her by surprise. Her eyes flickered, she paled visibly, and she glanced imploringly at defence counsel, and then, very vociferously, denied any such thing.

I didn't say anything. Under my breath, I simply hummed the tune "Tell us another one, just like the other one, tell us another one, do-ooh."

Much to the anger of the party-goers, I preferred the testimony of the three police officers. I found the defendant guilty of possession of cannabis, and resisting arrest, and intentionally damaging the shirt. I fined him $300 for the cannabis oil, $100 on each of the resisting charges, and ordered him to pay $40.00 to replacing the police shirt. I let him off the singlet charge because I had a reasonable doubt as to whether he even knew the constable was wearing one, let alone whether it was intentional.

More Party Time

As I have said, these cases are often similar. Young partygoers are always sober, rational and observant. The police are always heavy-handed Rambos spoiling for a fight. The reality is very different. Fights at parties are nearly always caused by excessive drinking or drug abuse. Police officers start by making polite enquiries. They are then usually subjected to verbal abuse. If they make an immediate arrest the crowd may become agitated and anti-authority.

> *"Why should this brutal cop arrest my mate just because he has cannabis plant blossoming from his pockets, is cursing and swearing like a madman, and refuses to turn down a stereo amplifier that has already shattered fifteen windows in the next block, and driven three elderly neighbours to telephone the Mayor, Prime Minister, and Ministers of Police and Immigration?"*

Another factor is that most front-line policemen are also young. They are also fit; in much better shape than most young revellers. They have learned by experience that a mob may turn on them, and most nights of the week they are threatened, abused, spat upon, or punched by drunken, irrational, and anti-authority youth.

I see it as only human nature for some young officers to react physically from time to time. Self-restraint is a relative concept. Even policemen have their breaking point. While this young constable should not have punched the defendant in the eye (the photograph arranged by defence counsel the next day showed a textbook "shiner"), in the circumstances it was perfectly understandable.

In cases like this a judge must tread a difficult path. The judge must not be seen to unquestioningly side with the police; neither must the police feel that the court is not supportive of them. In reality, a very delicate public relations exercise is in progress.

In my decision, I always refer to the difficulty of sifting through the facts in such cases: the emotional and heated situation, the short timeframe, and the perception problems witnesses face when trying to recall exactly what happened. I often comment that it is not helpful for girlfriends to become abusive and to scream provocative challenges from the side-line.

I then refer to the consumption of alcohol, the difficulties facing police officers in such circumstances, and the need for everyone in such situations to take a deep breath and step backwards.

And then, (unless someone is badly injured) I never go overboard on penalty.

Rock 'n Coke

Coca Cola caused a tall, slack-jawed, poorly dressed 50-year-old carpenter without previous convictions to blow his stack in a corner dairy not far from my home. He purchased a can of coke and then found there was an inscription on the bottom of the can indicating that he was entitled to one further can of Coca Cola free. It was a "Rock 'n Coke" competition promoted by the Coca-Cola Corporation. He asked the shopkeeper for his free coke. The owner told him that his shop was not a participating store and pointed to the conditions on the sticker which read only in participating stores.

The sturdy carpenter, never having won Lotto, never having won at a casino, never having even won a pig in a barrow, stood his ground and said that he was not going to leave the shop until he received his prize. The shopkeeper refused. Consequently, the usually affable fellow, became angry and pushed over two large confectionary display stands. The contents scattered everywhere. Both to the police, and to me, he maintained he was in the right that he was entitled to the can. He said the shop owner would not listen to reason. (Was he the pot calling the kettle black?). One of the witnesses, an elderly lady, said she was physically shaken by the incident.

He would have been eligible for diversion but two days after this incident had yelled abuse at the shopkeeper from a neighbouring building site. The defendant became quite heated in court. I intervened. I quietly explained to him that whether or not he was entitled to a free can of coke was not the issue I had to decide. The question for me, I said, was whether he had behaved in a disorderly way in the grocery shop. Angrily pushing over two large confectionery stands in front of other shoppers was not a reasonable response to the shopkeeper's refusal to give him the can. He calmed down and seemed to understand what I was saying. I gave my decision. Guilty.

I fined him $75 and ordered him to pay reparation for the damaged goods, court costs, and witnesses expenses. I was told he had only one previous unrelated traffic conviction. I wondered whether he had some underlying mental health condition, or perhaps an addiction to the drink. But I was not prepared to take the matter further by ordering a psychological assessment on such a minor matter. I told him not to get in a fizz over a can of coke.

Someone Else

Identification was the issue in the case of Williams, who elected to defend himself (with the help of a McKenzie friend kaumatua) on a most serious, almost capital, criminal charge: wilfully damaging a clothesline!

He and two unemployed longhaired mates attended a party hosted by two employed shorthaired schoolteachers. When it was noticed that their language and booze consumption exceeded commonly accepted quotas, an investigation proved that no one had actually invited them to the party.

The police arrived to evict them. The defendant was last to leave. The constable followed him out the door. The defendant deliberately went to the clothesline and pulled one of the wires until a stay broke off and the line collapsed onto the lawn. He was immediately arrested and made no comment. But by court day he had convinced himself that it must have been someone else. He cross-examined somewhat shyly using questions muttered to him first by the McKenzie friend. I did not think they were very effective.

"Can you see in the dark, Constable?"

"Were you really one metre behind me, Constable?"

"Were you and I really the only two people in the yard?"

"Are you sure it was me you arrested?"

The Constable robustly replied affirmatively to all questions. The defendant testified. He said he couldn't remember much but didn't think it was him.

"How much drink had you had?"

"Heaps, but I was still pretty sober – half sober!"

Convicted and fined $150 and to pay the $30 repair bill!

Wrong Dairy

For much of the time I was a judge in Auckland I lived in the attractive bush-clad suburb of Titirangi. I purchased my daily newspaper and milk from the Scenic Dairy at 412 Titirangi Road. One day, I was presiding in the Henderson District Court (now Waitakere District Court) Ratanui Street, when a young man appeared in court charged with offensive behaviour. The police had found him at 2:00 a.m. drunkenly urinating on the empty milk crates stacked outside the dairy. He pleaded guilty. I fined him for his disgusting behaviour and observed to him:

"You chose the wrong dairy, young fellow. That is where I buy my milk!"

He just looked at me and gasped. Despite that, I imposed a fine in the usual range, not increasing it for personal reasons!

Another Rose

Wouldn't it be nice if the local paper for once said "Bon vivant, raconteur and man-about-town questioned by authorities" instead of "Town drunk busted again."[1]

Quadriplegic

How do I sentence a small-time cannabis dealer who is 28, a quadriplegic, married with 4 children, and living on an invalid's benefit?[2]

Demolition Party

Some boozy lads were caught red-handed having a party at Munt Maunganui – with 16 bottles of whisky, 9 of rum and 10 cartons of beer – all stolen the day before from a liquor store. Some party!

In another case that same day, a young man was charged with intentionally damaging a house in Rata Street near the port buildings at the Mount.

On a Tuesday afternoon, clerical staff at the Harbour Board heard loud banging noises and observed three young men who seemed to be demolishing the house. The defendant denied that he was part of the demolition squad. He was a tenant of the house, had been away for a long weekend and had returned on the Monday evening to find all the windows broken and most of the internal walls torn down. His own bed and property were covered with rubble.

Some of his mates had enjoyed an excessively exuberant party over the weekend. All he was doing, he said, was throwing lengths of timber through what had been his bedroom wall into what had been the laundry. He was trying to clear up so as to remove his belongings. His two mates were helping him. The noise came from the timber hitting a disused washing machine.

The two mates and his girlfriend confirmed that he had been away for the weekend. The girl's maiden name, interestingly, was Matahaere. It was pronounced almost the same as the exotic dancer Mata Hari executed by a British firing squad as a supposed

---

[1]From a cartoon by Joe Martin: '*Unclear on the concept*' 1989.

[2] Place him on probation for 6 months and warn him about future imprisonment.

German spy in 1917. When I heard her name called by the court crier, I expected to see a slinky, sensuous espionage agent. Instead I got a chubby, nervous little part-Māori teenager who kept groaning throughout her testimony. I found her boyfriend not guilty.

We Know Our Rights

A couple defended themselves on a charge of trespassing at the police station. The husband, Brian, was a very aggressive, macho, heavily built man described in the papers as a manager. It didn't say what he managed but his powerful, tattooed arms indicated that he wasn't managing a florist shoppe. His lady partner, Betty, was quite attractive until the flattened Kiwi vowels and garbled language enunciation revealed more about her. She was also very stroppy and determined to convince me of how right her claims were. She knew these things. She was a receptionist for a Government Department.

I have had many such cases over the years. The defendants and a male friend had spent five hours drinking at a local hotel. The friend, Marty, opted to drive them all home. He had only driven a few hundred metres up Commerce Street, when a police officer stopped him. The officer, instantly overwhelmed by alcohol fumes as he leaned in the car window, immediately commenced breath-testing procedure. But Marty and his friend Brian (the male defendant) protested both vigorously and obscenely that Marty had been unfairly singled out from among the hotel patrons, especially as many were more drunk than Marty. The unfortunate officer, his ears burning from the insulting invective hurled at him, and undoubtedly noticing the size of the defendant's bi- and triceps, prudently used his car radio-telephone to summons reinforcements.

Three police patrol cars were on the scene in a matter of minutes. The presence of six enforcement officers did little to deter the defendant from his angered perception that the officers were all acting unlawfully, unfairly, and illegally, and used some further Anglo-Saxon language to give them the message.

Surprisingly, and most leniently, Police Sergeant Pedersen elected not to arrest him for obstruction or using indecent language. Instead, the police left the two defendants in Commerce Street to polish up their adjectives, while Marty was taken to the police station for breath testing. But Brian was not going to let the police get away with such brutish and fascist behaviour. And neither, for that matter, was Betty. The quaffing of many ales throws prudence and discretion to the wind. Fired up, in his case, by six jugs of Lion Red beer and, in her case, by a modest three jugs of the same amber restorative ("unaffected by alcohol were we!") they decided to visit the police station to bail out Marty and remind the constabulary that the citizenry of a democracy has its rights too.

At the police station, Brian confronted a young policeman. He flexed his biceps and demanded to see Marty, who by then was being processed in the watch house behind the counter. The policeman warned Brian that he was not permitted in the watch house and to please leave. But, as a fervent liberal democrat, Brian protested his rights. He asserted that as a citizen taxpayer he had free access anywhere in a police station. So, uninvited, into the watch house he went. The constable again told him to leave. He did so, but since being left on Commerce Street alone with Betty, he had remembered a few more Old Anglo-Saxon phrases that he tried out on the constable to show him who really was boss.

The constable could see he was dealing with no average citizen: Brian had a bigger vocabulary and bigger triceps. So, Constable Gordon asked Sergeant Pedersen to explain the true legal position to Brian. The sergeant explained that no one was allowed into the watch house to see a prisoner without permission and that no-one is permitted to use such foul language in a police station. He suggested that Brian and Betty sit down calmly and wait until Marty had completed the drink/drive procedures.

This was too much for Brian. He had secret knowledge that both the constable and the sergeant were really SS Storm troopers masquerading as New Zealand Police. He said he had waited long enough and reminded the police that they were public servants: he was the public and Q.E.D. they must be the servants. He would not wait patiently in the foyer and would not shut his mouth. He demanded his rights. A further three times the exasperated and patient sergeant told him to leave the police station or he would be arrested for trespass.

"Trespass! How can the public trespass on its own property? You arrogant swine. No way!"

Brian was arrested. But not without a struggle. He ended up on the floor with four policemen trying to handcuff him. He received bruising and red eyes.

Betty had never seen such things happen in her workplace. She knew how proper public servants are meant to behave. She was convinced that her belligerent partner was correct in all he had said. And now she had living proof that the police were brutal sadists. They had just beaten her man to the floor. She gave them a tongue-lashing. She reminded them of her rights. She was told to be quiet. She turned up her amplifier. She had also remembered some of the words she had been taught by Brian on Commerce Street. She used them in the police foyer. They were very effective: she was instantly told to leave or suffer the fate of her boyfriend and be arrested for trespass. After several repeat warnings, she steadfastly refused to leave. She met her martyrdom fearlessly and spent the night in the cells without blanket, food or friend.

They did not have a lawyer. Why have a lawyer? There was no need to waste their money. They knew their rights. They needed no representation from some ignorant legal lackey. Over the intervening two months they had become even more resolute. They recalled the events of that night with extraordinary accuracy. The police were liars and thugs. They were quite unaffected by liquor. They used no bad language. They were not aggressive. They did not refuse to leave the police station. There was no need for them to be arrested. They knew their rights. And what is more the police were gangsters and any sensible judge worthy of his pay could see that was the case.

When the case was over, and my decision given, they left the court disenchanted with the police, disillusioned with me, and disheartened with the $250 fines. I thought then that video cameras like those used in banks should be set up in police stations.[1] I felt sure that if offenders were shown a technicolour replay of how atrocious and outrageous they behaved after six jugs of beer, they would change their plea to guilty with alacrity.

"How do you plead?"

"Guilty, with alacrity."

Smirnoff Amnesia

Vodka can be problematic. There is the story of a man who had a few too many vodkas and was driving home when he was stopped by the police. A breath test showed he was way over the limit. The officer started writing out a ticket when a collision occurred in the opposite lane. The officer rushed over to the scene of the accident. The drunk driver, seizing the opportunity, sidled away, drove home and went to bed.

The next day there was a knock at his door. Two police officers confronted him.

"Are you Mr. Rodnik?" one of them asked. He admitted that he was.

"Were you pulled over at Main Street last night for driving under the influence?"

Again, the man admitted he was.

"And what did you do then?" the officer asked.

The man replied that he drove his car home and went to bed.

"Where is your car now?"

The man answered that it was in his garage.

"May we see the car?" asked the officer.

"Sure", said the man, and opened the garage.

Inside the garage was the police patrol car.

Christmas Beer

I sent Buck to prison for nine months on two charges of assaulting his de facto wife and a charge of driving while disqualified. Although he pleaded guilty, the facts were disputed, so I heard them.

On Christmas Day 1990, Buck had too little Christmas cheer and too much Christmas beer. After a social function on Christmas afternoon the couple returned

---

[1] They now are.

home. They argued. Booze being booze, memory being memory, and love being love, neither could remember what they argued about.

He became enraged and punched the complainant in the face, knocking her to the ground. He then kicked her often in the head and ribs, and punched her on the shoulder and face. She fled from the house on foot, but the defendant caught up with her. He then dragged her back to the house, and gave her more of the same. As it happens, he was truly remorseful. He has done it all before. But she loves him still. He needs both punishment and help. I also directed counselling for anger management and alcohol abuse when he is released from his nine months in prison.

Under-age Liquor Sale

Paul Mabey[1] defended two charges against a wine shop proprietor named Ramsay for selling liquor to a 16-year-old youth. The boy's mother had been to the police, complaining that her boy had a drink problem but was continuing to be sold alcohol by the defendant. On his birthday, the boy had been sold three 750 ml bottles of vodka! I don't blame the mother for being worried. But the police case was not well prepared and Mabey did a good job in raising the necessary doubts. There was no doubt about the boy's age. The doubts were as to the days on which the sales were said to have taken place. The witnesses got the dates hopelessly wrong and I had no option but to dismiss the charges as, where a specific date is alleged, it must be proved. If the police charge that an offence took place "on or about" a given date, then the situation is different. Hopefully Mr Ramsay has been punished enough with Mabey's fee and will be more prudent in the future.

Some "purveyors of spirituous and alcoholic liquors"[2] let their greed overcome their sense of responsibility. No doubt the police will keep an eye on him from now on, so justice may have been done.

---

[1] A very competent and thorough barrister. Deservedly, he became a QC in 2000, and a District Court judge in 2016.

[2] When I was young, the sign "purveyors of spirituous and alcoholic liquors" was displayed in the door of all public houses. "Spirituous" had no religious connotation. It meant "distilled".

Drugs

Where the Poppies Grow

A wretched heroin addict grew over 100 very attractive and healthy poppy plants (papaver somniferum) in his girlfriend's well fertilised backyard. It looked like Flanders Field. The blooms were so colourful and striking that neighbours and passers-by often stopped to admire them. As did the detective, walking his bloodhound around the block. When the detective ran up the garden path towards the kitchen door, a hypodermic syringe landed at his feet. So did a teaspoon with brown crud on it. The accused, hearing the vulgar, turkey-like distress calls of his girlfriend (which all seemed to start with the letter "F"), had tossed his "gear" out the wrong window right on top of the cop!

The man had pleaded guilty to possession of opium, which he had extracted from some of the pods. He denied cultivating the plants.

Juries aren't greatly enamoured of the drug world. This jury quickly decided he was the gardener and down he went like a Scud missile

The pathetic and inept prisoner (with a very predictable list of previous drug convictions) had gone cold turkey since conviction and was making sturdy and commendable efforts to sort himself out. I gave him six months' periodic detention, and six months' probationary supervision with counselling and treatment conditions.

Incidentally, the term "cold turkey" comes from piloerection. And if you are worried about piloerections, that is just the scientific term for goose bumps. These goose bumps develop when someone abruptly withdraws from taking opioids. The skin on such shivering addicts looks like the skin of a plucked turkey.

Smoked Stupid

Ongoing drug use helps people believe as many as "six impossible things before breakfast!"[1] It augments native stupidity with an almost irreversible progression. Cannabis is the main trigger. I realise that the pro-cannabis lobby and many casual users of cannabis disagree with this and say the negative effects are only temporary. But what I am talking about are the effects of early onset, long-term heavy cannabis use.

Peter Hitchens[2] concurs with my view in his article in the *Mail on Sunday* entitled *We'll go down as the nation that smoked itself stupid.*[3] He writes:

> *Cannabis makes you stupid. I know this already, from the feeble arguments and moronic insults that I get from the dope lobby when I argue for harsher, more effective laws against this dangerous, unpredictable poison.*

He refers to our famous New Zealand Dunedin longitudinal study[4] of over 1000 people over 38 years from birth. Putting aside all other variable cannabis was "…the consistent factor in the lives of those whose IQ shrank and stayed shrunk forever...".

> *When future Chinese historians ponder our national collapse, laughing softly as they do so, I think they may well note that this was the society that banned T-bone steaks while it decriminalised cannabis, and that it was the country that smoked itself stupid. They will conclude that we deserved the irreversible national decline that followed. And they will be right.*

Schizophrenia

I have spoken with two psychiatrists both working with young people hospitalised in Auckland with a diagnosis of schizophrenia. Both doctors had no doubt that pre-adolescent cannabis smoking was the trigger for their currently incurable psychosis.

---

[1] As the Queen said to Alice in *Alice in Wonderland by* Charles Lutwidge Dodgson, better known by his pen name Lewis Carroll,

[2] British journalist, author, and Christian. Brother of Christopher Hitchens, author, columnist, essayist, orator and illuminating atheist.

[3] Daily Mail newspaper,1 September 2012.

[4] The *Dunedin Multidisciplinary Health and Development Study* has studied 1037 people born between 1 April 1972 and 31 March 1973 in Dunedin, New Zealand. As at 2015 the findings have generated over 1,200 publications of various sorts. The multidisciplinary findings have shed new light on cardiovascular, respiratory, physical, digestive, oral, sexual, mental and psychosocial health and risks.

They said the more patients with schizophrenia use cannabis, the worse their condition becomes.

Peter Hitchens also referred to the Dunedin Research Unit report on the Health consequences of cannabis use.

> *The findings of that 38-year longitudinal study of about 1000 people was that:*
> *Adolescent-onset cannabis users, but not adult-onset cannabis users, showed marked IQ decline from childhood to adulthood. For example, individuals who started using cannabis in adolescence and used it for years thereafter showed an average eight-point IQ decline.*
> *Quitting or reducing cannabis use did not appear to fully restore intellectual functioning among adolescent-onset former persistent cannabis users.*
> *IQ decline could not be explained by alcohol or other dr use or by reduced years of education among persistent cannabis users.*

Mellow Fellow

I warned a goofy, gawky 17-year-old that he was off to prison if he ever came back to court again on further cannabis matters. He was caught with 18 cannabis bullets, which he admitted he would have probably sold for $18 each. According to the book, he should have gone to prison for a short spell, but on this occasion I relented because of his age and the fact that he received a favourable probation report. I also felt six months' periodic detention would, in his case, be a fairly salutary lesson, as, from the look of him, 26 long Saturdays of physical labour would really rattle his dags.[1]

I also gave him a final warning and did my usual hollow sermon about the "evils of dope" and how many young people ruin their lives. He grinned back with an ingenuous look on his face:

> *"I've been there, done that. All I do is smoke dope. I'm as mellow as now!"*

I looked at him closer. He was stoned. I thought he had looked somewhat unruffled about his court appearance!

Stoned

A defended case in the Thames Court made me smile, but also made me think about the harm caused by long-term cannabis use. The defendant, a gaunt, bearded, dishevelled 55-year-old was charged with possession of cannabis for supply. When the court-taker called the case I watched him stagger from the foyer into the courtroom and slump heavily into the chair next to his lawyer. At the same time, I saw three

---

[1] I am told this expression is now archaic. Young people, especially city kids, have no idea that dried faeces on a running sheep's backside actually do rattle. That's why farmers "dag" such sheep with shears to clean them up. As the Australian classic says *"Click go the shears, boys, click, click, click. Off go the dags, boys, quick and slick."*

unkempt and "stoned" citizens of similar age glide into seats in the public gallery. His fellow travellers, I guessed.

Three months earlier, at about 1:30 pm, two police drug squad officers with a warrant searched a camp in a remote bush area of the Coromandel. The camp was ramshackle and primitive. The sergeant told me it consisted of a broken-down bus with no wheels, a rusty caravan with peeling paint, two canvas tents that looked like Army surplus from WWII, and a long-drop dunny so ferociously odoriferous as to keep all but the most daring intruders at bay. Nearby was a large plot of healthy cannabis plants in various stages of maturity, all lovingly tended. In the caravan was 1.5 kilos of dry cannabis heads and the glass bongs used by seasoned dope-smokers.

All four middle-aged residents were "high", and had trouble comprehending the purpose of the police raid. They all admitted smoking cannabis daily over the several years they had lived there. Progenies of the hippie era, it seems they did little else in life apart from hitch-hiking to Thames every week to cash their welfare benefit and buy supplies.

Adrian was the only one charged: he had somewhat foolishly admitted the 1.5 kilos was his, when it obviously belonged to all four.

Anyone caught in possession of at least 28 grams (1 ounce) of cannabis or 100 cannabis joints is presumed to be a supplier, unless the defendant can prove to the contrary. The penalty for dealing in cannabis carries a maximum prison sentence of eight years, whereas for simply possessing the drug, the penalty is imprisonment for a term not exceeding 3 months or to a fine not exceeding $500 or to both. But imprisonment is only imposed if there has been serious previous convictions or exceptional circumstances.

Because of the large amount, he was deemed by law to have possessed it for supply to others and not to have it for his own personal use.

The prosecution case was over in 40 minutes, there being no real challenge to the testimony of the two officers.

Then the fun began. Counsel called the defendant to the witness box. Adrian struggled to his feet, had difficulty finding his way, but finally stood in the box, his cheerful grin enhanced by three missing teeth.

Counsel: "Please tell His Honour your full, name, occupation, and place of residence."
Defendant: "Uhh! Say that again?"
Counsel: "Please tell His Honour your full, name, occupation, and place of residence."
Defendant: "Ahh! Yeah! My full name is ... Umm... my full name is... What is my full name...Ahh, yes, I'm Adrian."
Counsel: "And your family name?"
Defendant: "My what?"
Counsel: "Your family name, your surname?"
Defendant: "Well, my name is Adrian. Not a sir."

Another happy, gummy grin in my direction. Red eyes dull from the joint he must have had only minutes before court.

Counsel: "What do they call you? Adrian who?"
Defendant: "Adrian."
Counsel: "Adrian who?"
Defendant: "I am Adrian from the bush."

At that point, I could see that his plugs weren't sparking and there was no fuel in his tank. Poor red eyed Adrian didn't know his name!

Counsel: "Well, skip that. Where do you live? Your address?"
Defendant: "My what?"
Counsel: "Where do you live?"
Defendant: "I live in the bush."
Counsel: "But where?"

Time to blow the whistle and close the game, I thought. I gently suggested to counsel that she might be wise to acknowledge defeat. I called an adjournment, and invited counsel and prosecuting sergeant into my chambers for a coffee.

"I have made up my mind," I said. "It is clear to us all that Adrian is going to take a while to reach the starter's gate. It is also obvious that he and his friends do little else in life but smoke cannabis. The large amount of it found in the caravan belonged to them all, and was all for their own use. I have decided to reduce the charge to one of simple possession and let Adrian and his mates all smoke their happy way back to their camp."

The sergeant grinned in agreement. He had other more important cases that day. Even a fine would be a waste of time. Defence counsel smiled in appreciation. She had achieved a forensic triumph, and as her fame spread, would soon have many new (and stoned) clients from all over the peninsula.

Specialist Drug Court

Judges in the criminal courts are not there to engage in political or academic arguments about cannabis or its legalisation. That is a political argument. Daily, we see the destructive impact of drug abuse. It is no mirage. It is real. The NZ drug harm index 2016 estimated the social cost of all drug-related harms and intervention at $1.8 billion.

A positive development, since 2012, is the creation of dedicated courts called Alcohol and Other Drug Treatment (AODT) Courts where a team of specialist judges, lawyers, counsellors and therapists use all-inclusive means to rehabilitate rather than punish offenders who have acknowledged addictive issues that have contributed to their criminal offending.

Many of these mainly young offenders openly acknowledge their serious dependency on drugs and want help. Why would that be if, as the pro-cannabis lobby argue, there was no problem?

A Dozen Previous Offences

A bearded, gaunt, reclusive fellow of 38, from the back-blocks of Erewhon had been caught with a kilogram of good quality cannabis – 1½ Kleensacks full. The police knew him of old. They accepted that he had the cannabis for his own use because they knew his years of smoking the stuff meant he was quite capable of puffing his way through the lot without sale or supply to anyone else. The problem was that he had twelve previous convictions. He was charged with growing the cannabis as well as possessing it. The pre-sentence report made it clear that the fellow was hardly a public menace. He had simply spent the last decade smoking dope. He said he smoked in order to keep his aggression under control.

The probation report indicated there had been some very violent episodes in his youth. He had only been to prison once before. I couldn't see much point in imprisoning him but gave him four months because I am not really allowed to simply ignore the proper approach to sentencing as directed by the Court of Appeal. He told me the law was nonsense and that most New Zealanders believed cannabis should be made legal. He said I was wasting national resources by sending him to prison. I pointed out that the Massey University study of New Zealand attitudes (Dr. Webster) the previous year proved that he was wrong and that a very large majority of New Zealanders did not believe in more liberalisation of the Misuse of Drugs legislation.

Finally, he gave me a wan little grin and said:

"Well, at least I'll eat better in prison than I am at the moment!"

Space Cake

An enterprising woman with a broad jolly smile and pleasant features had been charged indictably with cultivating cannabis and possession of cannabis for supply. She pleaded guilty and I had to decide whether I should decline jurisdiction and send her to the High Court. This decision required consideration of whether she was likely to receive a sentence of over three years imprisonment. Her counsel finally persuaded me to keep her in the District Court jurisdiction. But he had to work for it because the green-fingered naughty-culturalist was caught with 52 well-tended plants – one for each week of the year. Most of the healthy plants were about two metres tall - and there were eight pounds of cannabis drying out in the ceiling cavity.

When the police arrived at her house, she was in the kitchen baking a "space cake". She should have been singing the catchy song:

Well, well, well, look who's here.
I haven't seen you in many a year.
If I knew you were comin' there'd have been no cake,
Been no cake, been no cake.
If I knew you were comin' there'd have been no cake.
How-ja do. How-ja do, How-ja do.

She had already mixed the cannabis oil with the butter preparatory to adding the flour, eggs, milk, vanilla, and lemon extract. She had the oven heating and the wooden spoon in hand. The cake was to share with her friends. Imagine what hilarious afternoon teas grandma might have had with a cannabis space cake!!

I sentenced her to two years imprisonment followed by an intensive rehabilitation programme.

Coromandel Cannabinoids

Robert Reid, the Thames bailiff, kindly drove me to Waihi one morning. He was very interesting with his tales of life on the Coromandel. He had been a bailiff only two years but already knew the cannabis communities on the Coromandel well. He had a pleasant manner and was treated well by most of his clientele. His main (and at time very onerous) duty was to collect fines. He had only been assaulted three times, none of them serious.

On one occasion, after a perilous trip in his four-wheel drive vehicle up a tortuous track to a house in the bush, he was nearly speared (literally) by the occupant who hadn't heard him coming. The man panicked when he thought it was the police and charged poor Robert with a spear. The fellow calmed down and a few days later arrived at the court with a bundle of bank notes, peeled off his $2000, paid his outstanding fines, and went bush.

Austerity reasons had been provided to Robert, requiring that he hand in his cellular car phone. I would have thought that as a protective measure such communication equipment would be crucial for anyone working in the back-blocks of the Coromandel, as the police may be quite distant and a phone would be the only way to contact them. Surely Justice Department administrators needed to be realistic about such needs. The area had more than its share of criminals, as the murder of the two Swedish tourists on the Coromandel clearly illustrated. Robert said the economy of the Coromandel would break down but for the trade in cannabis. I thought he may well be correct.

Bashers, Beaters, Punchers, Stabbers & Killers

Vicious Cycle

In a busy daily list court, it is rare not to have at least one case involving family violence. A major part of police work involves attending at and resolving domestic violence incidents. Sometimes the offender or even the victimised woman turn on the attending police officers and abuse or assault them.

The psychology is interesting. Domestic violence is very repetitive. Violence erupts, the woman calls the police, the man is arrested, the woman doesn't want him to go to prison, she forgives him, he is contrite and remorseful, and all goes well for three months until the next drunken or violent episode. Then the whole scenario is repeated. It is rarely a one-off situation. Men who beat up women usually do so again. The cycle must be broken. The basic psychology appears to be a man's need to dominate and control his woman. Sometimes this is based on jealousy. It is not so much a question of "anger management" as it is the need to control. Frequently the man is insecure. Men often feel justified in what they have done. Some feel they are entitled, as husband, to have their needs met. Self-entitlement and self-centredness are commonplace. Some see a woman and children as "personal property". They blame the woman for what has happened.

> *She deserved it! The bitch nags me. She is a hopeless housewife. She gives me crap for dinner – and it's never ready when I get home from the pub. She is a bad mother. She never listens to me. Doesn't she realise I am the boss? What does she expect? If she gives me lip, she gets the bash!*

Men often minimise what they have done or deny it altogether. They refuse to accept their offending behaviour.

> *She ran into the wall. She fell on the floor by accident. It certainly wasn't me who gave her the black eye.*[1]

Emotional, physical or sexual abuse are all common factors. Often, offenders have a family history of violence. The domination of women and children can be cultural or based on religious beliefs. Psychological and probation reports frequently disclose that the offender had a childhood marred by physical and sexual abuse.

Fortunately, there are excellent programs both in the community and in prison to rehabilitate men who are violent on the home front. Expert counsellors teach them to respond in a non-aggressive way. They learn to respond responsibly, respectfully and honestly, and to resolve problems by negotiation and good communication. They are provided with tools as to how to respond when a situation becomes heated and potentially violent. They are taught to walk away, go for a walk or drive, and use calming techniques to simmer down.

Family violence remains a festering sore on our society. I have not seen any comparative figures, but my feeling is that the incidence of domestic violence remains undiminished and is a major societal problem. The emergence of methamphetamine has been sinister. That pernicious drugs unquestionably heightens the likelihood of violence. Studies prove that. Police arrests show that.

As with all human behaviour there are always exceptions to the general rule.[2] Not all chronic meth users are violent. Similarly, while most users seem to become quickly addicted, I have seen exceptions. Some people appear capable of using meth on an irregular and controlled way without progressing to addiction or showing the serious dysfunction evident in the majority of users.

---

[1] Over the years I have been surprised by the number of women who get black eyes from walking into walls. Physiologically that is impossible. Only the eyebrow or forehead can be bruised. The eye is set in a socket for good reason!

[2] I have formed the perhaps jaundiced view that telling the truth in court is now the exception rather than the rule.

Bouncing the Bouncer

I gave a prisoner 18 months' jail for attacking and injuring a bouncer in a local hotel by hitting him from behind with a large handled beer glass. It pierced the bouncer's jugular vein and caused much ruddigore, but, thank goodness, and most surprisingly, no serious ill-effects. To worsen his already precarious legal predicament, the man then left the bar and, with his mates, smashed in the front bar windows of the hotel with a boat oar, shouting much verbal abuse, including the not uncommon African American epithet "fucking honky" which seems now to be a rather standard, if somewhat unimaginative, term of ethnic abuse used by disgruntled patrons in public bars.

Vasectomised Cuckold

A robust and tough-looking man very nearly ended up in prison. He had assaulted his de facto wife while both were heavily intoxicated. Her injuries from the assault were minimal but at one point in the eight-hour drinking session, he scared her sufficiently that she jumped from a second-floor window and broke her leg. The argument started because, unbeknown to her, he had sneaked off to the doctor and had a vasectomy. When she found out, believing that fecundity is all, and with many rum and cokes igniting her maternal wrath, she became incensed with his deceit. In order to get one back on him, about halfway through the party, she hopped into bed with one of his friends for a little coition, with the added excitement consequent upon the increased risk of detection.

And detected she was! And added excitement there was!

Hubby caught them both, as they say in high school, "hard at it" and hell hath no fury like a vasectomised cuckold. He undoubtedly thought she deserved to be bitten and half-strangled, for that is what he proceeded to do. I did not agree with him. But by the time of the trial, after a summer break, she loved him again. And he loved her. And it was all really just foreplay! So, I gave him periodic detention for 3 months with a direction to attend counselling for his fairly impressive drinking problem.

Head Strong

For four years two young Whitianga fellows had been arguing over who owned a set of car tools. The tools were worth $400.00. It exploded into a violent donnybrook[1] outside Snappy Jack's Takeaway Bar in Whitianga. The defendant ended up head-locking the other young man and ramming his head:

---

[1] Called after a town of that name near Dublin, since 1204 so notorious for the concussive playfulness of its annual fair that the fair was permanently banned in the 19th century.

(1) into a corrugated iron fence, and

(2) into the side panel of an adjacent car.

This caused damage to all three hard surfaces. The victim also suffered broken spectacles, a broken wristwatch, an inedible Snappy Jack takeaway meal, and a naturopath's fee for spinal re-adjustment. Also, witnesses' expenses. Total: just under $750, which, for an unemployed youth (who couldn't see anything wrong in what he had done because the dispute had now been "sorted out!"), I thought an immediate order for payment of that reparation was punishment enough.

Tantrums and Rage

Rage reactions are commonly seen in children, but, sadly, I have had scores of cases where individuals land themselves in serious trouble with the law because of their inability to control their temper. The anger does not just stop with the crime. It often resurfaces months later in the courtroom. I have even seen lawyers lose their temper with opposing counsel or with an obstinate witness. An angry witness or accused usually sends a negative message to the judge or jury. While the witnesses may feel justified in their anger – and it may be legitimate anger – it is still damaging when exhibited in court. We never know the full story, the history, and background circumstances. We must reach our decision on our impression of the credibility of those who testify.

People who are angry lose credibility. We are less likely to give weight to the testimony of an indignant, argumentative or furious witness. That is because we know, through experience, that hot-tempered people are irrational and blame everyone but themselves for their problem. They are unable to see the other side; the only side is their side. They want instant gratification or approval of their own desires or beliefs to the exclusion of all else.

Road rage

Road rage is another example of uncontrolled anger. A few years ago, two young men on the western motorway, angered by another motorist and fuelled with alcohol, stopped and beat him to death. They were tried for murder but found guilty of manslaughter.

Farewell White Boy

"Fuck off, honky!" the angry, intoxicated young woman screamed outside the pub. "Get to hell out of my country and go back to where you bloody came from!"

"I'm from Auckland", said the angry, intoxicated pakeha youth.

"I don't mean Auckland, you turd. I mean England or Holland or wherever overseas."

"Well, you stupid bitch, why don't you bugger off to where you came from."

"I'm from here. This is our land."

"No, it's not. You lot came from Tahiti or Rarotonga or somewhere you are too thick to remember. Don't tell me to fuck off."

At that, she ran up to him and dropped him to the footpath with a massive king hit. She had a minor history of nuisance offending and no job. I gave her 75 hours of community work. I felt like reminding them both that we are all immigrants from East Africa. We are all boat people of one sort or another, and that as Paul McCartney tells us,[1] "Ebony and ivory need to live together in harmony". Instead, perhaps prudently, I said nothing.

Paua Plunderer

Manu Bay is a typically wild West Coast beach, near Raglan. The black, rocky coast may not be attractive to those who prefer golden sands, but it is well-known to surfers and those fishermen, who dive for paua or kina. Some overdo it. The claim that Māori are natural conservationists is no truer than most stereotypical tags pasted upon social groups.

Jake Wiremu Potaka, the accused in a jury trial, did not look to me like a conservationist. Apparently, he made a similar impression on the local honorary fisheries ranger, Mr Van Dijk.

As Potaka emerged from the sea with his bag of paua, Van Dijk approached and said that he wanted to ask a few questions. According to Van Dijk, the accused immediately became nasty and said:

"I don't give a fuck who you are. If you don't fuck off I'll stick this knife up your arse and slit you to the throat and chuck you in the sea."

He removed a knife from a sheath on his leg and held it in his right hand. He then said.

"I'll fuckin' do you. I'll fuckin' kill you. Now piss off."

Mr Van Dijk needed no second thought. Prudently, he took one look at the large, angry man threatening him with a knife and hastily retreated to his car. He then left and phoned the police.

---

[1] Written by him and performed with Stevie Wonder in 1983, it became a number one hit in USA, U.K. and elsewhere, but not in NZ.

"We all know that people are the same wherever we go
There is good and bad in everyone
We learn to live, we learn to give
Each other what we need to survive together alive."

The accused, of course, denied all this. He admitted to the jury that he didn't like fisheries officers. He also admitted having told the ranger to piss off. However, he said he did not have a knife and doesn't even own a knife. He called as his witnesses an 11-year-old nephew and another adult mate to confirm that he had no knife and to say that, although they were present, neither of them observed the incident in question.

For decades, there have been limits as to how many paua may be taken. Currently, for recreational divers, the limit is 10 paua per person per day. They also must reach a minimum defined size. It is illegal for divers to use scuba gear. They can only be caught by free divers.

The poaching of paua has been a significant clandestine illegal activity for many years. The meat is illegally exported and fetches high prices, particularly in Asia. Under our law, there is a special customary right for Māori to harvest more than the statutory limits, provided the molluscs are to be used for traditional feasts and festivities. There is an extensive global black market in the collection and export of paua meat. Fisheries officers, with the help of police, enforce the law.

There was a recent television program in New Zealand focusing on this topic. It is clear from contemporary sources, both in court and on television, that the poachers frequently react angrily, and sometimes violently, when apprehended with under-size or too many paua.

Patrolling fishery officers, with the backing of police, can issue on the spot infringement notices of between $250 and $500 for minor offences, such as having one or two more pāua than permitted. Over the last decade, legitimate exports have been worth between $35 and $50 million per annum. A paua industry Council was created some years ago to support and regulate the industry. In parts of Asia, dried paua can fetch between $500-$1000 per kilogram.

In May 2008, there was a major police and fisheries office operation in various parts of the North Island to detect and arrest criminals who were illegally taking and exporting paua. Many of the arrested men are recidivist offenders who have made good money from flouting the law and seriously damaging an important fisheries resource. 130 fisheries officers, supported by 70 police, arrested 65 individuals after an undercover investigation lasting well over a year. 35 motor vehicles and other equipment, including boats and scuba gear, were seized and forfeited to the Crown.

The addresses and summing up to the jury were speedy. The jury retired to consider its verdict at 11.15 a.m. They returned at 3.40 p.m. after a surprisingly long retirement.

I had no doubt at all that he blew his lid and threatened the complainant in the manner claimed. It all rang very true. The accused's evidence lacked credibility. While the jury was out, I heard that the accused had been asking representatives of Maatua

Whangai[1] to set up some supervision programme for him. So, he must have expected he would be found guilty, as indeed he was. This implies that he perjured himself by swearing on oath that prosecution witnesses were liars. Probably! But he may have been simply realistic enough to see that his chances of acquittal were thin.

After the guilty verdict, I found that he had four previous convictions for assaults and two convictions for threatening and refusing to comply with the requests of a fisheries officer! I sought a pre-sentence report with a view to anger management and a month later sentenced him to nine months imprisonment with anger management to follow. What he did was very frightening. More so because he threatened an enforcement officer. He hadn't learned from previous convictions for similar offending.

Forgiving Murder

One of the most remarkable instances of forgiveness is illustrated by the response of a former Australian army colonel, Sandy MacGregor, to the schizophrenic young man who murdered his three daughters. In 1987, the three daughters, 19-year-old twins Jenny and Kirstie and their 16-year-old sister Lexie, were at home on the north shore of Sydney. Richard Maddrell, a student obsessed with Jenny, whom he had met at university, knocked on the door. Maddrell declared his love for her and then shot her at close range. He then wounded Jenny's girlfriend, and then killed Lexie, and Kirstie. Maddrell was arrested but was acquitted of murder because it was clear that he was a paranoid schizophrenic and insane.

After the initial horror, trauma, and shock, Sandy MacGregor decided that if he was to retain his own sanity he needed to change his thinking by accepting what had happened, and forgiving Maddrell for his monstrous acts. He used a meditation technique he had been learning for a few years before his three girls were killed. The method involved tapping into the subconscious mind through meditation. I still have his book Piece of Mind, published in 1992. It dovetailed nicely with the Transcendental Meditation techniques I had been taught years before in Palmerston North. Those techniques were made worldwide by the Maharishi Mahesh Yogi and all the partners of my law firm, Fitzherbert, Abraham, Crossley & Evans did the programme in 1976.

Colonel MacGregor said that the technique taught him that if he remained bitter, angry and vengeful he would end up yet another victim. And that is what people have reiterated to me both in court and on the Parole Board. The ultimate forgiveness was when MacGregor visited Maddrell in prison and spoke to him. He said: "Richard

---

[1] Maatua Whangai is a Maori community-based social service provider which provides free assistance to Maori adversely affected by the justice system.

Maddrell, I unconditionally forgive you for the murder of Jenny, Kirsty and Lexie." He later wrote:

> *"I had to teach him that I wasn't condoning his actions or making the offence any the lesser. But I was bringing to mind the part of him that was in me. That was pretty emotional. I could hardly gasp out their names but at the end of it I felt euphoric, lighter, I felt the monkeys were off my back…*
> *I realised in meditation that hatred, anger and revenge will only make me another victim. That's when I started to work within meditation, acceptance, co-operation, unconditional love and forgiveness."*

Colonel MacGregor is clearly a cut above the ordinary. During the Vietnam War, he was the first anti-communist soldier to explore the Cu Chi tunnels. Instead of simply blowing up the complex and cramped passageways (as the US Army did), MacGregor and his men entered and mapped the tunnels, providing very valuable information about the Viet Cong and their tactics and supplies.

As commander of 3 Field Troop, he and his brave team of Australian army engineers defused thousands of Viet Cong booby traps. He was later awarded the Military Cross, and the US Bronze Star for his leadership and courage. Until 2015 he continued to write and lecture on his meditation technique and the need to forgive.

Sports Rage

Sports rage is a similar and equally disturbing example of unrestrained anger. Often it is not just the players who lose their temper, but fans, parents or other onlookers. Referees are often the victims, sometimes even killed. In Brazil, in 2013, a young referee of an amateur soccer game, sent off a player, who refused to leave. The player attacked the ref. The ref pulled a knife and fatally stabbed the player. Fans reacted insanely, invading the ground, and stoning the referee. Then they decapitated him, cut him in quarters and put his head on a boundary stake.

While in Samoa, I presided over a murder trial of three men who had bludgeoned to death the umpire of their cricket match. To my astonishment, they were acquitted of murder despite yelling "Kill him!" as they ran across the pitch and beat him to death with their lethal three-sided Samoan kilikiti bats. The jury told me they only found it was manslaughter "because he was such a bad umpire." The philosopher Emperor Marcus Aurelius of Rome summed it up: "How much more grievous are the consequences of anger than the causes of it."

Court Rage

I have witnessed several instances of aggression and anger in my courtroom. Often members of the public jeer at an accused or a witness. Once or twice punches were thrown. On only one occasion I was the target. A very large woman – a nutritional over-achiever – entered the dock draped with a grey prison blanket. She was dishevelled, purple-skinned, and either mentally disturbed or affected by drink or drugs. I deduced that under the blanket she was not wearing much. As the prosecutor was telling me that she had been smashing shop windows and cursing at passers-by, she suddenly bellowed at me and jumped right up on the wooden rail restraining her in the dock. That in itself was an extraordinary physical feat, given her size and condition. But there she was, suddenly a metre off the floor, eyeing me with wild anger. She then bent her legs as if to squat, and with another loud roar she launched herself at me on the bench. For an instant I could see myself ignominiously crushed to death by this agile colossus. But that was not my fate! The designers of courtrooms have had many centuries of practice. My bench was a carefully designed distance and height from her position on the dock rail. Her charge of the heavy brigade failed miserably: all she achieved was a painful belly flop onto the wooden floor of the courtroom. She was seized by the court orderly, helped to her feet, and dragged down to the cells looking terribly distressed. I adjourned the court. As they say, it ain't over till the fat lady springs.

The Jealousy Affliction

The defendant was tough, lean, and mean, and had just been released from prison after having competed intensive alcohol treatment, without much effect! His main line of defence was that as the child was his own flesh and blood, he was entitled to see her when and where he wanted. The fact that he had never contributed to the upkeep of the child was irrelevant. But the Family Court judge had recognised the man's dire alcoholism and aggression and properly granted a non-molestation order.

The defendant said his partner was intoxicated when she arrived home at 7:00 a.m. – "lushed up", he said. He denied the choking, the kick and the punches through the van window. Under cross-examination he admitted that he wanted to choke, kick and punch her and had threatened to do so. He was annoyed she had been to the pub "and started sculling lush".

He admitted ripping a pendant from her neck because "I was aggro – cos I thought some other guy had given it to her". Then she became upset and "started freaking out on me". He was sure some other guy must have inflicted the bruises noted by the police that night.

"She has a bad name, you know."

Jealousy is a terrible affliction. Usually produced by insecurity, low esteem and possessiveness, it warps the ability to think rationally and to see the reality of relationships

I sentenced the young man to six months in jail. He was caught by the Criminal Justice Act provision that requires imprisonment for people who use serious violence. He had previously twice breached the non-molestation order. He had cut up her clothes with a knife. He must have needed a lot of careful counselling before he finished his sentence.

Pool Rules

At Tairua there is only one hotel. It is an elderly hostelry called the Sir George Grey.[1] On the 16th August 1990, two young strangers appeared there. They said "Howdy" and they drank. They played pool. They had a dispute about whether there had been a "scratch on the break" (whatever that may mean!) and one suddenly stormed from the bar, went to their car, took out a shotgun and fired it into the air. This I took to indicate an unconventional protest to the breach of the pool rule.

Mr Douch, the prosecutor, asked one of the locals, a brawny truckie with mutton chop whiskers:

"What did you do when the gun was fired?"

He grinned at the appreciative jury and replied:

"I nearly shat myself!"

The jurors clearly empathised with him. They laughed. I laughed. The accused laughed, because he was not the man who fired the gun. It was his mate. The accused faced a charge of assaulting another hotel patron who had tried to calm things down. I convicted him and sentenced him to community work.

Killings at the Mount

Mount Maunganui[2] is a beautiful port and seaside resort where Suzanne and I lived for a year while we built a house across the harbour at Te Puna. The city is on a peninsula that fingers out to Mount Maunganui, a 232-metre extinct volcanic cone that dominates the landscape. The extinct volcano was an ideal location for Māori to build and occupy fortified villages with wide views, sea on three sides, steep cliffs, and abundant fish and shellfish to feed the occupants. Curiously, this historic and geographically significant landmark has been the scene of much bloodshed. Twice the incumbent Māori tribe was attacked, overwhelmed and ejected from its fortress. But it wasn't just Māori who did the killing. When I was living there, I was to deal with two madmen who killed on the mountain.

---

[1] Named for the tough-minded fellow, twice Governor, and once Prime Minister of New Zealand.

[2] Known by Maori as Mauao – "caught by the morning sun".

The first was the tragic rape and strangulation of Monica Cantwell, a 25-year-old English tourist who was killed on 20 November 1989. She was about to return to England after a short visit to New Zealand, having lived and worked in Australia for some time. She stayed the night at a local youth hostel and was dropped off by friends at the thermal swimming pools at the base of the mountain. It was her intention to walk the picturesque surf-washed track around the base of the mountain and then to climb to the summit to enjoy the amazing panoramic view. She had planned on re-joining her friends in the early afternoon. When she failed to appear, her friends reported her missing to the police and a search was undertaken. On the morning of 22 November, her body was found in regenerating native bush. She was only partially clad. Her clothing, handbag and shoes had been placed alongside her body. She had been raped and strangled.

She was killed by a 20-year-old Aucklander, Charles John Coulam, the adopted son of an Auckland lawyer. Before he left Auckland for Mount Maunganui, he had told a flatmate that he had planned something which involved rape and death.

He made a full confession to the police. He admitted killing the young woman and then swimming in the surf to clean himself. He caught a bus to Taupo under a false name. Learning of the murder from the media, the flatmate went to the police. The police located Coulam and he was arrested within hours. He appeared before me in the Tauranga District Court. I remanded him to a psychiatric hospital for a report. He was found to be a paranoid schizophrenic and insane. After many years in a mental hospital, he was transferred to a prison.

Several years later he appeared before my parole board panel. He was still an undue risk to the safety of the community. Since then he has appeared before the parole board several times but is still considered to be an undue risk.

I witnessed part of the second killing, although I didn't realise what was happening until the killer appeared in my court three days later. Suzanne and I were staying at her parents' beach house on Marine Parade, overlooking the main surf beach, when in the early morning of Boxing Day 1991 we saw a disturbance in the water just off the shore. Two men were splashing in the water. A small crowd gathered, wondering what was happening. Tragically, it was Donald Munro, a devout but psychotic Christian, baptizing his friend Graham Neil by holding him under the surf until he drowned. I remanded him for a psychiatric report. The police said that he had been trying to exorcise the Devil from his friend. He held Neil under the water with fatal results. There was no divine intervention. It seems that the Devil won. The accused also spent years in a mental institution. Despite some research, I've been unable to learn of his later life.

Uncontrolled anger

A frenzied anger response has put many men before me both in court and at the Parole Board. Many are angry if they do not get their own way. Nobody matters but themselves, and if they are thwarted by other people, employers, or the police, they react angrily often with instant, uncontrollable, sometimes fatal violence. Their distorted and often fragile sense of self-worth makes them hit out at anyone who challenges their "entitlement" to anything. They like to think they are powerful and in control when the reality is that they are mental and emotional weaklings, frightened cowards, very much out of control. The use of violence and aggression is their attempt to stay in control. Peel off the first layer of their onion and you find a weak, scared and sometimes depressed person who refuses to be accountable for his destructive behaviour.

Earless

A young man who had appeared before me briefly one day on an unrelated matter, appeared again the next day, charged with disfiguring his best friend at a party. There was a drunken fight. The defendant allegedly pulled a knife. There was a furious struggle during which the friend's ear was slashed off. Counsel said only part of the ear was cut off but the police said the lot.[1]

The police initially opposed bail because the defendant is still awaiting disposition and was on bail on an unconnected charge of throwing a full can of beer through the window of a passing car and hitting the woman motorist in the neck and injuring her. He had an obvious alcohol/drug problem, which he was already addressing, so I finally, with some concerned reluctance, agreed to bail him – but with a curfew and other restrictions. After a hearing, I sentenced him to three years imprisonment.

Slob

> *Yes, I did punch him. He really pisses me off. When we married, he was a handsome and helpful hunk. But now he is a fat, useless, unemployed, drunken slob. A pathetic husband and sad excuse for a father. I know I shouldn't have whacked him, but he drives me crazy."*

This colourful description by a frustrated wife was probably accurate, but she shouldn't have whacked him. I convicted and discharged her without penalty. Surprisingly, despite his negative attributes, she seemed to overlook his many faults, and they were still living together.

---

[1] There has been a similar debate about whether Vincent Van Gogh cut off his whole ear or part of it. It was actually the lower quarter of his left ear.

Teenage Truant

Disturbing, but far from a unique case: a man charged with assaulting his 14-year-old daughter with a vacuum cleaner hose. She ended up with bruises and welts and told a teacher at school what had happened. His young woman lawyer did a very good job cross-examining the 14-year-old. As the case unfolded it first looked as though Dad was some sort of brutal sadist. He was certainly a powerfully built man with triceps like Popeye the sailor. His daughter, the complainant, was a cheeky-looking teenager with an eye for the main chance. She told me her father lost his temper and assaulted her because she had not returned home at the correct time.

Under cross-examination, it was established that she was a very disobedient young girl. She finally admitted that she had:

(a) been playing truant on a regular basis – and at the time of the assault, unknown to her parents, had missed three consecutive weeks schooling.

(b) spent the previous four nights sleeping at a friend's home while her parents had been anxiously trying to find where she was.

(c) been sleeping with her 19-year-old boyfriend, a young man, whom her parents considered most undesirable.

The girl's body language gave her away. She pouted, she rolled her eyes heavenward, she jaunted her chin, and she almost stuck out her tongue at counsel. She was cheeky, rude, and was convinced that there was no justice in the world if her activities were to be curtailed in any way.

It is a common attitude of some teenagers that everyone is wrong but them, and she was a very good example of just how difficult some offspring can be during their adolescent years. After hearing her cross-examined, I called Sergeant Glover and Miss Taylor into chambers and explained that what was really necessary here was some counselling, if that could be obtained in her small rural community. I suggested that Popeye had certainly gone too far with the discipline, but that his overreaction in disciplining the girl was understandable given her quite insufferable behaviour.

Miss Taylor said that she was quite happy to have her client plead guilty now that the court had clearly seen his viewpoint. The sergeant agreed that a severe admonition would do the trick. I returned to court, convicted him and ordered him to come up for sentence if called upon within the next six months.

I warned him against using physical punishment (since 2007 it has been a crime to smack children, with the police having a discretion not to prosecute if the offence is considered to be inconsequential) and made some suggestions as to counselling. While I was talking, I noticed the girl totally ignoring me and chatting to a girlfriend in the back of the court. Angrily, I gave her a shot across the bows, and pointed out that her rudeness in not bothering to listen to me was symptomatic of her narcissism and lack of manners. Of course, I didn't put it in such complex words, but she was looking somewhat red-faced by the time I had finished.

Sibling Rivalry

I reduced the prison sentence of a man from the East Cape because the severe hiding he gave his sister had been partly provoked by her making racist comments about his European partner. It had happened before. He was very remorseful and had a positive pre-sentence report.

Up on the Cape there is no periodic detention centre. He was 30 years old, had very little work, and was on the dole along with just about everyone else in that remote region.

The Victim Impact Statement was interesting. His sister complained of bruises and sore ribs (he had punched and kicked her ten times) and angrily told the Constable,

> *"I hate his guts and have always hated his guts".*

This reaction raises an interesting issue of what we now call sibling rivalry. There are many reasons for antipathy between siblings. Ever since Cain and Abel fell out with each other, sibling rivalry has led to mayhem and even murder. Sometimes it starts with the arrival of a new baby. The older child feels threatened and supplanted by all the attention given to baby.

> *Why does my young brother get all the attention? Why am I disciplined and he isn't? They love him more than me, the little shit. They always say he is smarter, better behaved, and better looking. He is their favourite. The little bastard. Dad spends more time with him than with me. I bit him when Mum wasn't looking. He deserved what he got.*

As parents, we must be vigilant to ensure each of our children feel equally loved, respected and cherished. We must never play favourites, make comparisons, or typecast our children. We should give them equal time and affection, focusing on their individuality and special needs. It is sometimes hard to do because, like it or not, not all our children or grandchildren are as appealing as others.

Dylan Thomas[1] and his brother were better managed than Cain and Abel. Thomas said:

> *"It snowed last year too: I made a snowman and my brother knocked it down and I knocked my brother down and then we had tea."*

According to Karen Doherty and Georgia Coleridge, authors of *Sibling Rivalry: Seven Simple Solutions to Stop Fights, Prevent Jealousy and Help Your Children Get On Better*,[2] rivalry

---

[1] Welsh poet and writer, (1914 – 1953).

[2] London, Bantam Press, 2010.

is the rule, not the exception. "Four out of five siblings will torment, kick, punch, fight and annoy one another at some point during childhood." The trick is how to handle it without it turning homicidal.

In the case before me, the sister had been very provocative but he went over the edge. I noted with some concern that some years back he had been sentenced to three years' imprisonment for manslaughter. On inquiry, I was told it was as the result of a motor accident. I gave him 21 days' imprisonment with a stern warning to keep his temper under control.

Hitler, Stalin or Mao?

I have spent much of my adult life trying to comprehend how the three dictators of the 20th century committed such monstrous atrocities. They never faced a court of justice, but if they had the trials would have been prolonged and unbearable.

Putting deliberate starvation by famine to one side, some historians debate who was the worst. There is much argument about the numbers, but I nominate the Führer for his cold-blooded, genocidal, industrial murder of over 15 million Jews, Slavs, Gypsies, Homosexuals, Soviet Prisoners of War, and Germans who opposed his Nazi insanities. Stalin comes a close second with about 13 million executions, and deaths in the Soviet gulags. Chairman Mao Zedong was also a heartless murderer of an estimated 10 million Chinese citizens.

Our murderous human species seems disposed to use genocide to eliminate victims of targeted demographic groups seen as undesirable: Jews, Ukrainians, Armenians, Gypsies, American Indians, Tutsi, Kurds, Chechens, Tibetans, Tasmanian Aborigines, and even Moriori on the Chatham Islands.

And these are just genocides over the last two centuries. There were many more in ancient times. The Romans may have killed 100,000 and totally wiped out the Dacians, as commemorated very graphically on Trajan's column still to be seen in Rome. And 1200 years before the Dacians, the Israelites, with God's blessing or direction wiped out the Midianites[1] and Canaanites.

[1] Except for 32,000 virgins who survived as war booty

Holocaust

This word is first recorded by the ancient Greeks and ancient Israelites. In Greek, it means "sacrifice by fire." After the Second World War, and the horrifying exposure of the Nazi death camps, everyone knows the word.

Jews use the word Shoah - "catastrophe"- to specifically identify the murders of nearly six million Jews by the Nazis during that barbaric time.

A gentle friend of mine, Victor Ziegler[1], and his wife Lilli, survived the horrors of Auschwitz[2]. After the war, they emigrated to New Zealand and Victor became a greatly admired legal executive in Auckland. We had several unforgettable discussions about these dreadful events. I asked him why, especially as the Jews were said to be God's chosen people, God had not intervened to prevent such pure evil? Could any rational person, after such monstrosities, believe in God? Why did God not intervene to destroy Hitler and his evil legions?

Victor simply said "For me, God died in Auschwitz. If not, where was he?"

He explained this to me. He said that by saying this he was in no way abandoning his Jewish identity. He loved the culture, festivals, ethics, learning, dignity and history of his people. He saw striving for justice and equality as the key to the future for us all; a secular tikkun olam[3] that needed no belief in God.

I read of a Hasidic rabbi who was the only survivor of his large family. His wife and 11 children were all murdered. He was questioned.

"Why did miracles occur only during biblical times? Why don't they happen in our time?"

His extraordinary reply: "The fact that there are Holocaust survivors who, after all they endured, can still keep faith, is itself, the greatest miracle of all."

Given his status and faith, I assumed this was not tongue in cheek, but that he really meant what he said.

Since Victor's death, I have studied other Jewish answers to the same disturbing questions. I find most responses incomprehensible.

- The holocaust was punishment for the disobedience and faithlessness of the Jewish people or because of the emergence of Reform and other non-Orthodox forms of Judaism.

---

[1] Victor died in 1996.

[2] The largest and worst of the death camps where 1,200,000 murders were committed.

[3] Literally "repair of the world." It includes the concept of behaving in a kind and constructive way to everyone, Jew or non-Jew. Orthodox and other religious Jews see such behaviour as ordained by God; secular Jews see it as rational social justice.

- We humans have free-will to achieve good or evil. The Holocaust had nothing to do with God. It was all the fault of humans. God is just a passive onlooker.
- The Holocaust was necessary to enable Jews to wake up and better comprehend God's plan.
- It is wrong to question why God chose not to intervene or to challenge that decision. God knows best.
- God suffered in the death camps along with the human victims.
- God caused the Holocaust to stimulate Zionism so that the State of Israel could be born.
- Or the complete opposite: Zionism caused the Holocaust because it was wrong to create the State of Israel before the Messiah came to the world.
- God is not all-powerful and all-knowing, and thus incapable of stopping the slaughter of innocents.
- God does what he likes and answers to no one.

> *"All the peoples of the earth are regarded as nothing. He does as he pleases with the powers of heaven and the peoples of the earth. No one can hold back his hand or say to him: 'What have you done?'" (Daniel 4:3).*

These arguments are unconvincing, if not nonsensical. The reality is that the perfect, almighty Judge and Lawgiver ignored millions of innocent men, women and children, Jews and Gentiles alike. For Victor, God died in Auschwitz. For many, God did not die there; he had never lived.

Cruelty to Animals

Public Horror

Some years ago, a colleague of mine in Huntly dealt with a very nasty case of cruelty to animals. Two Huntly teenage boys were arrested for burning three feral cats to death. The cats had been caught in a council trap and the teenagers rode up on their bicycles and poured glue onto the cats. One ignited the highly flammable glue and both youths departed as the cats suffered a cruel and painful death. The actions of these sadistic delinquents were recorded on a hidden video camera in a shop window, and a clip from the recording was played on national television. When they appeared in court the two youths showed no remorse and laughed and postured before the cameras in court. Many members of their family were appalled.

Such bravado and perverse behaviour caused grave public disquiet. There was a suggestion that the boys had committed the awful crime in order to gain patch membership of the Black Power gang. The Black Power gang, however, immediately disassociated itself from the two boys, making it clear that while some of its members committed murders, rapes and robberies, cruelty to animals was contrary to their credo. In the event the youth who lit the glue received 2 years' imprisonment and his mate 9 months.

Starting with Animals

One disturbing feature of offenders who are cruel to animals, is that some of our worst killers have animal cruelty convictions before their murder offences. Often offenders who are cruel to animals have themselves been abused and neglected as children. Sometimes the perpetrators burn or torture animals with firecrackers, air guns or spray paint because they are disadvantaged people from dysfunctional families and have not developed empathy for anyone – animal or human.

In 2001, a study of school shootings in the USA found 45% of those murderers had a history of cruelty to animals. An earlier FBI study found a similar percentage in murderers generally. Studies of rapists and violent criminals also showed disturbing incidence of animal cruelty when the offender was a child or adolescent.

Martin Bryant, the young mass murderer who shot and killed 35 people in Port Arthur, Tasmania in 1996, was found to have tortured and harassed animals when he was seven years old.

Such animal cruelty is a strong predictor of later violent criminal offending.

Traffic Court

More people appear on traffic charges than any other. It is a very rare individual who drives for long without sin! Defendants in the traffic and police courts are cosmopolitan, multi-cultural, multi-ethnic and multi-national. No matter who they are, great or small, they are worried bilious at the prospect of losing their driver's licence. Avoiding such disaster leads to all manner of ruses, lies, expense and nonsense. The most common offences are driving under the influence of alcohol and speeding. Many are the excuses put to the judge in the hope that a light sentence will be imposed. Many of the excuses are fabricated or exaggerated.

Just a couple

A burly plumber, with a tell-tale ruddy face and a breath alcohol count of twice the permitted limit, solemnly told me he had only had two glasses of wine and could not comprehend how he was over the limit. I raised my judicial eyebrows and started to comment.

He quickly added: "Of course, Judge, they were mighty big glasses!"

Stick up

Another man, embittered at being charged with driving with excess breath/blood alcohol didn't answer his summons. He returned it to our court Registrar by post.

On it he scrawled: "You know where you can stick this!"

Stupid as…

I sentenced a tall, gangly, young man to 15 months' imprisonment on charges of driving in a dangerous manner, driving with excess breath alcohol, and driving while disqualified. At age 21, he already had six previous convictions for driving while disqualified and four for excess breath/blood alcohol. After a row with his wife, he drove like a maniac from his home and into the nearby Bridge Street intersection. He was so enraged that he didn't see the other car. A high-speed collision wrote off both cars and it was very lucky that serious injury or death did not occur.

Not waiting to see if that was the case, he decamped from the accident scene on foot. But drunken curiosity got the better of him later. He returned to the scene of the crime, was breath tested and found to have a level of 900 micrograms of alcohol per litre of breath. When spoken to, he said

"I was as stupid as..."

I didn't ask what the full simile was. He caused major damage to the other car. A report from the Auckland NSAD[1] suggested a 12-week term of inpatient treatment, as he clearly had a history of severe alcohol dependency. I told him I fully agreed with the submission made by his lawyer that such a course of treatment should be tried despite his apparent past lack of motivation. I also pointed out that treatment was not the only thing. Punishment is also part of the learning process. It is in the public interest to emphasise to him, and to others, that drunken and dangerous driving, and disobedience of court orders, must be dealt with in a robust way. Rehabilitation is one thing; deterrence and retribution are another.

Aussie Rules

An Australian seaman appeared on a charge of driving with excess breath alcohol. His name, unfortunate maritime denizen of the heads, was Crapper. He might even be descended from the famous inventor! He was found to have an alcohol level of only 325 micrograms of alcohol per litre of breath, which is below the usual limit point of 400. Unfortunately for Crapper, there is a special provision that drops the permitted maximum down to 150 where the driver is not the holder of a current or appropriate driver's licence. Seaman Crapper did hold a driver's licence. In fact, he had two. He held one from Western Australia and one from New South Wales. Both were valid at the time he was breath tested. He produced them to the Police the next day. The problem is that we only recognise Australian licences until the end of our own licensing year, and our year had expired at the time of his alleged offending. The breath alcohol reading was accepted, and I heard brief evidence as to whether the defendant honestly and reasonably believed he held a current licence. I believed him. While the legal position was against him, I ignored the strict rules in the interest of trans-Tasman brotherhood, and let him off.

Hard lesson

A man in his mid-twenties – barrel-chested, pleasant-looking – came into court on crutches on his second excess breath/blood alcohol charge. Last year he received a heavy fine for a similar offence. His sentence should have been periodic detention this time, but his drinking caused a collision in which he lost his right leg. He also lost his job. No one else was hurt. An irreversible lifelong lesson learnt. Convicted and disqualified for 12 months.

---

[1] New Zealand Society on Alcohol and Drug Dependence.

Guinness Record

A 26-year-old man pleaded guilty to his 19th charge of driving while disqualified! I asked him if he was trying to get into the Guinness Book of Records. On an earlier conviction, another judge gave him a three-year prison term. But the last two or three sentences were for lengthy periods of periodic detention, working for the community. The man has no other criminal record; his only sin was his obsession for driving! I gave him my usual "grow up and be a mature adult not a teenager" lecture (which usually goes in one ear and out the other) and told him I had reached the stage where I had no idea what to do with him. Everything had been tried. Even the recent three-year jail term hadn't worked. I first asked him whether he wanted to say anything. He gave me a pleasant smile and simply said it was his intention to give up driving.

"Yeah, right!" I thought.

I commenced my sentencing by staring at him, looking down at my papers, banging my stamp down, while saying in a loud reproving voice:

"Five years."

I intoned it again: "five years" ... [Lengthy pause. Defendant's Adam's apple rises perceptively, and his eyes widen] "…is the maximum term of imprisonment provided by law for subsequent offences of this type. The maximum is always reserved for the worst possible case of its type. This is one of those cases." [Pause] "But I have decided in your case..."

A bit mean of me, but the shock tactic might have some impact and stick between his ears at least for a while. I sentenced him to 12 months' imprisonment, with a further six months' disqualification. It seemed a waste of money and prison resources to give him longer.

At dinner that night, I asked my wife Suzanne and my good friends and neighbours what they would have done. Ingrid Thomas, a senior hospital administrator, said "Five years!"

Her husband, Richard Thomas, years ago a prison officer, said: "Make him work, forever, if necessary, for the elderly – in the community."

Suzanne agreed with Richard that it was pointless to waste the taxpayers' money by locking him up. Who is right?

Fitness

A striking, fit, young athlete (an instructor at a fitness centre) was stopped in her car for weaving across the highway. She and a girlfriend had been to a party. She was well up on the Richter scale. She was given a summons and warned not to drive for 12 hours. Her friend drove the car away from the police station. Thirty minutes later, the same officer saw the car again, with the defendant once more behind the wheel! The friend had driven to her own home and the defendant had announced that she was fit to drive the rest of the way. She must have a short memory or have been buoyed up by the bubbly. Her friend had warned her not to drive, but alas! Her second breath test showed a slightly lower score. I told her I would give her a "bulk discount"- $500 on the first charge, $600 on the second, and 8 months' disqualification on both.

Killed his cousin

Peter Verano was a miserable, scrawny, young fellow trying to grow a wispy, unhappy excuse for a moustache and beard. His arms had been mutilated with ugly, inelegant, inartistic tattoos that will horrify his mortician. He was facing miscellaneous traffic matters, including a charge of dangerous driving causing death. He had been arrested on a warrant, having failed to appear on a remand date. In the meantime, he had allegedly committed a burglary of business premises and had been charged with that as well. His counsel pleaded for me to grant him bail for a week with an intimated plea of guilty then. He had a sick child and was soon to marry. (How any young woman could overlook his hideous tattoos I cannot comprehend. He must have an appealing personality or a huge income, and neither were apparent.)

The person killed in his car was his cousin, so he had to make the peace with members of his extended family. A month later, having read the probation report, I sentenced him to six months' periodic detention and 12 months' supervision.

Feel good

A young man, from that village of the delightful name, Bunnythorpe[1], was caught driving while disqualified. When asked why he had done it, he replied: "Because it felt good!"

The fact summary, written by an officer who should perhaps have expressed himself with more felicity, went on to say: "The defendant was then observed to have had his left arm amputated."

Which, there on the side of the road, even with the anaesthetic effect of 990 micrograms of alcohol per litre of breath, would certainly not have "felt so good"! But further enquiry showed he had lost his arm two years before in a forestry accident.

[1] Named after Henry Bunny, a Wellington Provincial Councillor, who purchased land in the area in the 1850s. In 1904, the Nathan family from Wellington built a milk powder factory there. A fire destroyed the factory two years later. It was rebuilt, but a stick of gelignite blew up the boiler shortly after the re-build. John Gillies, a competitor, was arrested and tried for wilful damage. The jury acquitted him. The milk powder produced at the factory was named Glaxo and became a renowned product in the UK. Many decades and mergers later, the descendant is GlaxoSmithKline a multinational pharmaceutical corporation employing 100,000 people and worth $NZ160 billion.

It is routine for some judges to give a stern lecture to drink drivers in the vain hope that others in the court room, or reading the court news in the local paper, will take the message aboard and learn a lesson. My experience is that such pulpit-banging is usually a waste of time and the judge's words mean little to most defendants or the public at large. All the defendant wants to hear, is how long or how much he or she is going to get. Every year, in the less serious cases at least, I found I was saying less and less, knowing that my comments were only of relevance for appeal purposes.

But in 1979, I was only in the second of my 35 years on the bench and was prone to over-exuberant and unnecessarily verbose judicial diatribes. Sometimes I look back on my comments and cringe with embarrassment. My remarks were to a motorist who was appearing for the second time on a drink-drive charge. His alcohol level was high. I have changed his name, because on the day in question I was the idiot, not him. Many people in the back of the court started laughing during my diatribe. They were laughing at me, not at the Defendant. I couldn't think why they were laughing. Later, I saw the written record and understood why. This is the relevant part:

> *"You have just got to get it into your head, Mr McHooch, that if you value your driver's licence and your job you must not drink and drive. This is a lesson and a sermon we preach daily in these courts. It is a sermon that may have something to do with the fact that there are well over 100 people alive*
> *on New Zealand roads this year who were dead this time last year. And that is what it is all about."*

I was the idiot, and it reminded me of Casey Stengel's[1] classic line:
"A lot of people of my age are dead at the present time."

Final adjournment

Fortunately, it is often not me, but the offender, who shows stupidity. It is very common in December for defendants in the traffic court to try to put cases off until late January. This enables them to put off the evil day of disqualification, and enables them to drive over the festive holiday season.

This story isn't humorous. It is tragic, although the hapless defendant thought he was funny and a winner. In December, the young fellow had successfully conned a judge into such an adjournment. He walked out of court beaming. A court clerk heard him say to his mate:

---

[1] Charles Dillon "Casey" Stengel, was an American Major League Baseball manager.

"The silly old bastard believed me!" he laughed. "There's a sucker born every minute."

Indeed, there is. The young man never made it before me on the adjourned date in January. He was killed in his car on New Year's Eve while driving from a party. His blood alcohol limit was over twice the limit. Had he been disqualified in December; he would still be here.

Race day

Alcohol is seductive. Drunk drivers take risks and do not think of the consequences of conviction upon their family or job. One traffic court day I had 33 drunk drivers appear before me! One of those was a very worried jockey appearing on his third drink/drive offence. He was distraught about being ordered to do periodic detention, because Saturday is the usual big horse-race day and a sentence of periodic detention would prohibit him from riding on most race-days and affect his occupation and income. His last conviction was five years ago, so I accepted his counsel's plea and fined him $1,500 and disqualified him for 15 months instead. Prison next time.

Different strokes

Our drink-driver reimprisonment rate is about 34%, which shows that many people don't get the message. 154 people in New Zealand were killed by drink drivers in 2017. But, interestingly, more people were killed by drink drivers *under* the legal limit than were killed by drivers over the limit. The total number of road deaths was 378. In the USA in 2017, 10,874 people died in drink-driving crashes – one every 48 minutes – and more than 300,000 were injured.

Our penalties are modest compared to some other countries: In Turkey, drivers are taken 30 km out of town and made to walk back. In Malaysia, the driver is jailed and so is the spouse! In the Russia, drunk drivers are disqualified for life. In Japan, all passengers in the car are liable if the driver is drunk - as accessories to the crime. In Poland, those convicted are required to attend several political lectures. In Norway, offenders are sentenced to three weeks in jail, with hard labour. In Saudi Arabia, offences are punishable by lashes in the public square. In South Africa, they are fined $10,000 and/or a ten-year prison sentence. The bottom line is that drink-driving causes massive di stress and loss of lives. A sober friend, taxi, bus, or train can prevent that.

Blast

A sign of the times: A young man did not hear the siren on the patrol car because he had his car stereo turned up so loud it just about decapitated the constable when the driver's window was wound down!

Dying for a drink

When the drink/drive legislation based on blood testing was introduced in 1968, the New Zealand Parliament nominated 80 milligrams of alcohol per 100 millilitres of blood as the test of whether a motorist was materially impaired by alcohol consumption to the extent that they should not drive. Scientists resolutely declared that the courts would not have to worry about people with levels much in excess of 280-300 milligrams of alcohol per 100 millilitres of blood, because at about that point the individual would have died of alcohol poisoning.

The Herald reported a decision from the Auckland Coroner's court, where the coroner Stephen Osborne found that a 16-year-old youth had died of alcohol poisoning after heavy drinking of straight spirits at a party. His alcohol level was 338 milligrams of alcohol per 100 millilitres of blood.

However, standing before me one day was living proof that for every rule there is an exception. Death did not intervene to prevent this attractive, well-dressed, hotel manager from driving. Her score was 336 milligrams of alcohol per 100 millilitres of blood. This is the highest blood alcohol level I can ever remember being mentioned in my court. But there was more to come.

"She has previous convictions, Sir", said the Prosecutor.

I was handed up the computer print-out. She had four previous convictions; all for excess breath alcohol. The last three scores were, respectively, massive counts of 1100, 1250, and 1183 micrograms of alcohol per litre of breath. All of which resulted in the defendant being indefinitely disqualified. As is probably obvious, she had also been convicted of driving while disqualified. She was also appearing before me on such a further charge. I remanded her back to her home in Wellington for a further probation report and for sentence. She was dealt with there and given a lengthy prison term.

Femme fatale

Achieving notoriety after her arrest for drink-driving (with two small children in the car) was a young mother who had one of the highest alcohol scores recorded in court – 1568 micrograms per litre of breath (nearly four times the 400-mg legal limit for adults). She must have consumed the equivalent of 25 standard drinks or more. Oblivious to the danger to her two little ones, she was swerving into other lanes and driving off the shoulder of the road. I sent her away for a pre-sentence report. She was clearly an alcoholic. She had no prior convictions. I placed her on probation for 2 years, sentenced her to 6 months home detention, and disqualified her from driving for 2 years.

In 2006, a female Auckland schoolteacher was convicted of driving with a breath-alcohol level of 1583 micrograms per litre of breath, and two other women were caught driving with alcohol levels which surpassed the 2000 mg maximum limit of breath-testing equipment. A woman from Dunedin blew over 2000 mcg and a blood test recorded 426 milligrams per litre of blood, almost five times the legal limit of 80 mg. Three months later, a Tauranga woman was convicted of driving with an identical blood-alcohol level. You would not want to stand next to them with a lighted match!

Drinking the Max

We think we have problems but, compared to the Russians, we are not even in the race. In 2012, I noted an article from Moscow reporting official statistics that showed 23,000 Russians die of alcohol poisoning annually, with 500,000 deaths from alcohol-related diseases, crimes, accidents and illnesses. Rospotrebnadzor, a Russian consumer advocacy group, estimates there are more than 2 million alcoholics in Russia.[1] Drunk drivers killed 2,103 people that year, compared to 57 people being killed by terrorists. About 30,000 people die annually on Russian roads, often due to alcohol consumption by motorists. This contrasts with British statistics, where a similar 30,000 people died on Britain's roads, but that was over a full decade between 2000 and 2010.

Some Russian MPs are seeking life imprisonment for drunk drivers, following public outcry over a drunk Muscovite who, speeding at 200 kilometres per hour, lost control and smashed his car into a bus shelter in Moscow, killing seven people, including five teenage orphans. The offender, named Maximov, had been drinking solidly for two days. Maximov was sentenced to the maximum of 9 years' imprisonment. Here, he would have faced a manslaughter charge and probably have received a life sentence, or very close to that.

Millions

This may seem like fake news, but it is not. Across the planet, well over a million people die on the roads each year (2,750 each day) and over 20 million others are seriously affected by road traffic accidents. Road crashes are the leading cause of death among young people ages 15-29. Each year nearly 400,000 people under 25 die on the world's roads, on average over 1,000 a day. Road traffic accidents are thought to cost roughly USD $500 billion globally. Over 37,000 Americans die in road crashes each year

---

[1] Russia has a population of 145 million (2019)

Exhaustion

Some years ago, the media reported on my state of "judicial exhaustion" in sentencing a man on his 19th charge of driving while disqualified, and another example was the case of a large, grotesquely tattooed, Black Power gang member, 29, before me on his 18th conviction. I also gave him 12 months' jail time.

Just before sentencing, his little daughter, aged about three, ran up to him in the dock calling "Daddy!" His lawyer seized on this tender moment of childhood affection by egregiously submitting that this unrehearsed display of infant love showed how much his client cared for his daughter. My immediate riposte was that if he really cared for his daughter, he might like to think about the impact his frequent offending and many terms of imprisonment was having on the little girl, and that his irresponsibility proved just the opposite. The defendant scowled angrily at me, but at least it might slowly dawn on him that he is not the wonderful, loving parent he and his lawyer would have me believe!

Artistic licence

A cunning young man was charged under an obscure section of the Transport Act with falsely displaying a certificate purporting to be a car registration sticker (Maximum fine: $500). He had used ink on last year's blue registration sticker, and then over the blue he had carefully painted brown - this year's colour. He had also amended the year. But, unlike Han van Meegeren,[1] his masterpiece was sufficiently flawed to be noticed by the local constable. He was lucky that he wasn't charged with forgery (Maximum: 10 years imprisonment).

The case illustrates the point that not everyone can afford to re-register their cars. The current annual fee (2018) to register a private motor car is over $250.00.[2] The cost of a warrant of fitness is $63.00 (payable 6 monthly for cars over 3 years old.) Given that the dole for a person under age 24 with the maximum additional accommodation benefit is $368.00 per week, the reality is that unemployed young people simply cannot afford to run a car or motorcycle. Fuel, maintenance, and tyres are all additional costs!

---

[1] The Dutch Master forger of Vermeer paintings who was tried for collaboration with the Nazis in 1947. He pleaded guilty, but because he had successfully defrauded Herman Goering, he was sentenced to only one year in prison. He never served the sentence. He died of a heart attack two months into his sentence. It is estimated he made (in today's dollars) about $20 million from his forgeries.

[2] Large motorcycles(over 601cc) $586.

No problem

I gave a surly and stupid young man 15 months' imprisonment on his sixth drink/drive charge. All five previous offences were within the last 18 months! He had been remanded for a probation report and substance abuse assessment. He refused to have anything to do with the local NSAD representative, and told the probation officer: "Alcohol is no problem to me!" He is Churchillian in his belief that he has taken more out of alcohol than alcohol has taken out of him.

He is like the alcoholic I had before me in Auckland who gave me a toothless smile when I observed that alcohol was causing him problems. He replied: "It's not the alcohol that causes me problems. It is the lack of alcohol that does that!"

I didn't care much for what he thought. My job is to protect other road-users from the awful carnage caused by drunk drivers.

Why do we break the law by speeding?

Because we enjoy the thrill of speed, are running late, want to show off, see speed limits as a challenge, want to race the other driver, don't think speeding is a serious offence, are in a bad mood, are in a good mood, didn't see the road sign, had one drink too many, don't think we'll get caught, think we have a right to drive as we please, think we are superb drivers, hate being stuck behind a slow driver, didn't notice our speed creeping up, want to keep surgeons, therapists and undertakers in gainful employment, or are psychopathic maniacs.

Mohawk

I remanded a young man for a report on his 4th driving while disqualified charge. I advised him to get a lawyer, as he would need one to save him from prison. He was caught the very day after I had given him 6 months' periodic detention for the same thing. Is it stupidity? Is it risk-taking? Is it that he couldn't care less? He was a heavily tattooed, bearded, 24-year-old, with a Mohawk haircut, and a ring in his nose. He would have sent a chill down the spine of Hiawatha, and sent Minnehaha scurrying for a tepee.

Reckless

A very bad example of reckless driving was that of a first offender defendant, aged 23, who pleaded guilty. He overtook a patrol car at 122 kmph in a Mitsubishi at Ngatea. The traffic officer activated both flashing red and blue lights and siren and gave chase. At the Canal Bridge, on a completely blind right-hand bend, the defendant pulled to the wrong side of the road and overtook a slower car at 140 kmph (87 miles per hour). He stayed on the incorrect side of the road for 200 metres. The patrol car pulled alongside but had to pull back to avoid an oncoming car. The defendant failed to stop. The chase continued for several kilometres, still at 140 kmph and with the defendant often on the incorrect side of the road. At the intersection with the main highway No 2 (past the Hauraki Golf Club), the Mitsubishi mounted the traffic island and demolished all the road signs. The defendant then braked hard, slid sideways through the intersection, and continued towards Auckland at 120 kmph. Oncoming cars were forced to take evasive action by pulling off the road.

In order to save his own skin, the traffic officer pulled back. He told me over 30 cars had to swerve to avoid a head-on collision. Every right-hand bend was negotiated on the wrong side of the road.

But the collision with the road signs had caused problems. By the time the defendant reached the Red Fox Tavern,[1] the Mitsubishi was smoking badly, and its speed started to slowly decrease until it finally juddered to a standstill outside the Mobil Service Station at the western end of Maramarua. There, the Mitsubishi was lost to sight in a huge cloud of smoke and steam. The defendant emerged. He was arrested at 2:00 p.m. He was unemployed, and driving his parent's car. The car was seriously damaged. His parents were not amused.

The traffic officer told me it was the worst driving he had seen over his career of 20 years. The defendant's parents were present in court. They were equally appalled. Interestingly, the young man had been sober. It seems he had panicked when he saw the patrol car. Why? Because he only had a learner's licence and was worried what his folks would think. I know what they now think…

I remanded him for a report. I should have sought a psychiatric report! Madness! Motorcar Mania! A month later I sentenced him to 9 months' periodic detention and disqualified him for 2 years.

Flat out

A 21-year-old – driving with 1600/400 micrograms of alcohol per litre of breath– four times the legal limit - fell flat on his face when he got out of the car for breath testing. He didn't move again until he blew into the Evidential Breath Tester 20 minutes later!

---

[1] Where, in October 1987, the proprietor Chris Bush was murdered in a $20,000 robbery. It took 30 years to catch the two alleged killers. They are currently awaiting trial.

Insurance

A stroppy, wild-eyed young man became quite nasty when I remanded him for a reparation report. He had tried a wheel spin in his car at Mount Maunganui, lost control, and smashed through a block wall fence, causing an estimated $3,500 in damage.

"Why should I have to pay for that?" he asked with a truculent smirk.

"Because you damaged it," I responded.

"But isn't the owner insured?"

"That is irrelevant. Even if there is insurance, you have to make good the damage you did. Why should the insurance company pay? That just increases the insurance premiums the rest of us have to pay."

He was in employment. I made him pay the lot – and a fine. And removed his driver's licence for 12 months.

Slow learner

A headstrong young delinquent, who I sentenced to seven months' periodic detention for his 3rd driving while disqualified conviction, was caught again two days later driving up the street by a neighbour who is a police officer. He said he was just checking his car out because his wife is expecting their second child within a few weeks. Unfortunately, he won't be attending the birth. He will be in prison for four months. I pointed out that he should have had more consideration for his wife and family, as I am sure she will not be happy that the father of her child is so brainless.

Timber!

An elderly motorist had a lucky escape as he was driving across the Maungatapu causeway on a bright and pleasant morning. A young Swedish exchange student was in the passenger seat.

Suddenly, a long wooden 4"x 2" cut timber plank shattered the windscreen and struck the driver on the head and chest. He was temporarily blinded but managed to keep his wits about him and keep his car from plunging into the estuary. Both him and his young passenger were hurt, but thankfully, not seriously.

The defendant was the driver of a large articulated truck and trailer unit that was heading towards the wharf at Mount Maunganui. The injured car driver was proceeding in the opposite direction. It was contended by the prosecutor that the wooden plank was from a kiwi-fruit pallet being carried on the rear of the trailer. The driver acknowledged that he was probably passing the complainant at the time of the accident although he was unaware of any problem with his load. No one actually saw what happened, including the car driver and his young Swedish companion. It was all a question of what proper inferences could be drawn from the available facts. The prosecution case was not helped by the fact that a thoughtful bystander threw the timber into the estuary tide. An examination of the kiwi fruit pallets showed them all to be securely fastened with draw-straps, but that one pallet had one board missing. It looked as if it had been missing for some time because the remaining timbers were aged and dark.

The charge was one of driving with a load not properly secured. I had to be satisfied beyond reasonable doubt:

(a) That the load was not secured properly;

(b) That the wood had come off the pallet on the defendant's truck.

It was unlikely that the wood had come from the two other vehicles passing about that time (a tarpaulined truck and a horse float), but there was simply insufficient direct and compelling evidence that the plank was off the defendant's truck. To convict him would have been to resort to speculation. Suspicions, yes. But the load was secured even if one piece of timber had inadvertently blown off in the wind. A stray timber from some other source may have been on the road and have been thrown up into the front on the complainant's car. I found the defendant not guilty and expressed my pleasure to the elderly driver that he had survived, and that I hoped he had purchased a Lotto ticket. His reply, which rather threw me, was that it was more like Lotto being in Court. From his demeanour, I couldn't tell whether that was an indication that he thought I lived in fairyland and that all my decisions were based on the flip of a coin!

Stung

O'Meagher, a craggy and cork-screwed 60-year-old sickness beneficiary had just enough left in his welfare benefit envelope to drive from Morrinsville to Puriri to drink two jugs of beer and four Bacardi Rums over three hours. Before he left in his utility vehicle, he wisely ate two meat pies. He told me a wasp had stung him three times above the collar line and he had lost control of his ute on Puriri Station Road. He hit a farm fence and had to be cut out of his car by a farmer. He said that, while waiting to be rescued, he opened a fresh bottle of Bacardi and drank 2/3 of the 40-ounce bottle. He admitted swearing at the farmer because the farmer seemed more concerned over the fence than about him. drinking after an accident is no defence. I convicted, fined and disqualified him for a year because of his high blood alcohol reading.

Last race

A somewhat haunted, grey-skinned, liverish horse trainer of 35, with a hoarse voice[1] appeared on his fourth excess breath/blood alcohol charge – with a blood alcohol concentration of 317 milligrams of alcohol per litre of blood! This was the highest I had seen for quite a while (for me, although not perhaps for him!). A substance abuse report clearly showed alcoholism. I sent him to residential alcohol treatment and disqualified him for 2 years.

Vampire

Tony Balme defended a 22-year old former navy gunner named Caine on charges of refusing to allow a blood specimen be taken, and possession of cannabis oil. His client had the style and good looks that Hollywood seeks these days. He was a young man with an affable personality and was not cowed by authority. He asserted his views in a forthright fashion. He had been arrested just after midnight for assaulting the proprietor of the Hong Kong Chinese takeaway bar for insisting on pre-payment. He was affected by liquor.

Constable Corbett took him to the police station after a roadside breath test proved positive. There, young Citizen Caine said he didn't want to undergo a breath test. He said he wanted a blood test, and the constable telephoned "the vampire" to come to take the blood specimen. The vampire was Mrs. Nabney, wife of Police Sergeant Bill Nabney,[2] who prosecuted in my court. She was a qualified laboratory technician and was authorised to take specimens under the provisions of the Transport Act.

She made a mistake. She didn't bring any identification with her. The defendant took one look at the petite and smartly dressed lady and asked her for her identification. He had been warned in the navy never to give blood to a stranger. Who knows whether the needle might be contaminated with AIDS? Both Constable Corbett and Mrs. Nabney took quite some pains to explain her status to him. She offered to go home and get her I.D. The constable told her not to, and that he would simply charge the defendant with refusing to provide the specimen of blood.

Citizen Caine was undeterred. He said that he was quite happy to give a sample but first wanted to be satisfied that she was who she said. After all, doesn't a policeman have to show his police card or badge of authority? Tax men and dog rangers, too? But this logic fell on deaf ears. He was arrested, searched, and found to have a capsule containing an oily blackish green substance later proving to be cannabis oil. The

---

[1] Hoarse Whisperer?

[2] He later qualified in law and is still in Tauranga, practicing as a highly regarded criminal defence barrister.

defendant became heated. He leapt to his feet in the holding cell and rather colourfully exclaimed: "You slimy cunt, you planted that there!"

That was grossly unfair, uncouth and unreasonable, but it did show his immediate and instinctive reaction to the find, and I felt he was genuine when, in his sober testimony in court, he absolutely denied any knowledge of the capsule and vigorously explained that he did not take dugs of any sort. Tony Balme relied on *MOT v Goodgame* [1986] 2CRNZ, in which a man refused to believe that a little chap in sun hat, shorts and jandals was a medical practitioner. Provided the belief was honestly held, it could be a defence. Mr Goodgame was believed. I would also have believed Mr Goodgame, because I have looked sideways at many young doctors who appear in court looking like hippies, insurance clerks, used car salesmen, disbarred solicitors, or fruit pickers from the Hawkes Bay.

It would be much simpler if they "looked" the part. I found Caine not guilty.

Smart Alec

Alec, a trade union official was not mean-spirited, selfish, or nasty. He was just obstructive, arrogant, verbose and impossibly difficult. He was the sort of fellow who would make any normal non-judicial human being feel like punching him in the nose! He was speed-checked in Cameron Road, Tauranga with the Hawk Radar. The officer followed him down a private driveway. And there the fun started

The case went like this. The officer asked the defendant for his name and address. He received no reply. He asked to see the man's driver's licence.[1] The defendant rapidly flashed it in front of the officer so fast no one without the Krypton factor could have read it. When testifying, he said in his broad East London accent: "He asked to see it. He saw it. He didn't ask to read it. If he had asked to read it, I would have let him."

The officer then twice repeated his request. He warned that a refusal to answer could result in his arrest.

Alec replied "Don't take me on, Sonny."

The transcript of the defendant's evidence makes interesting reading:

> *He just approached and said, "Why didn't you stop?" I just opened my licence and closed it quickly twice. At least he could see I had a licence. He then asked for my name and address. I*

---

[1] It is an offence to not "produce a driver's licence for inspection without delay after being required to do so by an enforcement officer." All drivers must also give a properly identified officer "their full name, full address, date of birth, occupation, and telephone number, or such of those particulars as the enforcement officer may specify, and give any other particulars required as to the person's identity."

said, "Why, are you arresting me?' He said, "No." He asked me my job. I said, "Union official." He said – "One of those commie bastards eh". I said, "Yeah and you are the sort that gets right up my nose when I have to defend you". I said "I want to know what my rights are? Are you arresting me?". "No", he said. He asked if I had been drinking. I said, "A couple of glasses of wine an hour or two ago." He said, "Now I know why you are performing the way you are". He poked his nose right into my face and said, "Make my day and have a poke at me". I didn't come down in the last shower. I said, "Take your uniform off and I might take you up on it". He said, "Forget the uniform have a go at me."
I got into his patrol car. He took off his cap and said "Now I've got you, you bastard!" So, I jumped out of the car. I said, "I'm not refusing you, but I want a witness and I want to get advice from my solicitor". He never said why I was meant to be going to the station. I wasn't under arrest at that point. After that he did put me under arrest. He didn't tell me the consequence of that such as that I would be entitled to bail. He said if that's the case I'll get someone else and he went on his radio-telephone. Several patrol cars arrived – police. A police officer said, "Smart arse eh?" - with reference to me being a union officer.
I was arm-locked and forced into the patrol car. He said nothing during the trip to the station. At the station, they asked me my name and address. I said, "I'm not refusing to give my address but I want to know my rights and I want to speak to my solicitor." There was a sign with arrested persons' rights on them, so I started reading them and an officer tore them down. I then phoned my solicitor. He advised me to take a breath test. The police said they now wanted a blood test. I was then asked for my name and address and I gave it in full. The officer then asked if I had a middle name and I said, "I have just given it to you".

This transcript is fairly typical of what we hear during defended traffic cases. People fail to realise that by resisting and being abusive to the police they simply dig themselves a much bigger grave. Bloody minded people get into bloody awful trouble. Why do people hold to their beliefs so stubbornly and resist any attempt by others to consider other more sensible considerations? A month later, after considering written submissions, I convicted the defendant. I preferred the evidence of the officer and found he was acting within the law. I imposed a substantial fine.

Lies, all lies

Johnny Pirana is a dangerous and surly young man who looks like old photos of the prophet Rua.[1] He was charged with dangerous driving. He was unrepresented. I could not understand why he defended the charge. After the first police officer had testified to a crazy car chase around the residential streets of his town at speeds in excess

[1] Rua Kenana Hepetipa was a long-haired Māori prophet, faith healer and land rights activist. He called himself the "New Messiah" and he built a new community in the heart of the isolated Urewera bush country. In 1916, police mounted an armed expedition to arrest Rua for sedition. He was acquitted but imprisoned for resisting arrest.

of 120 kmph with flashing lights and screeching sirens, I asked Johnny if he wished to ask the officer any questions. He grunted in the negative.

I then pointed out to him that unless he challenged any part of the officer's evidence with which he disagreed then I would be likely to accept the evidence as accurate and reliable. He then growled the words "He's a Liar!"

I repeated my advice that he tackle the witness over anything he thought was a lie. He just folded his arms and stared back at me with dark angry eyes. The second officer in the patrol car then gave very similar evidence. I again asked Johnny if he wished to cross-examine the witness. He said nothing. That was the conclusion of the police case, so I then asked the defendant if he wished to give evidence. He said "Nah!"

I asked if he wished to call any witnesses. He shrugged the negative. I then pointed out that unless he gave evidence, I would be obliged to decide the case solely on the unchallenged evidence of the two policemen and that he might think it sensible to tell me his side of things from the witness box. He said he wouldn't. So, I gave my decision, found him guilty, fined him $600.00 and disqualified him from driving for 6 months. I pointed out that he had really wasted everyone's time by not putting forward a defence or challenging the police. He then got very nasty with me. He stood up and said, "I told you my defence. He's a liar."

He is a nasty, frightening bit of work. Some years back, he received a sentence of eight years' imprisonment for raping and sodomising a woman. Some other members of his family have equally bad reputations. A court clerk tells me the name is notorious at the local High School where family members have been wilful, dishonest, and obstructive three generations.

Motorbikes

My mother never wanted me to have a motorcycle. I ended up with a NSU Prima motor scooter instead. Mum and Dad bought it for me while I was at University. I think they mistakenly felt that if I fell off the scooter I would be bruised and possibly broken but not killed. I doubt they were clear with the concept.

We mourned for Ross Blair, a son of one of our dearest friends – Mary Blair – from Matamata. Ross was killed on Saturday, 8 March 2014, after colliding with a truck that had negligently pulled out of a side road in front of him. Aged 45, he left a wife and four children. Suzanne and I drove down to the funeral on Friday, 14 March. It was a secular service held at the Manawaru Hall in Shaftesbury Road, 13 km south of Te Aroha. There was a very large crowd. I am not good at assessing crowd numbers, but I would guess at least 500 and 600 people. Apart from some elderly people like me wearing suits, most of the congregation were very casually dressed and there were many "bikers". None were gang members. All were men who enjoyed riding motorcycles. When the hearse left to drive to Te Aroha for a private cremation, all the men on bikes revved their growling engines and followed the hearse in procession. There were at least 30 motorcycles. Ross would have been proud to have such a cortège.

It was all very sad. And it brought home to me, personally, the tragedy and heartbreak of death on the highway. Ross was a share-milker. His wife, Karyn, and her four children, would need to look elsewhere for a place to live. That is because the farmhouse goes with the job. The farmer would need to contract another man to milk his herd. That new milker would need the house as the usual part of the standard share-milking agreement. The farmer and landowner – an intelligent, well-meaning man – spoke at the funeral. He was devastated to lose such a good man. He had never had a share-milker who worked as hard and as efficiently as had Ross.

The consequences of death on the highway are terrible, long-lasting and various. And yet, this happens day after day, year after year. We read the death notices, we see and hear media reports on accidents, we intellectually understand the trauma and grief caused by such accidents, but it is not until the old man with the scythe arrives at our own doorstep that we fully appreciate how awful road deaths are. Motor-cyclists are 22 times more likely to die in road accidents than motorists. Motorcycles are less stable, less visible, have no real protection in the event of a crash.

I spoke to two "bikers" at the reception in Te Aroha after Ross's funeral.

"Why," I asked, "do you guys love riding bikes so much?"

They said it was the exhilaration and feeling of freedom, speed and power they experienced on a motorbike. They all understood the risks but were undeterred. One man told me what was the first thing a biker asks after an accident?

"Is my bike OK?"

It seems to me riding motorcycles may lead to an adrenalin addiction. It is what I might call a motorbike addiction syndrome (my acronym: MBAS). As with many recreational pursuits, it is the fear factor that is compelling. Dicing with death is addictive, a passion. There is a strong element of the macho male archetype. Only real men ride bikes.

One man joked to me that it was a great way to get away from the wife and kids. Was he joking?

This part of New Zealand has long been famed for its thoroughbred horse breeding. In earlier times, young men rode horses. The offence of 'riding a horse furiously' was a provision in the Police Offences until 1981. Some men, and occasionally women, have swapped the fast, powerful horse with the faster, more powerful Harley. Both are beasts that need taming. Of course, horse riding can also be fatal; you might be thrown off the animal, kicked by a bucking horse, or even (as I once read) killed by a horse bite in the neck. I conceded to my mother's concern by not riding a motorbike, although the stability and visibility factors still put me at risk! Maybe some of these biker guys weren't so amenable and deliberately ignored mum?

Showered

Police entering a house to apprehend a drunk driver found him cringing in a shower cubicle, looking suspicious: he was fully dressed.

Impairment

Drink driving offences are widespread. It is important for judges to consider the individual circumstances of each offence and of each offender. It is easy just to have a sliding scale based on the alcohol reading and whether the motorist has previous convictions, but that is not always justice.

Under New Zealand law for those under 20 there is a zero tolerance for blood alcohol concentration. Even one small drink will put a youth before the judge. If the young person's alcohol level is less than 150 micrograms per litre of breath and less than 30 milligrams per 100 millilitres of blood there will be a fine and 50 demerit points. If the alcohol limit is higher, there will be a disqualification from driving, 50 demerit points and either fined or imprisoned.

Adults (20 and over) must not drive with a blood alcohol concentration more than the legal alcohol limit, which is 250 micrograms per litre of breath or 50 milligrams per 100 millilitres of blood.

The maximum penalty for first offenders is up to 3 months imprisonment, a fine up to $4500 or both. More severe penalties apply to repeat offenders or those driving with very high blood alcohol concentration.

I found it helpful to focus on how impaired the driver was – not just on the amount of alcohol consumed. Some people can hold their liquor. Some cannot. It depends upon body size, emotional state, personality, exhaustion and other factors. The important factor is the effect alcohol has on behaviour and impairment. I always look to see whether the driving was dangerous, whether road rules were breached, whether there was an accident, and whether the public was in danger. In brief, how great was the risk to the safety of others. Obviously repeat offenders are in a different and more serious category.

Distractions

A study reported in the British Medical Journal in 2005 found that talking on a cell phone, even hands-free, causes more driver impairment than an 80/100 excess breath/blood alcohol. A study conducted by the American Automobile Association in 2001 found other distractions also caused more impairment: eating, adjusting radio dials, having children in the backseat. Today we should add texting and talking on smart phones.

Boil on Backside

It is not often that a court case centres around a boil on a backside, but that was a significant issue in one of my cases. A young fellow from Kawerau was charged with driving while disqualified. The police spotted his car and followed him up the road until he turned into the car park of the Kawerau Hotel. They recognised him as the driver and said he was the only person in the car. They saw him get out of the driver's door of the Honda Civic and walk to the door of the hotel. The police used the patrol car's public address system to call him back to where they were parked. He was asked why he was driving while he was disqualified. He said, "Because I've got a boil on my arse!"

He was taken to the police station and charged. He called a very respectable witness, a local Kawerau baker, who said that he, not the defendant, was the driver of the car. He said he had been asked by the defendant to take him to the hotel to get some papers from his father. The baker said he had at first declined to do this and to avoid being the driver had told the defendant that he didn't have a licence. Eventually, however, he agreed to drive. He said the defendant sat next to him in the front of the car, but had the seat pushed back so that he was in a reclining position to avoid pain from the boil on his posterior. I gave him the perjury warning. But the witness insisted he was telling the truth, despite the fact that the police said they had only seen the defendant in the car, and no one else.

The baker testified that he had got out of the car and gone into a video shop. He said when he returned, he couldn't find the defendant, so he walked home. It seemed most unlikely, even bizarre, but I could not see any reason for him to lie as he was not a friend of the defendant and would not sensibly risk imprisonment for perjury. The police may not have seen the reclining defendant. Saved by a boil!

Road Rage

One unpleasant feature of today's society is the tendency of certain people to react violently after incidents on the highway. They attack other motorists, with fists, baseball bats, wheel braces and anything else they can lay their hands on - and often as the result of nothing more than some minor affront to their perceived driving rights.

I remanded an 18-year-old youth, who had no history of offending, for a pre-sentence report. With three mates, he had rammed his car into the rear of a stationary vehicle. After the accident, the defendant and his mates began yelling and threatening the complainant and his three friends.

The complainant feared for his safety. He rapidly left the scene, pursued by the defendant who tried to overtake and force the complainant's car off the road. In town, he rammed the rear of the complainant's car on three separate occasions. When interviewed three days later, he simply said he was "pissed off that the guy didn't stop". I must admit, in today's aggressive world, I wouldn't have stopped either.

Over the years, I have dealt with many instances of road rage. They come to court only when there is an allegation of a crime, or a breach of the traffic regulations has occurred. Some years ago, I even presided over a preliminary hearing where two young men were charged with murder in West Auckland as the result of a very ugly road rage incident. Ultimately, they were acquitted of the murder charge, but convicted of manslaughter and sentenced to a lengthy term of imprisonment.

As someone has said, something about driving cars "releases the inner alligator".

Triune Brains

The American Neuroscientist Paul MacLean endorsed the alligator concept. In 1990, he published a controversial book *The Triune Brain in Evolution*[1], arguing, among other things, that a primitive reptilian part of our brain governs our sense of survival and the fight-or-flight reaction we have to danger. He argues that the reptilian brain is "inflexible, compulsive, ritualistic and incapable of learning from previous experience".

The reasoning is that road rage is basically uncontrollable, because we feel threatened and our reptilian brain forces us to react antagonistically to ensure survival. It is, I imagine, similar to the primitive territorial protection instincts that are aroused when our house or private space is invaded or threatened.

We also see things only from our own perspective. Of course, we have driven properly. The other driver has not, and is solely to blame. It is best to take a deep breath and not respond to the other driver in a road rage incident. Let it pass. Even if you think the other driver is some kind of maniac, let it pass. It is better to forgive and forget than to end up bashed senseless, or with your car smashed by the maniac! Don't give the other motorist the finger sign or yell obscenities at him or her.

In my experience, young men are the most likely to be aggressive. It goes with the gender/age macho male factor. But I have occasionally had cases where even older women have lost their self-control and vented their anger in most unladylike ways.

Getting Stoned

In Samoa, only the foolhardy stopped after an accident involving injury to a pedestrian. If you did, you were likely to be stoned to death. When I was there, I remember a very distressed Australian woman, married to a member of the High

---

[1] Springer, 1990.

Commission staff, telling me that she struck a child who ran out under her wheels as she was driving to Apia from the Faleolo Airport 40 km away. She immediately stopped to render assistance, but the villagers started stoning her car and trying to tip it over. She wisely drove to the police station, where she was praised for her good sense. The High Commission then took over and a formal ifoga[1] was arranged after the funeral. By then the family had calmed down.

The Buff Yeoman

The defendant was the very model of a modern yeoman, although he probably does not realise that fact. Short in stature, muscular of build, and square of chin, he was a hard-working, heart of oak, rural contractor.2 He had spent the day cleaning oxidation ponds and laying some road metal on a country road. He rewarded himself for his hard work that day, firstly, by buying a dozen cans of Lion Red beer at the local country pub and, secondly, by visiting an old flame on a neighbouring property.

But the flame had flickered out. She had a new boyfriend, who became somewhat terse and unfriendly when he learned that our yeoman had in the past held more than his girlfriend's hand. Thus, rejected, the defendant, with stolid Saxon reluctance, headed off home in his car.

At about 9.30 p.m. he was dazzled by oncoming vehicle lights. He flipped his Mitsubishi car into a ditch but was unhurt. He made his way home on foot where some tipsy friends comforted him. They did not recognise him as a yeoman. They thought he was a Cossack! They poured him two vodkas that would have knocked Grigori Rasputin off the Tsarina's couch.

One of the now sober friends brought me the vodka glass to show me in court. It was a very large, dimpled beer glass. More than sufficient to hold a walloping Smirnoff.

A police officer had found the wrecked Mitsubishi. He noticed an empty beer can on the ground and four full cans inside the car. There was some mail in the vehicle. It identified Mr Yeoman as the likely driver. Fifteen minutes later a very inquisitive constable disturbed the Russian Revellers. The defendant sensibly admitted that he had

---

[1] A formal ceremony of contrition and forgiveness.

[2] At my Palmerston North Boys High School music classes, we boys would sing with patriotic gusto:
"Where are the Yeomen, the Yeomen of England?
In homestead and cottage, they still dwell in England,
Stained with the ruddy tan,
God's air doth give a man,
Free as the winds that fan
the broad breast of England!"

been the driver, and explained how the accident had happened. But in so doing he showed obvious signs of intoxication. He was breath tested. He scored 750/400.

The issue for me to decide was whether he had consumed the liquor before or after the accident. I gained the distinct impression that Mr Yeoman's lawyer had not studied the Transport Act.[1] It has a provision designed to cover cases like this. The provision says:

> *It shall be conclusively presumed that the proportion of alcohol in the defendant's breath (or blood) at the time of the alleged offence was the same as the proportion of alcohol in the defendant's breath indicated by the test.*

The law was specifically designed to stop motorists "having a few" after an accident to thwart a possible prosecution, and motorists in New Zealand have ever since quaffed a nervous brandy or three after an accident at their peril. This was the situation being argued by Yeoman's lawyer. But there was a problem: Constable Park testified that he had considered this very possibility and had consequently asked Mr Yeoman as to whether he had downed a few after the accident. He was adamant that Yeoman told him that he had "only been home a half an hour and had nothing to drink since". These words were recorded that night on the Constable's checklist.

The defendant was adamant that he had said no such thing. He called the constable a liar. The constable quivered with anger. Yeoman then thumped the Bible on the bar of the witness box. Dust and bits of biblical binding half hid his hand.

He exclaimed with some passion, "I am telling the truth. I am a Buff man! Like most people, I tell lies sometimes. But in Court here I am telling the truth!"

Later, I was amused when he said to the Prosecutor: "Are you calling me a dummy? You are trying to put words in my mouth and I won't let you. Not on your Nelly!"[2]

I wondered what a "Buff Man" might be. I thought I had misheard him and that he meant "rough", not "buff". He did not look a likely nudist! Later in the case he told me was a member of a Buffalo Lodge, which I gather is similar to a Masonic Order. The abbreviation is "Buff". We live and learn![3]

I was concerned that the notes made by the constable at the time clearly contradicted him, but there was the possibility of mistake or that the defendant was so traumatised by his massive Smirnoffs that he didn't know what he was saying.

---

[1] I often politely suggest to lawyers that a good starting point is to first read the instruction manual. A failure to study the legislation can be fatal.

[2] An expression not heard much these days, except from Kiwi yeomen, a direly threatened species. It was originally a cockney term "Not on your Nelly Duff" (rhymes with puff (breath, life).

[3] The Order (oddly called the "Royal" (it was not) "Antediluvian" (it was not) Order of "Buffaloes" (they are not) has as its motto "No Man Is at All Times Wise" (Latin: *Nemo Mortalium Omnibus Horis Sapit*). How true!

His two friends gave testimony confirming the vodka drinking. They looked like vodka drinkers. The woman looked like a Māori clone of Nikita Khrushchev's frumpy wife, Nina. Remember her?

They both said Yeoman looked sober when he arrived home. One of the Russians had been a barman for eleven years so I thought he should know. I believed him and his lady shot putter. I found special circumstances, fined him $500, and did not take his driver's licence. Perhaps I was wrong? I have a soft spot for solid folk with no previous convictions.

No Entry

The Greenlane motorway off-ramp proved too much for a rustic farmer who was visiting Auckland for only the second time in his life. He was seen just before midnight, doing a U-turn on the onramp. In his bucolic, addled innocence, he had somehow missed the signs and went up the off-ramp instead of down! He was totally bewildered and I had sympathy for him, being a reluctant big-city driver myself.

His case reminded me of a case I had in the Auckland traffic court some years ago which caused much more mayhem because it happened midmorning and not near midnight. An elderly car, driven by an even more elderly lady driver, somehow managed to drive up the motorway leading to the Harbour Bridge the wrong way. It only took seconds before there was a mass motorway mix-up, with traffic backed up for miles, while the traffic officers got to the old lady and backed her car down the motorway. The sergeant told me the old lady was quite unruffled and wondered what all the fuss was about!

"Marie, are you still driving?"

A Spot of Bother

When I was in law practice, I acted for a well-known speech and drama teacher much beloved by about three generations of Palmerstonians. She was well into her 80's when she was referred to me by one of my partners. She told me, in her beautifully enunciated words, "a spot of bother" while driving her ancient Austin tourer.

She had failed to see a compulsory stop sign on Victoria Avenue. She didn't see the traffic approaching her from both sides of the intersection with Church Street. On she went. She hit two cars. One rolled on its roof. The other hit a plane (sycamore) tree on the side of the road and was badly damaged. Thrown somewhat off her planned course of travel, her car toppled a power pole, went through a fence, and came to rest on the front lawn of an adjacent house occupied by a Salvation Army Major.

She emerged from the wreck, her pink feathered hat a little askew, and her thick bifocals somewhat steamed up, but otherwise unaffected by her experience. She was charged with careless driving and wished to defend the charge. After all, she protested, it was not her fault!

"Those other motorists should have seen me coming."

After about three intense and difficult consultations with the dear old lady and her very worried nephew, I finally managed to persuade her to plead guilty and get the case over without too much fuss. I saw the nephew a day or two before the traffic court hearing. He asked whether anything could be done to have her fail her annual driving test and allow her the dignity of retiring from behind the wheel without the mortifying imposition of a disqualification.

I said I thought it rather a tall order, but that I would have a word to the prosecuting sergeant and see what I could do. As luck would have it, my client had taught elocution to members of the sergeant's family, and he agreed with the nephew's suggestion.

The sergeant was very benevolent in his presentation of the facts to His Worship "Gentleman Jack" Horn.[1] He suggested that she be ordered to re-sit her licence as part of the penalty.

I then made my plea in mitigation, pointing out her remarkable service to many now articulate and eloquent members of the community and that she was appearing in court for the first time in her life and had learned a very traumatic lesson. Jack Horn fined her, and with a wink and a nod, exercised his discretion not to disqualify her. But he made the proposed order that she re-sit her driver's licence.

After sentence had been pronounced, she gave a very brief but courteous curtsey to the Bench, turned around and, whether from nervousness or poor eyesight, missed the

---

[1] Jack Raymond Poppleton Horn, S.M. An excellent, courteous, well-regarded Magistrate who later became Chief Judge of the Arbitration Court.

We often think, as did the Heaven's Gate team, that our team is morally superior to all others. We take great pleasure in believing that our people are the best and that everyone else is inferior. We are suspicious of anyone who is different from us, in ethnicity, culture, religious beliefs, or social status. We see and accept only that information that accords with our own belief system. Without bothering to think or analyse, we reject contrary views. Even eminent scientists and jurists, who pride themselves on their ability to logically and rationally analyse information, can be led astray by their own idiosyncratic beliefs. It is very difficult to calmly and rationally question both evidence and current belief philosophies.

Difficult Parentage

Many people are conceived in circumstances that, with some degree of predictability, may affect and colour the rest of their lives. I had before me a handsome young man of 20 on a theft charge. He was conceived as the result of his 17-year-old crippled mother having been raped by a 70-year-old man.

Killing Wanda

A former de facto husband became spiteful to his lately lamented love. He knew she had a "fish named Wanda".[1] He broke into her house and, among other acts of vandalism, killed Wanda and her aquarium friends with a surfeit of fish food: he emptied the whole packet of fish food into the water. "Get stuffed" he is said to have exclaimed.

[1] Named after the 1988 movie of that name starring John Cleese, Kevin Kline, Jamie Lee Curtis and Michael Palin.

Decisions & Procedure

Sometimes I look back on my comments of a decade ago and cringe with embarrassment. I seemed then to be like the cartoon judge in Punch magazine who, scowling and majestic in scarlet, and horse-hair wig, growled: "Before passing sentence, I would like to indulge in a few random right-wing observations, some character assassination, and a little foaming at the mouth."

Suppressing Names

To suppress publication or not? A colleague came under intense media criticism for making a total suppression order in the Auckland Court. She made what was called a "blanket order" by which I understand she suppressed all details of the case.

The Summary Proceedings Act allows us to ban publication of details which might lead to the identification of the defendant, complainant or witnesses but does not, I believe, enable a complete muzzling of that angry growling media-monster. She had some type of protest case and she said she did not want her court turned into a forum for self-advertisers or some such thing.

Often, I read some media "summary" of a judge's decision and wonder why such a decision was made. Then, after learning the full facts of the case I can fully understand the decision and would have done just the same myself.

One of my cases was much simpler and much more illustrative of the normal application for a suppression order. The defendant, a small, sad, bespectacled lady had stolen just over $5000 from the insurance company she worked for. Her husband was unemployed and very ill. He had a rare and untreatable bowel disorder, was neurasthenic (chronic fatigue syndrome) and depressive as well. I was handed a medical certificate advising that his condition could worsen and he could become suicidal if he learned of his wife's embezzling.

I was urged not imprison her, but place her on periodic detention and order her to pay reparation. I had no problem with that as a punishment because the woman had major psychological and financial problems. But I was surprised at the application to suppress publication of her name and details.

How, I thought, could she attend periodic detention one day a week for five months without her house-bound husband not wondering where she was?

I asked both her and her counsel. Surprisingly, neither seemed to have thought about that. I finally made the suppression order but pointed out that I thought it would be prudent for her to tell her husband the truth, as I felt sure it would never remain a secret without major deceit on her part.

Hard Day at the Factory

Some days are exhausting. By 5:00 p.m. one day, I still had two defended cases to hear. But I threw up my hands in horror and pointed out to counsel and defendants that I had just dealt with nine people on difficult sentencing matters (six went to prison) and 30 others on miscellaneous matters. In between, I had a Youth Court and various chambers applications. I explained that I was in no fit state to properly deal with other important matters. I then adjourned both hearings. I was too tired to do justice to man or beast and the thought of the hour-long drive home and the need to read 23 probation reports for the following day did not help. Sometimes we need a three-day weekend.

Appeals

I kept a copy of the first appeal judgment against my sentence. It is of interest in that it is, by today's long-winded standards, so remarkably short.

It was a decision of Mr Justice Perry[1] dated 1 June 1978.

---

[1] Justice Sir Clifford Perry. Died, 1983

C.J. Field for the Appellant
G.E. Lane for the Respondent.

"I read this file last night and I have listened with interest to what you have said Mr Field, but I do not think that the sentence is excessive. Magistrates, in my view, are entitled to take a serious view of the use of heroin, which was the case here, and the learned Magistrate in imposing half the sentence which is permitted under the Act, in my view viewed the matter correctly. The appeal is dismissed."

Often the appeal judge would rely on the fact that the Magistrate had "the advantage of seeing and hearing the witness". One frustrated lawyer, who thought this was a cop-out, responded by saying: "But I had the advantage of seeing and hearing the Magistrate!"

Mental pictures

Before a jury trial commences, the judge reads the evidence taken before justices at a preliminary hearing. The typewritten transcripts from the preliminary hearing are referred to as "depositions" or "deps" to use the vernacular. The preliminary hearing takes place to decide whether there is enough evidence against the accused to put them on trial. If the evidence is insufficient, the justices may discharge the accused at that point.

As I sit in my chambers reading the deps, I try to form a mental picture of the various witnesses, particularly the accused. Often my mental picture proves to be far from accurate. I can thus understand why little old ladies are traumatised after a burglary of their home. Their mental picture of a huge eight-foot ugly troglodyte with sharpened incisors remains with them forever. They would be staggered to see the undernourished little wimp who actually broke in and stole their television.

Achtung!

A drunk German tourist appeared in my court charged with some nuisance offence. The prosecutor told me the man spoke little English. I asked if anyone in the courtroom spoke German. A fresh-faced young man raised his hand, stood up, smiled and said "Jawohl".

I thanked him and asked him forward to act as interpreter. He stood next to the prisoner, and the prosecuting sergeant asked of the German, "What is your name?"

The young volunteer interpreter commenced his duties.

"Vot ist your nam?" he said.

"Excuse me, Sir!" I interrupted, "Where did you learn your German?"

"From war comics" he proudly replied.

"Achtung! Die Englander!" I thought, but never said.

"Thank you, Sir," I said, "we need an interpreter with a more extensive vocabulary. Please take your seat." I did not add the "schnell".

I thought I heard him mutter "Eat lead, Fritz!" as he walked away. But I may be mistaken.

The Paper Jungle

In 1993, a disgruntled male dog owner appealed from the Auckland District Court to the High Court against a fine of $100 imposed upon him for keeping an unregistered dog. Such cases are usually dealt with in the judge's chambers, not in open court. My colleague, Judge Allan Lawson, had imposed the fine. The High Court judge requested details as to why the fine had been imposed. Judge Lawson had dealt with scores of similar cases and could not remember the actual case. Nevertheless, he prepared a memorandum. The memorable memo neatly summarises the mass of paperwork that must be processed by judges of our court. The memo read:

> *Your Honour may not be familiar with the manner in which "minor offences" are dealt with in this court. Notices of Prosecution for minor offences are surreptitiously placed in the Judge's "in tray" at frequent and irritating intervals usually in his or her absence. They come in stacks or bundles and are usually accompanied by numerous other prosecutions instigated by Government Departments, Local and other Statutory Bodies. At or about the same time there will also appear, equally mysteriously, applications for Second Hand Dealers' Licences, Auctioneers' Licences, Share brokers' Licences, Massage Parlour Licences, Immigration Removal Warrants and many others. Also, not to be overlooked are stacks of fines enforcement files, applications for re-hearings of minor offences such as over parking, and all manner of similar misdemeanours. These are often carefully concealed beneath a pile of civil interlocutory applications and miscellaneous outpourings of our criminal, quasi-criminal and civil system*
>
> *The aforesaid offence of non-registration of a male German Shepherd Cross of a greater age than three months is, of course, merely one particular example of a minor offence. The range of minor turpitude is enormous. To mention but a few: Electrical Wiring Regulations, By-Law breaches, under-age drinking, failure to send child to school (Truancy). Others may be found scattered like grains of wheat amongst statutes and regulations.*
>
> *The Disposal Thereof:*
>
> *The Judge peruses the mountain of files with great care, and then imposes whatever penalty he or she deems appropriate. No hearing is held. No defendant or counsel is present. No submissions are made. No tears are shed. No howls of derision are heard from the gallery. Fellow miscreants do not suddenly awake from slumber and, bleary eyed, stagger drunkenly forward, or in such other direction as their condition impels. No anxious mother suckles a fretful child. There are no sideways glances or rolling back of eyes from Counsel's table, and certainly no titters are heard to run around the Court.*

The Judge sits alone in his Chambers and affixes his facsimile signature to the information sheet, perhaps muttering silent curses to himself, as he does so. He does not deliver a condemnatory monologue, at least not one that is recorded or intended for the ears of others. I hope this short Memorandum may assist Your Honour in dealing with this appeal.

Transparency

The Philpott Case[1] raised a storm of public anger when it was found Philpott was on work release so soon after being sentenced for massive company fraud as managing director of the old and solid firm of Cory Wright & Salmon Ltd. The Minister had intervened, cancelled the work release, and set in motion a complete review of the criteria for such releases. It does make somewhat a farce of it. The same can be said of the automatic release after serving half a sentence with good behaviour. Thus, when in court we say twelve years it only means six, which is really a deceit on the public. Why not sentence to a finite six years imprisonment and say that a further third will be added to that sentence if there is misbehaviour?

De-spotting Leopards

Can we change our evil ways? Modern social science indicates that, with effort and resolve, we can make significant changes to our behaviour and thinking, but it isn't easy. Modifying moral decision-making is a problem. In brief, if we were devious, cheating, and dishonest as children, it is likely we will be the same as a mature adult. The spots don't wash off with normal laundering. This is reflected in what is called recidivism and desistance, two rather awkward words that mean backsliding into further offending or not committing further crimes.

We have very disturbing figures in New Zealand, with one of the highest imprisonment rates in the developed world, the highest percentage of prisoners locked up for interpersonal offences (mainly domestic offending involving physical or sexual assaults, threats, or damage to house or personal property) and the highest percentage of prisoners serving time for sexual offending. Currently 60 percent of prison inmates re-offend within two years of being released from jail. Despite great efforts, we have never reduced this re-offending rate. Ongoing unemployment, undiagnosed mental illness, and serious addictions all cause the backsliding.

In 2015, Dr. Beth Weaver, a Scots academic, authored a lengthy and sometimes unfathomable study of *Offending and Desistance*[2] It was reviewed by Dr. Peter Johnston,

---

[1] Robert Philpott, the chief executive, brought down the company with losses of $57 million, He was sentenced to two years imprisonment for fraud, forgery and false pretences for making an unauthorised $1.1 million company loan to his brother. Philpott was the son-in-law of Fred Turnovsky, respected patron of the arts, businessman and economist.

[2] Routledge, Abingdon, Oxfordshire, 2015.

our New Zealand Department of Corrections research director. He refers to a passage from Dr. Weaver's book, which quotes the clearly understood words of a recently paroled prisoner, and then, a not so understandable sentence from an academic analysis by the author.

> *I went down to London and started working the next day. I thought "F**king hell, it's f**king knackering", and I was thinking, "I wonder if I should just hand myself in, and go back to jail" – cos it's a lot better in jail than it is here, you know, working like a c**t!*

From this Dr. Weaver concludes:

> *It is through this process that they (the released prisoners) deliberate on the social solutions they confront, through the lens of their ultimate concerns, which necessarily challenges the exteriority and constraint assumptions of informal control theories.*

To which Dr. Johnston comments: "Errr … if you say so." And I respectfully concur!

Court Officers

As the Executive Judge I was reliant on Stuart Greenshields, the Deputy Registrar. He was a great help. He did most of the scheduling and basic organisational work for me. He was an excellent court officer, capable administrator, and a very agreeable man. The same can be said of our Registrar, Kevin Nally, a highly competent Court Manager, with a great relationship with the judges, and understanding of our role. He is an effective communicator, courteous and clear, a competent problem solver.

Over the years, I have been impressed by the dedication, intelligence and industry of the men and women who run the courts. Poorly paid, they are unstinting and always they do their duty, often quite late in the day.

In the mid 1980's the Secretary of Justice made a bizarre, incomprehensible and very detrimental decision. He decided to terminate the employment of all court managers, registrars and some deputy registrars who did not have university degrees. That applied to nearly every District Court registrar in New Zealand. The judges were in disbelief. We could not comprehend the irrational thinking behind the decision. Not only did we lose the senior management of nearly all our courts, but a vast, irreplaceable and exceptional resource of institutional knowledge. In my area – Tauranga, Gisborne, and Hamilton – we lost priceless and highly competent leadership leading to ongoing problems for many years as the new replacement registrars tried to cope with a role to which they had no training or ability.

Some years later I was overjoyed to find Dick Jopson, who had been lost to us as the capable and personable Courts Manager of the Waikato region, working at the Manukau District Court. He had been reluctantly persuaded, on a substantially higher salary, to return from retirement to help sort out the administrative disaster that had made South Auckland a laughing stock of judges and lawyers.

Workload

I crawled from court one day at 6:00 pm and made some notes. I was brain damaged after a long day. I looked at my desk. I had 20 dog prosecutions sitting on my desk to be dealt with as minor prosecutions. My clerk took one look at the hangdog look on my face and immediately volunteered to postpone them until the following week. I felt no remorse whatsoever as my list that day consisted of 131 people: 8 pre-trial conferences at 9:30 a.m.;13 drink/drive cases; 9 offenders for sentence; 7 diversions; 15 young people in the Youth Court at 2:00 pm; 10 fines defaulters; 3 work licences; 19 warrants of arrest; 47 general summary prosecutions.

Can there really be justice when people are pushed through the system as if they are sheep being dipped? I try. But I am sure I stagger somewhat by the end of the day and make mistakes. Thankfully there is an appellate system to correct the decisions made while in a state of exhaustion. The other exhausting factor is the sadness felt at watching well over 80 Māori facing justice: unemployed, ill-dressed, many over-weight, illiterate, badly tattooed, and lacking self-esteem. As Te Arikinui Dame Te Atairangikaahu[1] said on the occasion celebrating the 25th year of her accession to the Māori throne:

> *There have been many advances and many young Māori are achieving academic and other successes. But there is a long way to go. Undoubtedly, the pakeha is much to blame but then so is Māoridom itself. It seems to me that there is too much talk, too little do.*

Business as Usual

Week after week the usual parade of cannabis gaspers, quick-fingered shoplifters, and unhinged wife-beaters – all frustrated by unemployment, underachievement and undercapitalisation. The prosecutor, in a summary of facts not intended to be humorous or caustic, but just employing English in a somewhat old-fashioned usage said:

"The defendant is currently enjoying the Unemployment Benefit."

Some enjoyment! On a welfare benefit [2] one could get ecstatic with joy. The expression is like the wry one: "She is a woman who enjoys poor health!"

---

[1] The Maori Queen from 23 May 1966. She died on 15 August 2006.

[2] 25 years later it is still only subsistence. Today the welfare benefit for an unemployed single man over 25 without accommodation supplement is $335.00. On 1 April 2019 the hourly minimum wage rose to $17.70.

Traumatised

I felt sorry for an as yet invisible defendant charged with assault. His lawyer asked that his client be excused on medical grounds and that a not guilty plea be entered in his absence. After reading the medical certificate I immediately agreed. His doctor had certified that the man was so "frightened" by the thought of a court appearance that he was exhibiting "...a nervous bowel condition, eczema, and hyperventilation..."

It is sometimes easy to forget the trauma most people feel when they are obliged to give evidence in a court. For us it seems hard to contemplate such abject fear. It is our world: an environment with which we are familiar. But that is not so for most people coming to court. They feel just as I feel in my dentist's waiting room.

Holiday

The Queen's Birthday holiday meant a day of relaxation and pleasure. It also meant that all the cases that would normally have been disposed of that Monday were added to my traffic list the next day. Consequently, I ended up today with 95 people in court. Luckily, Dick Kearney's civil list was light so he did the one remaining defended case in my list. As a result, we both finished at about 5.30. I also had a mountain of accumulated paperwork on my desk: Land Settlement applications, fine enforcement files, civil files requiring minor minutes and notes, and two appeal files upon which I had to certify the notes of evidence and sign my decision. It was the usual traffic list of drunkenness, stupidity, irresponsibility and unreasonableness.

Lock-up

The Whakatane Court Registrar, Bob Gillon, visited me before lunch to tell me that the prison at Waikeria is full and cannot take any more prisoners, whether on remand or as sentenced prisoners. We had at least twelve candidates.

The police station in Whakatane, has a large and well-designed cell block, but the officer in charge refused to accommodate any prisoners as there are insufficient staff. Bob agreed with me that it is hardly my problem as I am certainly not going to release potentially dangerous criminals onto the street simply because there is no room at the Inn!

The problem lies with the Justice Department. We are obviously approaching the same situation that we have had before, with a lack of prison beds. I only relented with one man, who had sexually assaulted a nine-year-old niece, and I bailed him instead of remanding him for pre-sentence report in custody. I was satisfied he was no undue risk to the victim or her family.

I rather mischievously teased the prosecuting sergeant.

"Sergeant, do you have a lock-up car shed at your home?"

He blanched, then grinned.

All an Act

Many top trial lawyers and judges have well-honed acting skills. There are many similarities between a talented actor and a talented advocate. In essence it is about good communication skills and story-telling. As with music, singing, art and oratory, this may be an innate gift from birth, but to an important extent the skills can be learned and practiced.

As a young man, I enjoyed acting in plays, both at school and university. While I never showed the same talent as my grandson KJ Apa[1], I did acquire some techniques to deliver effective messages in court. I gained a modest ability to tell stories, improvise, and adapt character to differing audiences: juries, prisoners, witnesses, and the public gallery. In jury trials, I tried to ensure the jurors understood what I was saying by talking to them without notes, and trying to be relaxed, authentic and clear. I know I often failed, but I understand from occasional feedback that I sometimes succeeded in creating a meaningful rapport and comprehension.

Procrastination

District court judges are usually given one day every three months to consider and write reserve decisions. They are precious days, because they are few and far between. Often, we work at night, weekends or during gaps in a case, to finish reserve decisions. It is surprising how little can be achieved in one day! How easy it is to procrastinate? We only reserve decisions in cases presenting difficult legal issues. Our court is a summary court, which means we are normally expected to give decisions "on the spot". If needed, we do have the assistance of research counsel – bright young lawyers – who help analyse the legal issues, prepare a summary of the relevant law, and help sort out cases with complex facts.

I very rarely use research counsel. Unlike the research counsel in the High Court, many of our research counsel are newly admitted lawyers who, while bright, have little experience in focusing on the critical areas necessary to help create a reasoned reserved decision. I prefer to do my own research. I also use my computer word processor to type, edit and print my own decisions. That way I can't blame anyone but myself for any errors!

---

[1] Hollywood actor, best known for his starring role as "Archie Andrews" in the Warner Bros/CBS Netflix series *Riverdale*.

With reserve decisions, procrastination almost inevitably raises its slothful head. It is easy to make up excuses and delay the writing. I found the best thing was to start. I would type up the name of the case, record the names of counsel and start summarising the facts. It is surprising how that spurs the resolve to continue and finish the job.

Beast of Belsen

In 1982, I made the front page of the New Zealand Herald – complete with my photo – for sentencing a one-legged Samoan youth to prison for six weeks for contempt of court. He had waved a large cardboard sign reading '*Fuck Justice*' in the rear of my court.

Leaders of civil rights groups foamed at their mouths over my insensitivity and severity. I was condemned as if I was the Beast of Belsen. They wanted me sacked, and condemned my treatment of the pitiable, under-privileged young teenager. What they didn't know that the youth was far from faultless. They didn't know that I had warned him several times that he would be arrested if he refused to remove the sign and apologise. They didn't know he gave me a middle-finger salute. He was, to quote Dorothy Parker's wonderful words, "as pure as the driven slush".

I knew him well. He had appeared before me several times as a young delinquent in my youth court. I had sentenced him to a term of corrective training not long before, and was surprised he was already free. He was, to put it in the vernacular, a bad little bastard. He had lost his leg when he fell under a train after a glue sniffing session.

I finally granted him bail pending his appeal. It is the only time I have ever released a written bail decision. I gave copies to the assembled media.

I have lost the copy of it now, but I started off by reciting his previous convictions, and what had actually happened in court that day. I then recorded that, despite his grave antisocial behaviour I would grant him bail because the appeal might take some time and it would be unfair to have him serve his full six weeks while waiting a hearing. The reporters were visibly astonished. From that moment on, they dropped their interest in the case as if he was leprous. Nothing more was published. The media feeding frenzy evaporated when they learned that the innocent crippled boy was no angel.

A month or so later, Justice David Tompkins allowed the appeal and declined to impose any further sentence on the basis that the six days he had already spent in prison would be punishment enough. I accept that the six weeks was fairly robust, but I thought the High Court could have been more supportive when the contempt was so blatant an attack on "Justice". If someone waved a sign like that before some of the more precious High Court judges, followed by the "up you finger", they would swallow their tonsils, suffer fibrillation of both auricles, and need a month's leave to recover from such a blatant disregard for their status.

There were two consolations for the mincing I was given by the media, and the fact that only a few of my brethren on the District Court gave me any support:

(1) The radio talk back show calls ran 4 to 5 in my favour and said I should be cloned!

(2) Many of my personal friends telephoned to tell me I was the last bastion of discipline, good order, and justice!

(3) Gang members, yahoos and other species of thugs behaved themselves impeccably in my court from then on!

Date of Hearing

The Tasman Pulp and Paper Co. of Kawerau[1] was being prosecuted for pollution offences. The short hearing was simply to fix a date of hearing for the prosecution case.

Defence counsel, Robert Fardell,[2] from Russell McVeigh (the Auckland mega firm) had travelled all the way down for that short and simple purpose – with a junior associate to assist him! Terrible! Such unnecessary expense must cost big companies a fortune. A local solicitor could have organised the hearing date just as well and it wouldn't have cost a couple of thousand dollars. Just what the junior associate was meant to do I found it hard to imagine.

---

[1] Said to be the largest paper mill in the world.

[2] Robert Fardell was made a QC in 2002. He was found dead on Narrow Neck Beach, Devonport, in December 11, 2005. He had a large funeral, attended by many judges. He was described as New Zealand's "Rumpole of the Bailey".

Night Courts

In 2005, the possibility of using night courts was raised, discussed and rejected. The proponents of the concept thought such courts would alleviate the problems faced by defendants or witnesses who suffer financial and social hardship from having to appear in court during the day. There would be no loss of wages, parking would be easier, child care would be easier, case back-logs would be reduced, court facilities would be better used, and some court staff, police, social workers, and judges would rather work at night than in the day. But the negatives outweighed the positives. Security in and around the courthouse was seen as problematic. Drunkenness would be more significant. Most staff and others involved in the court process did not wish to work at night. Rostering cases and jury trials was too complicated. Few judges saw it as of value. The police preferred to have officers on crime prevention duties at night, when the need was greater. The idea was dropped, but in some overseas jurisdictions it seems to be beneficial.

Arson

Diesel Maxwell

Dick James Maxwell, of Ruatoria, Rastafarian, appeared before me in the Gisborne Court. He had appealed a sentence of periodic detention imposed upon him in June the previous year for possession of an offensive weapon. The Court of Appeal refused leave to appeal but nothing was done to serve him with the Periodic Detention Order. By that December, the 6-month term had elapsed, and he still hadn't done a scintilla of work. The Probation Service resolved it by asking for a re-sentencing on the same terms. He was brought down to Gisborne to me because the local judge didn't hold a jury warrant.

Dickie Maxwell, popularly known as "Diesel" for his propensity to use oil as a fire-starter, had become nationally notorious a year or two earlier as leader of the Rastafarians during a period of the dreadful arsons which destroyed many properties in the small East Cape community, and terrorised the locals. I was told in December that he had now been thrashed and expelled from the sect for raping another member's "missus". He is quite a good-looking man – with none of the glazed pot-eyed look about him – but the Rasta dreadlocks are as thick and mutton-fatty as they could be.

In 1987, five detectives were accused of kidnapping "Diesel". They were acquitted. Three years later, Luke Donnelly, a farmer, was charged with murdering Rastafarian Chris Campbell. Campbell and his Rasta mates had arrived on Donnelly's farm, with as they said in bygone times, "malice aforethought".

It was a triumph for the defence because the jury also found him not guilty of manslaughter, which is the usual alternative conviction for those acquitted of murder. He walked free. That didn't really surprise me, because on one occasion when I was relieving for a week at the Gisborne Court, Donnelly appeared before me on a bail issue. He had vast public support from the gallery. It was clear that many citizens believed Donnelly, in shooting Campbell, had done society a positive service

Rastafarians

I was a relieving judge helping out in Gisborne. The local judges were kept very busy with the criminal aftermath of Rastafarian madness. I was there to preside over some of the more serious trials by jury. The crimes were centred on the small East Coast town of Ruatoria[1] which became like the lawless wild west in Tombstone, Arizona. The

---

[1] Ruatoria is near 1752-metre high Mount Hikurangi, the first part of New Zealand to see sunrise. On 1 January 2000 it was internationally but inaccurately feted as the first place in the world to see the sun for the new millennium.

District Court summary cases were held there, and I visited three times to run the sessions. There were horse hitching rails outside, and a 'Kai Kart' over the road that did a great trade in meat pies whenever the court sat.

In the 1980's Ruatoria was a war zone. Our courthouse was burned down. So was the police station – and about 50 other properties including a church, marae and farm buildings. I had believed the dreadlocked followers of Jah, mellowed by the 'holy herb', were, like their Jamaican forebears, people of love and peace. Far, far from it! The Mount Zion Hikurangi Rastas, fuelled by religious fervour and marijuana, were angry at the historical loss of Māori land to pakeha colonists and violence erupted. Lance Kupenga was beheaded by paranoid fellow Rasta, Joe Nepe, and a police officer was kidnapped.

Journalist and television news producer, Angus Gillies, wrote an amazing trilogy[1] about these bizarre events. Apart from the arsons, there were burglaries, thefts, abductions, trespass, assaults, drug offences, and cruelty to animals. The police were very busy trying to prevent or detect crime.

There was a backlash. Not just from pakeha but from a majority of Māori who were appalled at the mayhem caused by the Rastas. Rasta beach cottages and caravans and were attacked and burned.

The killing of Chris Campbell and wounding of Billy Kaihi by Luke Donnelly (see above), while extreme and frightening, brought most of the problems to an end.

Burning down the Gym

In 2001 in the Hamilton District Court (on a transfer up from the Youth Court), I had a difficult case involving three intelligent, handsome young people aged 15 and 16 years, who for incomprehensible reasons decided to burn down an almost completed $5 million gymnasium at Hamilton's Fraser High School. It was a difficult sentencing as all three teenagers were first offenders and were represented by competent counsel.

It was a no-win situation. On the one hand, as a Youth Court judge, I know that sending young people to prison can be counter-productive and damaging, traumatizing, and negative. It often affects their later chances of employment, happy family relationships, and education. Nurturing support in the community with sensitive and constructive assistance is productive and far superior.

On the other, I had to satisfy the public interest and make the three young offenders accountable for the most damaging school arson in New Zealand's history.

---

[1] The first of which was *Footsteps of Fire* (*Ngāti dread, #1*), self-published by the author 2008

Given their youth, remorse, and lack of prior convictions I gave each of them 15 months' imprisonment. Usually the media howl at such sentences – too short, or too long depending upon the perspective. But I was pleased to see the report in the Herald was that I "got it right". For once? The journalist wrote:

> *The seriousness of the crime demanded nothing less. As did the fact that arson by young people is an increasing problem. So commonplace has the burning of schools become that the Court of Appeal has ruled it a matter of grave concern. Thus, noted Judge Callander, there was a clear need to deter others who might mimic the trio.*

The trio planned the arson, and two of them returned to the fire to fuel it with more paper and other debris. At first, they denied responsibility and showed no remorse. That had changed by the time they appeared before me. I asked the prison service to hold them in "circumstances appropriate for their age" and to keep them apart from adult prisoners where possible. The two young men would be kept in a new youth unit at Waikeria Prison and would spend about 30 hours a week on rehabilitation, counselling and compulsory schoolwork. That seems some distance from the drab, depressing existence portrayed by prison critics. I granted leave for them to apply for home detention.1

The school principal, Martin Elliott, is reported in the newspaper as being pleased with the sentence:

> *A slap on the wrist would have sent a message to the rest of New Zealand that you can commit what was almost an act of terrorism and get away with it.*

In sentencing the three, I referred to how, over the years I have sat down with members of service clubs and even Sixth Formers in High School groups and have given them an exercise to complete so that they could have some idea as to how complex it is to actually sentence someone for a given offence. What I did was to prepare in advance a written set of facts. I then talked to the group. They split up into tables, and I would explain the main principles of sentencing that applied to the crime that I had selected. I always chose a crime with complex and difficult variables, as often happens in real life. After that, I would ask each group to independently fix the sentence for the given offence. Often the responses were so wildly dissimilar you would wonder if we were talking about the same case.

In my sentencing notes of the three young arsonists, I recorded some observations about how judges and society often take differing views on sentencing:

> *There is an extraordinarily wide opinion by members of the public as to what is the appropriate punishment for a given offence. An analogy with the military is the contrast between the Hawks and the Doves. At one end of that spectrum we have hard-nosed punishers*

[1] They made no application. They served their sentence until granted early release on parole.

who want some sort of tough communal response to any form of crime, whether it is crime against the person or crime against property. They really are the group that are the "throw away the key" brigade and they say "lock everybody up".1At the other end of the spectrum are people who take a positive view. They are more forgiving and perhaps more caring. They see that criminals, especially young offenders, are a product of our particular social milieu and they want the Courts to emphasise the positive factors, and are perhaps more charitable and forgiving. It is always a question of focus and it is a question of who you are and where you stand in your personal philosophies.

A few years ago, I read a book about the Judges of the United States Supreme Court. It spoke of an analytical group in Washington DC, which said it could predict the outcome of any future decision of the Supreme Court, in most cases, to a 90% certainty.[2] *This was done on a computer analysis involving very careful algorithms and a complex study of the background of the twelve Judges on that Court. It analysed their previous decisions, their socio-economic, family and educational backgrounds, their political views and matters of that sort, and then it said from that information, it can predict what the decision in a given case will be. So again, that illustrates the fact that even Judges are going to differ in their worldview of a particular case – of a particular crime.*

That is the difficulty that the sentencing process presents to any Judge. There are really no absolutes. There are no scientific laws or principles that assist me in the process of choosing what, hopefully, is going to be the right sentence for you.

It is obvious from what we have heard this morning in your lawyers' analysis of the case law that no two cases are the same. The variables are enormous. The factors are complex and complicated, and that means that other cases such as the ones we have been talking about are of no direct assistance to me.

And you have heard it all here in Court. The Crown, representing the community through Ms Dunn, wants me to take into account the more aggravating features of the case, and defence counsel, (your lawyers), want me to take into account matters that they feel water down the gravity of the offending and focus on some of your personal circumstances.

All those matters have to be taken into account in assessing this case, and I want to talk about some of those factors. I simply want to make the basic point that this is not a scientific process. It is a well-meant attempt by society through the Courts to seek what is often somewhat elusive, and is called justice.

One of the arsonists was a 16-year-old girl who intrigued the media. She was blonde and very pretty in a Lolita-like way. One newspaper article unfairly called her a "manipulative seductress" and that she had somehow enticed the two boys to join her in burning the building. It was suggested that she was the ringleader and that the boys would not have done it without her involvement. It was hinted that she would reward them with sex if they did as she commanded.

---

[1] Just like the Trumpists now cry "Lock her up!".

[2] Recent studies by LexPredict (2018) analysing 7700 decisions of the court show a lower prediction of 70%.

She was unusual. She referred to herself as a "lone wolf". The school principal believed she was the prime mover and he blamed her more than the two boys. Psychological reports described her as emotionally detached and unrepentant, with one professional saying she was a "real piece of work". The girl's mother – a hard-working and protective solo mum – told of the girl's drunk and abusive father who left the family destitute five years earlier. There were protection orders against him. The mother said her daughter's "troubles" became apparent a month before the fire. She said health professionals were treating her and I was told she had a "major depressive episode" and was in counselling. Her mother said a recently acquired nose-ring was just an "expression of her individuality". That was all undoubtedly true, but for the reasons given, her personal circumstances were only marginally relevant.

Scorned and Sizzling

Haruru Falls[1] is a beautiful and picturesque location near Paihia in the Bay of Islands. Many of the local houses have a wonderful view of the waterfall. My last jury trial for arson related to one of those houses. After a three-day trial, the accused, a 34-year-old former prison officer, was found guilty, and I sentenced her the following week to four years' imprisonment.

In August 2009, the accused, angered by and jealous of her former partner ending their relationship in favour of another female prison officer, set fire to the rented house in which the two women were living.

The house was badly damaged and the Kiwi owner, then living and working in Canada, was uninsured for the $300,000 loss. His exceptional 30-year collection of Beatles memorabilia was destroyed, along with a large collection of photographic negatives and prints taken by him as a professional photographer. All the possessions of the two women renting the house were destroyed.

The accused had taken the day off work pretending she had a dental appointment. She borrowed a car that would not be recognised in Haruru. She drove to the house with a large can of petrol. She splashed petrol over the exterior of the house and car shed. After igniting the petrol, she left the property. No one saw her light the fires, but she was observed by an elderly neighbour. He was suspicious seeing her wearing rubber gloves so he recorded the car details. When the fire broke out ten minutes later, he phoned the fire brigade and police.

On sentencing her, I emphasised that arson was a serious crime punished vigorously by sentencing courts because of the potential to cause major property loss, injury and

[1] Haruru means "big noise".

even death. The effect on all victims was devastating. The house owner later filed in bankruptcy and could not even afford to fly back from Canada to visit his mother who was terminally ill.

Firearms

Firearm Figures

While any offences involving firearms are serious, we are fortunate in New Zealand that we do not have such open access to the purchase of firearms as they do in most parts of the USA. The American figures are horrific. In New Zealand, firearms are involved in only about 1.7% of all crimes. That figure has not changed significantly over many years. There are about 4000 firearms offences each year. That includes all firearms offences, not just those that involve threatening behaviour. For instance, it is a firearms offence not to have a firearms license. Nearly three quarters of all firearm-related deaths in New Zealand are suicides. Deaths related to crime are about 16 per cent and the rest are accidental deaths, such as those that happen with deerstalking or duck shooting.

The USA has the highest gun ownership rate in the world – there are 89 guns for every 100 Americans, compared to 6 in England and Wales, 15 in Australia and 22 in New Zealand. Firearms caused 9,146 deaths in the US in 2012. There were 7 in New Zealand[1], 30 in Australia, and 41 in England and Wales. About 40% of Americans say they own a gun or live in a household with one, according to a 2017 survey, and the rate of murder or manslaughter by firearm is the highest in the developed world. In the USA, a firearm is used in nearly 500,000 crimes, resulting in the deaths and injuries of more than 110,000 people. 36,383 people die from gun violence of whom 12,830 are murdered.

While it is difficult to know exactly how many guns civilians own around the world, by every estimate, the US with around 270 million is far out in front. Despite all this, almost incomprehensibly, Gallup polls in the USA show a substantial majority of Americans oppose a ban on handguns. They say "Guns don't kill people, people kill people".

That is nonsense. It is people with guns who kill people. President Obama tried to have Congress pass new gun control laws, but the Republicans voted it down. The NRA supports politicians who oppose gun controls. There is a glimmer of hope. Just as here, the United States has seen a long-term decline in crime, with firearms offences seeing a steeper fall than other crimes.

---

[1] The ghastly mosque massacre of 51 Moslem worshippers in Christchurch in March 2019 completely destroyed our previously good record.

Suicidal

One distressed and depressed young man was charged under the Arms Act. His parents called the police when he drunkenly kept pointing a gun to his head, distressed over his inability to relate well with girls. It is not a case of criminality. It is very much an instance where counselling and treatment are required to give assistance. I took such steps in his case.

We have by international standards a disturbingly high teenage male suicide rate in New Zealand. I am told there were about 40 such deaths in 2017, slightly more Māori youths than Pakeha. The most common method is hanging. New Zealand's has the highest youth suicide rate in 41 OECD and EU countries. The overall suicide rate is double that in the USA and five times that of the United Kingdom.

Why? Why? The answer is complex but it is clear that poverty, the high rate of teenage pregnancies, bullying in schools, drug abuse, domestic violence, and poor family functioning are all significant factors. The high suicide rate ties in with other data, showing for instance child poverty, high rates of teenage pregnancies or families where neither of the parents have work. The number of people who have taken their own lives in New Zealand is the highest since records began, with 668 dying by suicide in 2018, the highest toll since records began 110 years ago. Sadly, Māori figures are disproportionately high.

Through the Looking Glass

A very obese, sweaty fellow, unhappy it seems with his appearance, fired a sawn-off .22 rifle at the mirror in his bedroom. It scared the neighbours half witless and did nothing at all either for the looking glass or the bedroom wall. The Arms Act defines sawn-off rifles as "pistols" and thus the offence is viewed most gravely, and two-year jail as a maximum sanction. Alice, as I shall call him, had no Arms licence and also had a drink problem. After reviewing several reports as to his mental health and social disadvantage, I sentenced him to 12 months probationary supervision with counselling and other community assistance.

Shooting Best Friends

There have been 28 fatalities in deer hunting incidents in the past 24 years – often where the shooter mistakes a person for a deer. Accidentally killing a best friend while hunting is an awful and unforgettable event. I had two such cases.

One man, a highly-regarded teacher mistook his best man and lifelong friend for a deer, and fatally shot him in the chest.

The other death occurred in a punt in the Gulf of Thames when an elderly man shot his lifetime friend with a shotgun while duck hunting. The hearing took two painful days, with the widow and her best friend (the defendant's wife) weeping in the rear of the court. The outcome was inevitable. He was obviously negligent and guilty of discharging a firearm dangerously. He should have pleaded guilty, and not have hired a lawyer. Perhaps understandably, he couldn't face the reality of decapitating his friend.

Both defendants were severely traumatised by what had happened. I thought the fact of conviction was sufficient penalty and imposed no penalty other than the payment of court costs.

In 2003, my friend and colleague Judge Chris McGuire took a very different view. He imprisoned two hunters for nine months. In separate hunting tragedies, each had shot and killed two other hunters. He emphasised that hunting accidents were becoming too frequent and hunters needed to realise there would be dire repercussions when negligent identification of targets lead to death. On reflection, I now agree with him, and that I was wrong to be so lenient.

The NZ Forest Service had a slogan "Better No Meat than No Mate."

33 deer-hunting deaths from 1979 to 2002 were assessed. Not properly identifying the target was a factor in two-thirds of cases. 58 per cent of all deaths were of friends who had become separated in the bush and lost sight of each other.

Poor Little Bambi

I was about eight, when the slaughter of Bambi's mother in the Walt Disney movie put me off hunters for life. Like Stephen King, it was the first horror movie I saw. Since then I have questioned whether it can be called a sport to lie camouflaged in the bush waiting to fire a .303 bullet into the chest of an unarmed, defenceless stag. Perhaps it is a sport if the stag is also armed with a .303 rifle and knows that the referee's whistle has started the game. Why not throw away the weapons and have the man go hunting, naked and unarmed? Who would win the game? Perhaps John Cleese goes too far when he says of hunters:

> *The excitement they experience when they murder an unarmed animal is entirely due to their deep feelings of inadequacy and importance in ordinary life.*

But it rings a bell. Does the hunter feel big and strong after excitedly murdering a defenceless animal? I am a fan of Sir David Attenborough. Wear camouflage, for sure. But guns and death, never. Just cameras, still and movie, with him and his crews since 1969, exercising their stalking skills by creating superb records of wild creatures across our planet.

In saying this I in no way belittle the need to cull excessive numbers of some species that threaten the natural environment.

Immigration

Punjabis work hard

The Hon. Mr Bill Birch was attacked for having the Labour Department employ as spies two men who had earlier organised Punjabis to pick vegetables for a commercial grower. The men ended up arresting the same Punjabis for whom they had earlier illegally organised work. A spokesman for the employment agency said he was horrified that 2000 Punjabis were taking jobs from Kiwis when we have 200,000 unemployed in New Zealand.

A grower, who seemed to be supported by the Minister himself, made the point that many New Zealand horticulturalists can't get Kiwis to do the job. And that is still the same today. Unemployment is not working!

The Labour department sends Kiwis out to the farms and after half a day many leave, saying the jobs do not pay enough and that the work is too hard. Much easier, and with less strain on the cervical spine, is to stay home, draw the dole, and let the Indians do the hard graft. Indians know how to work.

I spent many days of my work life dealing with unemployed people who hated the very thought of work. And that is a classic symptom of the unemployment malaise. An inertia. A depression. A slothful indolence. Some try to make excuses, but the hard truth is that in Asia, India, and many other parts of the globe there is no welfare state, and people either work or starve.

Many of the people appearing before me won't even use their backyard to grow a cabbage or a carrot. Cannabis perhaps, but even that is labour intensive. Better to buy it at the pub than have to pay the chiropractor. I see scores of unemployed but strong young men whose ancestors were tough warriors and who bear the same fine physique. But this vigour and strength fades in their 20s when beer, laziness, and fatty diet turns them into obese and idle sluggards. Work, as Oscar Wilde aptly said "is the curse of the drinking classes".

Slavery

$3000 Sale

Ron Gilbert had an interesting case: a 42-year-old Thai man charged with slavery! The accused was alleged to have sold a woman to an Auckland undercover police officer for $3000. Mind-blowing!! It is interesting to ponder just how different our society is from many others, and how far we have gone to emancipate women from the stereotyped cages in which they were imprisoned for millennia.

Purchase

I remember a case in Auckland where a Meadowbank businessman was charged with buying a Filipina woman. A jury convicted him, as I recall the case, but he had the conviction overturned on appeal. But as my delightful neighbour Val Ensor would say:

"All bloody well! But I can't think of anyone who would want to buy Myra?"

This was very much tongue in cheek. He loved her greatly and in all respects. She was a treasure.

Cheap and Disposable

The law requires real slavery: people held against their will, forced to work and paid nothing, or very little. Sometimes the slave holder 'pays' a few grains of rice to keep the slaves alive or uses a bogus payment that the slave holder reclaims at the end of the month. But the end result is that slavery is today what it has always been; one person totally controlling others and forcing them to work.

All races over many millennia have kept slaves in some form or another. We know that the Roman Empire was built on slaves, but Christendom and Islam justified slavery in their holy books. The English and the Maori both kept slaves. Even now slavery still occurs in current day Asia and Europe.

Slavery, whether for moral or economic reasons, was the major cause of the Civil War in the United States in which over 600,000 people lost their lives. Abraham Lincoln said "If slavery is not wrong, nothing is wrong."

Anti-Slavery International, an organisation founded in 1839 in London, today estimates, almost unbelievably, that there are 40 million people in modern slavery around the world. That figure includes 10 million children, nearly 30 million in forced labour, and millions in forced marriage or sexual exploitation. This means that there are more people in slavery today than at any other time in human history. Slavery has existed for thousands of years, but changes in the world's economy and societies over the past 50 years have enabled a resurgence of slavery.

Three trends have contributed most to the rise of modern slavery:

(1) the population explosion.

(2) social and economic changes causing unemployment.

(3) corrupt governments turning a blind eye to the problem.

This new slavery has two main characteristics: slaves today are cheap, and they are disposable.

In 2015, when Suzanne and I toured two old Louisiana slave plantations, we learned that an average slave in the American South in 1850 cost the equivalent of $40,000 in today's money; today a slave costs an average of $90.

Human Trafficking

In 2016, the first prosecution in New Zealand for human trafficking was brought against Faroz Ali. He was convicted of 15 human trafficking charges and 15 charges of aiding and abetting a person to unlawfully enter New Zealand. He pleaded guilty to numerous charges of helping people breach their visa conditions and not paying the minimum wage. Justice Paul Heath1 sentenced him to nine years and six months' imprisonment. Ali's treatment of the complainants was terrible. He lied to them about getting work visas. Nearly all their visas were just for one month as visitors, and did not allow them to work in New Zealand. They paid fees of several thousand dollars to Ali for nothing. They were treated "shamefully" with disgusting accommodation and 11-hour workdays often without any pay. Ali saved $100,000 from his failure to pay minimum wages and holiday pay.

In 2018, a Samoan national, Viliamu Samu, known locally as Joe Matamata, faced charges of human trafficking and slavery. He was alleged to have treated other Samoans as virtual slaves in the horticulture industry for several decades. The allegations were that he threatened and assaulted the workers, held their passports, and did not pay them a living wage.

---

[1] Justice Paul Heath served as a High Court judge from 2002 to 2018 when he took early retirement at age 62. He was greatly respected by both the District Court bench and the bar. He is now a full-time arbitrator.

Canine Law

If there is one type of cases judges hate most, it is dog prosecutions. One court day I had four dog prosecutions before 1.00 p.m. Two changed their pleas to guilty and admitted that Rover had been uncontrollably disobedient. The other two fought the good fight like pit bulls.

A year later I had a jury trial where the accused was charged with theft by finding. Finding, wait for it! A dog! I should go to Rome. I am now an expert in canine law.

Death Penalty

The law says that if a dog is proved to have attacked and bitten a human, the penalty is death. We use the ominous term – "destruction order". When the life of their canine child is at stake people will fight to the last bitch. Often owners will hire the best legal brains in the country to defend such cases. If their teenage son is before the court, often they don't bother to even attend court. They tell young Wayne to go and apply for legal aid. But when it comes to Rover? They hire a Q.C.!

I had two cases involving rather large dogs that had rushed at passers-by. Fortunately, no one had been bitten ("savaged" is the very descriptive word used by dog rangers) or attacked. It was just the "rushing at" which was the subject of the charge. Both complainant citizens were very traumatized by their encounters with Rip and Bruno. I have only kept jottings about Bruno.

Bruno

Bruno's owner was a seedy, grey-skinned elderly man with an almost impenetrable dialect, caused not by some quirk of geography and birth, but by the lack of serviceable teeth and an abundance of gum. His looks, however, belied him. He was a tenacious fighter for canine justice. He was absolutely certain that his beloved Bruno could never have jumped his three-foot two-inch gate in order to age the passing complainants five years in two minutes. The fact that the dog was a Ridgeback/Labrador cross weighing 60 kilograms with four rows of canines and no molars and had scared the melanin out of the skin of two very reasonable Māori working men who lived nearby did not impress the defendant one iota.

"No!" said the defendant. "Not only are they lying, but they have also kicked a hole in the bottom board of my gate. They have thrown stones onto my front lawn with the express intention of upsetting my cherished Bruno and his loving companion Fang."

I ruminated for two seconds as to the likelihood of the two albino workingmen having the courage to kick in the defendant's gate and thus let the predators loose upon their good selves. I found the charge proved. The defendant then told me he had already increased the height of the gate to 4 foot 6 inches. He handed me a letter from his neighbour (which I was unable to accept during the course of the trial as the neighbour, most wisely, had opted to stay home rather than become embroiled in such turbulent proceedings).

The handwriting was clearly that of an elderly person. The neighbour had carefully penned the statement that she had never seen the two dogs on the footpath at any time, day or night. But for all I know the elderly lady was long overdue for cataract removal, slept 15 hours a day in an alcoholic haze, or had been living "in terrorem" for so long that she was fearful of what two massive dogs and one spindly neighbour might do to her if she refused to pick up her biro and write said letter of exculpation.

Guilt was found. Fines imposed. Restraining order made. And, despite all the anger and paranoia exhibited during the hearing, the defendant smiled, said "thank you", agreed to keep the dog under control, and padded out of court with tail wagging.

Starving Chihuahua

In 1979, my Auckland colleague, Judge Patrick Mahony,[1] had an all-day hearing involving alleged cruelty to animals. The defendant faced charges of ill-treating and starving several Chihuahua dogs. One of the witnesses for the SPCA was a little old lady who was a Chihuahua lover. She testified as to the physical condition of the dogs when she first visited them. Tears came to her eyes and she said:

"Sir, they were totally emancipated."

Barking Mad

A Hamilton Disputes Referee had an unusual case in 1983. A King County farmer had purchased a dog. He advertised that he wanted a dog that would bark on command. He did not want the dog to muster livestock, but to use as a foil to the months of annoyance he had from the incessant barking of his neighbour's dog! The problem was that Bess did not live up to the contractual representation of responding to the command "Bark!" or "No Bark!" She just looked happily in her new owner's direction and wagged her black tail. So, the frustrated farmer sued, and won modest damages.

"What happened to your neighbour's dog?" asked the Referee after the case.

"Oh!" grinned the farmer. "No problem. That dog is dead!"

---

[1] From 1985 to 2004 he was the Principal Family Court Judge. In 2009, he became Sir Patrick when the Government reinstated knighthoods. He was made a Distinguished Companion of the New Zealand Order of Merit on his retirement. He was appointed to the Auckland Magistrate's Court bench one week after me – in February 1978. While thus significantly junior to me in date of appointment, he was superior to me in most other respects.

Breeding

A judge asked the owner of an aggressive dog, "Why did you choose this breed of dog?"

The defendant replied: "I often ask myself the very same question."

Inhumane Treatment

One day I had three defended dog prosecutions. I shall never end up on the Court of Appeal this way, I thought.

A thin, angry young woman had left her dog locked up in her house for four days without food or water. The neighbours, driven to distraction by the howling, had phoned the SPCA who found the poor animal in a very distressed state.

"How did you allow that to happen?"

"It wasn't my fault. I went away for the day and my car broke down."

"But four days?"

"I couldn't get back because of the car?"

"Why not phone your family or friends?"

"None of them have phones?"

"The neighbours must have a phone. They phoned the SPCA!"

"Don't like them."

She didn't like the dog too much either. Despite the fact that she was a 20-year-old solo mum on a benefit with no whanau support, I fined her $200, costs $65, ordered her to pay the $368 SPCA charges for food, veterinary care, and transport charges and I forfeited the dog to the SPCA. I also gave the fine to the Society. Not that it would matter much. The woman was unlikely to pay the fine. She would end up doing Community Service, blaming the neighbours, the SPCA, the dog, and me for the fact that she had to pay a penalty. What she would never do is blame herself. Oh! Goodness Gracious me, no!

Abandoned

An uncaring, unkempt, unhealthy, unhappy man had good cause to look miserable. He had left his dog behind in Wainuiomata when he had shifted north before Christmas. The problem was he left his dog and her new pups in the car shed of his rented house and took off into the night without a kia ora. After a week, the neighbour became upset at the plight of the dogs and phoned the SPCA.

One puppy had died. The other just made it. The mother dog was given to a caring home. And the defendant, uncaring homo sapiens, was fined $300 together with similar expenses to those I have just related.

Maintain, Train, Restrain.

Dog owners have the advantage in court cases because many lie through their teeth in order to stop the not callous judge ordering an execution. Another difficulty is that these cases are hard to prosecute, and the cases are not helped by the fact that the prosecutors are usually City Council employees, not lawyers. There is always difficulty identifying the dog, identifying the owner, preventing hearsay evidence, proving service of notices and matters of that type.

I have noticed an upsurge in such prosecutions. There are too many people with dogs they can't maintain, train, or restrain. It seems to be a popular thing to own a dog as a property or personal protection device. The Staffordshire Bull Terrier, those ugly-snouted, pig-eyed, fighting dogs, are particularly popular, especially with the unemployed. And making matters worse, people become so emotional about their dogs! Dog fight days are not my favourite!

Despite the instances of cruelty or negligence against dogs that we see in court, most human beings have a very special relationship with man's best friend. As an old friend of my father told me, "Dogs love even real bastards". It is rare that a dog exhibits the madness, anger and savagery of humans and when they do, it is usually because of a lack of training or an absence of understanding the basic needs of the animal.

An illustration of the lengths to which a dog lover will go, and of the legal expenses incurred, was shown in the last dog prosecution case I did before my retirement. The whole sad saga cost the dog owner many thousands of dollars in legal and peripheral costs and resulted in considerable publicity, both positive and negative. As can be expected, there is often great antagonism between the victim of a dog attack and the owner of dear old Fido.

Dog Bites

Remember that our canine companions have extremely sharp teeth and very strong jaws. Not all dogs are man's, or more importantly, children's best friend. Dog bite statistics in New Zealand are horrific. A 2015 study,[1] showed 99,000 serious dog bite

---

[1] *The Burden of Dog bite Injuries in New Zealand: 2004-2014*. Authors: Plastic and Reconstructive surgeon, Johnny Mair; Medical Student, Zachary Moaveni – Middlemore Hospital.

injuries in the decade 2004-2014 with 5,842 cases requiring hospitalisation and surgical management. Our figures are higher than incidence rates in Australia, UK, and USA. Those at highest risk are small children, Māori and people living in poor socioeconomic areas. Most injuries occur on private property. Every year almost 12,000 people are bitten by dogs, including more than 1700 children – many left with permanent scars. No verifiable figures are readily available for how many dog attacks occur in New Zealand each year (most are probably not reported), but forecasts are for attacks to reach 16,000 a year by 2020 if no change happens. In fact, no-one has any idea how many bites there are each year, something which could only be rectified by compulsory reporting.

Family

Family Court

Before the District Court was created in 1981, I decided many family disputes. Just before the creation of the Family Court I was elected as the inaugural President of the newly formed Family Courts Association of New Zealand. Later, when I was appointed a jury trial judge rather than a family court judge, I was obliged to resign from the association. On reflection, I made the correct decision not to return to the Family Court later in my career. Deciding issues of family dispute is emotionally draining and highlights personal deficiencies as a husband and parent. But, just as a priest can give sensible advice to families despite living a life of celibacy, so a Family Court Judge can give sensible advice despite having personal domestic problems of his or her own.

Judging Families

But personal problems are irksome for a judge. "How can I resolve the problems of the family appearing before me in court, when I can't even solve my own?" Conflict and disagreement are part of our lives. Couples celebrating 70 years of marriage who tell fawning journalists that they've never had a cross word in all that time, are either hopeless liars or moronic cretins. It is only human for us to disagree. We all have different personalities and viewpoints. Life is a stressful process and misunderstandings, financial pressures, infidelity, anger, parental conflict, and sibling rivalry, all take their toll. In many families, alcohol, drugs, and mental illness make matters even worse. Physical, mental and sexual abuse may be commonplace. Kindness and love evaporate. Egotism, self-absorption, narcissism and even worse – psychopathy – can totally destroy relationships in the family, causing division, deceit, scapegoating and turning one family member against another.

Artful Dodger

A man applied to have his maintenance order reduced. He had fathered another child by another woman. Our local magistrate, D.G. Sinclair,[1] gave judgment:

> *I think you are just a dodger. That is all you are. But I will allow the application in part. I must face the fact that your de facto has now got a child so I will reduce the wife's maintenance by $10.00 per week. So, what you have got to face, in case you do not know it, you have got to keep on paying $20.00 per week instead of $30.00 And do not take on any more women!*

Bad Parenting

All too often, the problem starts with the parents. Bad parenting, or sometimes a total lack of parenting has a universally destructive impact on children and their development. Not ever knowing a father, or having little contact with a father, has a negative influence on a child's entire life. Probation, prison, and psychological reports reflect this sad reality. Solo parenting is all too common in New Zealand. Many boys raised without positive male role models struggle to develop their full potential. Children raised in an environment of parental conflict, tension, hostility, violence, and infidelity frequently struggle to have good meaningful relationships in their own lives. Studies show that such children have lower levels of well-being, struggle with relationships, and form fewer good peer relationships.

Most of us have problems with communication. Not just as spouses but also with our children, friends, work mates and others. Proper communication becomes difficult when we are emotionally upset.

Vindictive Hubby

Slandering, ridiculing and making unfair or exaggerated accusations against a spouse is often a tool used by litigants seeking custody of their children. Judges know this and

---

[1] Donald George Sinclair, Senior Stipendiary Magistrate, died 1981aged 72.

are watchful. One judge passed a photo around our common room table. It was an exhibit in the case he was hearing. It showed an attractive young woman lying naked in a field. Tastefully protruding between her legs was a daffodil. The husband said this showed how debauched and sinful she was – totally unsuitable to have custody of their little girl.

"Who took the photo?" asked the judge

"I did", said the husband.

Unquestionably the photographer hubby was a consensual and active participant. He was Oliver Mellors with Constance Chatterley, the daffodil replacing the daisy chain. Unless it's a 'selfie', a photo requires a person on both sides of the lens.

No Communication

In families and marriages, communication may be shallow and lack any real meaning. Yelling, screaming, swearing and blaming become the norm. Things are said that should never be said; things that are never forgiven or forgotten. Often the real issues remain hidden. The surface issue hides the real problem. Unspoken anger, unhealed wounds, and bitter resentment remain unsaid and thus unresolved.

Power and control are part of the human condition. Power clashes between parents and between siblings may lead to irreparable lasting harm. All families undergo stresses when adolescent children challenge parental controls and seek their own way in life. Generational and sometimes cultural differences raise additional concerns. Frequently in court, I see teenagers rejecting the religious and cultural beliefs of their parents to join gangs or engage in delinquent behaviour. One fairly common example of this is the Polynesian child, raised in a strict Christian household with strong cultural structures, breaking away to join a peer group in antisocial or criminal behaviour. Family cohesion is destroyed and family conflict increased.

Youthful Offending

Burglar Boy

The Youth Court prosecutor presented me with a 14-year-old who had allegedly committed eight burglaries while awaiting disposition on a charge of assault with intent to injure. He looked as though margarine wouldn't melt in his very youthful mouth. He was really just a kid! His small rural community clearly has its problems with unemployment, drunkenness, boredom, delinquency and lousy parents.

Another youth, aged 16, from the same town, got ratty about something, so he kicked in four shop windows, including the front window of the Salvation Army. Total Repair bill: $1,527.00. He had been unemployed since leaving school at 14. The police found him, very drunk, and bleeding from both hands.

I asked why he had smashed the windows.

"Dunno" he answered, rolling his eyes.

After years on the bench I still asked dumb questions! He was too drunk to remember. Frustration?

One Big Slip

Some years ago, in early May, Auckland University completed a day of its annual capping ceremony. Notoriously, the new graduates, wearing their gowns and hoods, descend on local bars and restaurants to celebrate the end of their studies and the commencement of a new life.

One brilliant young engineering graduate took things too far. He became very intoxicated and went alone to the Westhaven Marina, the largest boat marina in the southern hemisphere. He unchained a dinghy on the wharf edge and rowed out to a luxury yacht moored in the harbour. He boarded the stern of the yacht. He jimmied open the cabin door and stole liquor from the galley. He then sat on the back deck, like a young Onassis, and began to amplify the quantity of alcohol he had already consumed.

A neighbouring yachtie saw all this. He realised that the young man was a stranger and that the cabin door was smashed. He phoned the police. The harbour police arrived shortly thereafter in the Deodar II. The young man was charged with theft of the dinghy, breaking and entering the yacht, and stealing liquor from the galley.

The next day, in a sorry state, he appeared before the court and sought an adjournment without plea so that he could get help from a lawyer. He appeared before me several weeks later. He entered a plea of guilty to all charges. A very senior and competent lawyer, engaged by his distraught Waikato family, represented him.

The lawyer urged me to discharge the young man without conviction. He had no previous convictions, had paid reparation for the broken lock and the consumed liquor, and his brilliant passes at the Auckland University engineering school became the main topic of submission and mitigation.

It was established, with written and personal support in court from the Dean of the Faculty of Engineering, that he was the most brilliant young graduate the engineering school had seen in many years. The professor told me the young man had passed his exams with the highest of marks and had been awarded a prestigious scholarship at a famous engineering institution in Scandinavia. Given his undoubted and superior ability, this scholarship would potentially point him to a distinguished lifetime of achievement in the engineering world.

I posed the question:

> *If an unemployed young Māori lad from South Auckland had stolen the dinghy, broken into the yacht, and started drinking the alcohol, what with the court have done with him?*

Senior counsel squirmed somewhat. The young graduate squirmed more. His parents and the Prof looked alarmed. The barrister responded by pointing out that the young man from South Auckland would not face the same dire consequences to his future employment by reason of a conviction. I maintained a very grave demeanour. I indicated that I would take the lunch adjournment, would consider the submission further, and would give my decision after lunch.

I was not attempting to be sadistic in putting off the case for an hour and a quarter. I wanted the young man seriously to reflect upon the gravity of his situation. A few hours of drunken, youthful stupidity were threatening his entire occupational future. After lunch, I announced to the young man that I would not enter a conviction against him if he made a very substantial contribution to a local charity. In the Auckland court, the normal practice was that the donation should be to the local Salvation Army because its officers did excellent work in and around the court helping indigent, alcoholic or mentally ill defendants. No other churches did so.

I was aware that the young man had already paid full reparation for the damage to the yacht and for the alcohol that he had consumed. He was clearly very remorseful and it was unlikely he would ever repeat his offending. I stood the case down briefly until the lawyer presented me with a receipt for the $1,000.00 donation. I then made an order directing that he be discharged without conviction.

Over the years, I have discussed the facts of this case with friends. Some think I was very wrong and should have punished the young man by imposing a community-based sentence or a heavy fine. Others agreed that what I did was appropriate. Looking back, I am pleased that I did not play a part in wrecking the young man's life.

As the English rock band, Pink Floyd sang it:

One slip and down the hole we fall
It seems to take no time at all
A momentary lapse of reason
That binds a life for life
A small regret, you won't forget
There'll be no sleep in here tonight.

Sergeant Ropiha's Greenstone Ring

Sergeant Ropiha never went overseas with the 28th (Māori) Infantry Battalion in 1940. He did not exist. He was a figment of my imagination. I created him to get a message across to young Māori teenagers who burgled houses. Several police and parents told me it worked wonders. Sometimes the youth cried. Sometimes the mother or social worker cried. I would say this:

Wiremu, I want to tell you about a brave Māori soldier who went to war with the famous Māori Battalion. Do you know about the Māori Battalion? (They all did). Good.
Sergeant Ropiha had married a year before and had a baby daughter. His wife and baby took the train to Wellington to farewell the Sergeant on the wharf before the troop ship sailed overseas to the war. He kissed his young wife.
"Aroha ahau ki a koe", he smiled. "I love you."

From out of his tunic pocket, he pulled a tiny gift which he gave to her. It was a small greenstone ring. She put it on her finger and kissed him back. "Haere ra", he said, "Farewell."
The ring was not expensive. They had no money. But to her it was a taonga[1] beyond price. A gift of love.
Sergeant Ropiha was killed in the desert war and never returned to Aotearoa. Mrs. Ropiha grieved greatly. She raised her daughter. She never remarried. As an old kuia, the ring was still her greatest treasure. The ring became too small for her gnarled old finger so she kept it in a small saucer on her bedside table. One day, a young fellow like you climbed through her window to burgle her house. There wasn't much to steal because she was poor. But the boy saw the greenstone ring and stole it. Later, he threw it away because no-one wanted to buy it off him. Mrs. Ropiha was overwhelmed with sadness that her husband's precious gift was stolen. She died a few months later of a broken heart. All because of a young burglar and thief like you.

Sione's Toyota

Another of my fictional tales that seemed to get a message across to Samoan boys was this:

Ioane, did you hear the sad story about Sione's dying grandfather? (Of course, not). Well, Sione and his happy aiga[2] lived in Mangere. Sione was 19. He was the only one who owned a car. It was an old Toyota that he parked outside their house.
The aiga was going through a tough time because Sione's tamamatua[3] was dying at Middlemore Hospital. A nurse phoned them about midnight.
"Can you please come here as soon as possible, the old man is very ill and the doctor doesn't think he will live very long."
The family quickly dressed and ran out to go to the hospital. But to their dismay, Sione's Toyota had gone. Only a few pieces of smashed window glass remained. No-one had any cash for a taxi. Other family and friends were miles away. An hour went by before a cousin arrived to drive them to the hospital. But it was too late. Granddad was dead. They were unable to say their goodbyes or say a prayer with him. They were devastated. They were angry. All because a young fellow like you had stolen Sione's Toyota without thinking about the consequences.

Floating with Noah

Pre-adolescent marijuana use is clearly linked to schizophrenia. The experts say that the causative factors may be multi-factorial and sometimes hard to pinpoint. The

---

[1] A treasured possession
[2] Family
[3] Grandfather

amount of cannabis smoked and genetics seem to increase the likelihood. Scientists studying the AKT1 gene found that the risk for people with a particular variant of the gene was seven times higher for those who smoke cannabis daily when compared with infrequent or non-smokers. It will be interesting to see what future scientific research tells us. In any event, the psychiatrists I talk to say that the incidence of schizophrenia in young adults is noticeable and worrying. They all say that the brain damage is irreversible and only treatable with lifelong appropriate medication.

But try warning young people! They don't listen, don't care, and think we geriatrics are still floating along with Noah. Prehistoric old men?

Teen Court

In 1987, I dealt with four 15 year old boys from an Auckland boarding school, who had unlawfully taken a motor vehicle in order to travel into the city to a teenage party to meet some girls. They located a car on the roadside. They broke the door lock and opened the door. The boys were unable to get it started; the police arrested them a short distance away.

All four boys appeared before me in the Children and Young Persons Court charged with interfering with and converting a motor vehicle. Parents and a senior teacher were with them. All four admitted the charges. The boys were asked to describe the circumstances of their offending. Their versions were acknowledged by the police as being correct, and social welfare reports were ordered. Their cases were adjourned for two weeks for that purpose.

Before they left the court, I invited the teacher, a social worker, and representatives of the boys' families into my chambers. I told them I had been studying a teen court process in the USA and suggested that we could try the same system with the four teenagers. I explained that, if the information in the social worker's reports was positive (as seemed likely), I would consider having the punishment imposed by the boys' peers after a formal hearing at their school. It was agreed that full consent would be needed from the boys, their parents, and from the school authorities. Kaumatua[1] consent was also sought.

The reports from the social worker were very good. Three of the four boys were first offenders, although one had been expelled from another high school for selling marijuana. All boys came from caring homes. Three were popular with their peers. Two were talented at sports. Three were of average academic ability. One was an "A" student who hoped to become an air-force pilot after leaving school. He clearly had the potential to do so. A criminal record would jeopardise this ambition.

---

[1] Elders

Two weeks later, after the reports had been considered, consents were forthcoming from everyone. The school principal was very positive and agreed that the court be held in the school hall one evening. He agreed that time be made available for all participants to be tutored in their respective court duties. He agreed to select a jury of 15-year-old boys from the same class as the four offenders. He wished the anonymity of the school to be preserved and his wishes have been honoured. The anonymity of the boys under the Children and Young Persons Act was also ensured.

The boys, their parents, and senior family representatives all agreed that participation would be beneficial. I promised the boys that full performance of the sentence imposed upon the boys by their peers would result in them being discharged from the official proceedings without any conviction or punishment. A local lawyer, Mr. Richard Blackwood, generously volunteered his time to act as "training officer" for the boys and spent time with me discussing the ideas, and planning the procedures and techniques to be employed.

As no overseas training material was available, I prepared instruction sheets. There were separate sheets for the jurors, the prosecutor, and the defence advocate (all of whom were 15-year-olds). The information explained the basic principles of sentencing, the roles of the advocates, the importance of law and order, and suggested possible sentences. Earlier in the week, the boys spent an evening with Richard being trained in their roles and in the procedure to be adopted at the actual hearing. They were given the instruction sheets to study.

The sentencing hearing was heard in the school hall. I was the judge but played a very minor role. The "prosecutor" and "defence counsel" capably outlined the facts to the 12 young jurors and made their arguments.

The jury retired and returned 20 minutes later with a different punishment for each boy.

(a) BOY 1: Sentenced to write apology letters to three of the victims and to spend three Sunday afternoons mowing staff lawns for three hours.

(b) BOY 2: Sentenced to write two apology letters to victims and to spend two Sunday afternoons mowing staff lawns for three hours.

(c) BOY 3: Sentenced to spend four Sunday afternoons cleaning school vehicles and tending gardens for three hours.

(d) BOY 4: Sentenced to write apology letters to the three victims, to weed the school tennis courts (apparently quite a large undertaking) until completion and to read the lesson at a school church service the following Sunday.[49]

All punishments were appropriate, and in due course were properly completed. When the four boys came back before me in the real court, I commended them, warned them, and did not impose any further punishment. As far as I know, none of the boys subsequently appeared before the court. The "shaming" before their peers, teachers and parents had achieved the right result. The court received television and national radio news coverage. It was mentioned in the news and on talkback shows on all the Auckland stations but one. Other provincial stations also mentioned it. I received favourable and constructive correspondence from many sources: a university professor of psychology, the principal of a College of Education, teachers, social workers, several members of the Stokes Valley Methodist Church, members of other religious groups, lawyers and journalists.

After getting written feed-back from all participants and onlookers, I wrote a detailed report Teenage peer influences: a teenage sentencing court evaluation.[1] I submitted it to the Justice Department for consideration. Some months later, I was advised that such a sentencing court was not considered appropriate. I took it no further.[2]

All these years later I still believe that teenagers are powerfully influenced by the attitudes and actions of their friends. Peer influences may be good or bad, positive or deviant. My small experiment highlighted the pressures that result in delinquent offending. As we told the school that evening:

> *We all live in a community and must relate to other people in a caring and harmonious way. Offending is only offending because the vast majority of people prefer to lead orderly, peaceful, and honest lives, working together in a spirit of tolerance and cooperation. Crime causes people to be hurt. Crime is a symptom of the worst aspects of human behaviour: violence, intolerance, cruelty, inhumanity, dishonesty, selfishness, anger and greed.*

Starship Nurse

Judges can win big in the Youth Court. Lives can be changed for the better. Sadly, we seldom get feedback, positive or negative. My most positive outcome arose in the Youth Court in Otahuhu. A 15-year-old girl of Māori heritage appeared before me on a shoplifting charge. It was her first offence. She was personable, pretty and bright. I spent some time talking to her, asking what she wanted to do with her life.

"I want to be a nurse aid." she said.

"Why a nurse aid? Do you want to make beds and empty bedpans?" I asked. "Why not be a nurse?"

She seemed a bit taken aback, and upon further probing told me that she'd left school and didn't have the education to train as an actual nurse.

---

[1] Youth Justice Library, Wellington, 1987.

[2] The USA National Association of Youth Courts, reports that there are (2018) more than 1,000 youth court programs in 49 states and the District of Columbia. Several states have passed legislation providing for such Teen courts.

"Well, then, go back to school and get your School Certificate and University Entrance."

"I could never do that."

"Of course, you could. Why not? Kia kaha."[1]

About ten years later I, was working for a few weeks at the District Court in Auckland when a clerk phoned me in my chambers and said that a young woman wished to speak with me. For security reasons, judges and staff are always cautious about letting strangers into the judges' suite. I was assured that she looked genuine and showed none of the known hallmarks of an assassin. She was brought into my chambers. She was tall, elegant, with a lovely smile. She introduced herself as the same girl from the youth court I had dealt with a decade earlier. I didn't recognise her or her name. She was one of so many.

She said she wished to thank me and held out her registered nurse's medal. She said:

> *"I am now a ward sister at Starship Children's Hospital – I wanted to thank you because that would never have happened without you talking to me and spending time with me that day in Youth Court. I thought long and hard about what you said. I went back to school. I found studying very hard. But I made it. And I love my life, caring for sick children. Thank you."*

Wow! I felt as though I had won the lottery. I was delighted. Judges are rarely thanked. I am still purring all these years later.

The Lawyer's Widow

A murderer appeared before us at the Parole Board. He was already on Life Parole. I remembered the killing. It was diabolical. He and another 16-year-old youth, high from sniffing glue, broke into the Hamilton home of a lawyer's widow, Evelyn Orr, aged 84 years. Having previously been burgled several times, she was fearful. She kept her doors and windows locked both day and night. But this didn't deter the two youths who may have stolen a key. For some demented evil reason, the burglary led to a monstrous and sustained attack on her with an electric jug, broken milk bottle, dining room chair, garden hoe and rake. She suffered a broken spine, several broken ribs, a punctured lung and massive blood loss. Blood was found seven feet up one wall. All in the course of a burglary that profited the youths by some tins of food, groceries and various house keys.

---

[1] Be strong.

Why? Because the youth was never loved, committed other crimes from an early age, was raised in welfare institutions, associated with anti-social peers, was constantly drunk or stoned, and didn't give a stuff about anyone but himself.

Stubborn

An interesting comment in a pre-sentence report:

"Andy is 'forthright and non-concessional'."

Does this make him a difficult and stubborn young bastard?

Sloths

Laziness is increasingly something we often find. Some young people are so slothful and idle that they literally don't even know what day of the week it is. Unemployment and substance abuse sap the will to be productive, active and optimistic about life. Many seem in court to be "no-hopers" or useless layabouts when in fact it is often that life is not, and probably never will, be positive for them. It is a vicious cycle.

I remanded one young fellow for a report on his seventh driving while disqualified charge and fourth drink/drive charge. He had driven one block from his home to the local shop. The constable asked:

"Why didn't you walk to the shop?"

"Couldn't be bothered walking the distance," came the reply.

Imagine what hard work on periodic detention for 26 Saturdays must do for a youth like him?

A year or so earlier, I had a young man before me, and the issue was whether he went to prison or did periodic detention. It became an easy decision when he told me:

"I would rather go to prison. I don't want to do the work."

The mental images this conjured...?

Hormonal Temptation

All around the country, on billboards and in the windows of shops which retailed intimate lingerie, were photographs of Australian (later international) model Elle MacPherson, known affectionately in the trade as "The Body". And, if I might personally note herein, appropriately so!

Several of the billboards went missing (as might be expected as they are much bigger and better than Playboy centrefolds). But two culprits in Wellington were caught! The huge poster was difficult to conceal. Considering the billboard poster looks to be larger than the average student flat, I didn't find it surprising! They were hauled before a

Wellington beak – an unidentified colleague of mine. The lads were discharged without conviction because their mitigatory submission helped win the day. The two submitted:

"We only did it because we were controlled by our hormones!"

That could not have failed to impress even the hardest hearted and oldest judge!

As Dorothy Fuldheim[1] has written: "This is a youth-oriented society, and the joke is on them because youth is a disease from which we all recover."

Or as Oscar Wilde wrote in *Lady Windermere's Fan*: "The youth of the present day are quite monstrous. They have absolutely no respect for dyed hair."

Youthful exuberance and stupidity, especially with the male gender, is often displayed in court. Judges have the power, in special cases, not to enter convictions, but to discharge a youthful offender without conviction.

False Complaint

A nubile, naughty, nutty 15-year-old faced two charges: one of stealing from her grandfather and the other of making a false complaint to the police.

Jilly was a strange and troubled teenager. She stole $500 off her grandfather by forging his name and using his credit card. But the most serious matter was the false statement.

She told her mother, and later the police, that a well-known member of the Filthy Few Motor Cycle Gang had raped her outside a teenage nightclub.

The whole story was a fiction, a fantasy. She told me she made it all up because she was upset with her boyfriend who had left her outside the nightclub and was dancing with someone else.

She needs counselling or psychological investigation. For that reason, I placed her on supervision for six months

Deaf Facto

A 16-year-old in the Youth Court offered to pay for the damage he had caused to a car. I asked the thin, pimpled stripling the source of income. He said he was on a "marriage benefit".

"But," I said, taken aback by his youth, "at 16, surely you are not married?"

"Oh! Sort of. I'm in a 'deaf facto', but she mostly lives with her mum now that the baby has been born!"

I checked. He was on a domestic purposes benefit because Social Welfare thought he had daily care of the baby. Where are we going as a society when inept, incompetent

---

[1] American Journalist and TV personality, died 1989 aged 96.

16-year-olds father babies and expect us, the taxpayers, to do the paying – somctimes for decades?

Bad Little Burglar

In Youth Court, I had a bad little burglar – 14 years old. No one knew what to do with him. The social worker, in recommending supervision at the Boys Home at Auckland, listed the boy's problems as being:

(1) Poverty.
(2) Unemployment.
(3) Drugs and alcohol.
(4) Parenting – or lack of.
(5) Peer influence.
(6) Boredom.

Just about says it all, doesn't it?

Eccentrics

"Don't spread it around, but on the really tough ones, I just go with 'eenie, meenie, minie, moe.'"

Ambrose Tindall

It is interesting how seemingly minor cases can generate such anger and have dire consequences. That is why I always tell Justices of the Peace that their jurisdiction is so important. A 70-year-old appearing before the JPs on a defended but very minor traffic charge may find the whole experience extremely traumatic. It may be the first time in his life that he has ever appeared in court. He may have "stewed and simmered" for months or even years and if he viewed the decision as wrong, would, like Ambrose Tindall, stew for the rest of his life.

Ambrose Tindall appeared before me in the Henderson Magistrate's Court in July 1980 for a further remand. He had been arrested the previous month when he stabbed his local Member of Parliament, Dail Jones, in the chest, puncturing his lung. Tindall had visited Jones several times at his constituency clinic in Henderson. He went there to elicit support for his long-standing obsession over perceived injustices arising from a $15.00 traffic violation he had incurred back in 1972. Previous visits to the MP had been eccentric but non-violent. Jones had repeated his earlier advice that there was nothing he could do to help Tindall, as the legal process had run its course and there was no way to quash the conviction.

Tindall was a returned soldier. "Surrender" was not in his lexicon. He had no criminal convictions before or after the traffic ticket. He defended himself on the traffic violation which was, if memory serves me, for going through a give-way sign. Some say it was a parking ticket, but I don't think so.

The case was heard by a Justice of the Peace.[1] The JP heard testimony from the police officer. He then heard from Tindall, who said the officer was wrong in what he said he saw. The JP (as was usually the case with traffic cases) said he preferred the testimony of the officer. He convicted a very angry Ambrose. He fined him a modest fine of $15.00 and ordered him to pay the court costs.

Ambrose was livid. He was appalled that the JP had not believed him. He appealed. The appeal was heard in the Supreme Court (the present day High Court). Mr Justice Graham Speight[2] heard the appeal. It must have been apparent to him that Tindall was exceedingly distraught at the lower court verdict. But the judge was obliged to find that the JP had heard the witnesses, preferred the testimony of the officer, and entered the conviction. In law, he could not upset that finding. As a concession to an obviously over-wrought man, he allowed the appeal in part, cancelled the fine, but retained the conviction and costs.

But that was a lighted match thrown into a bag of fireworks. It was not the fine that mattered to Ambrose. It was the conviction. His name had been sullied. He had been unjustly dealt with, not just by the JP but also by the learned judge. The fireworks exploded. He went to prison for a few days for refusing to pay the costs.

That made matters worse. After his release from prison, he threw petrol onto the steps of the High Court. Later he hurled acid up onto the bench of Judge Peter Graham in the District Court in Henderson. He started a letter campaign seeking redress. He wrote to the Prime Minister and others. In 1977, he sent a threatening letter to the Attorney General, Peter Wilkinson. It included the disturbing threat:

> *The time has arrived for action… as I have tried every lawful means to correct this injustice. I now intend to go outside the law and tell you I shall physically bring you to your knees. If, in the fracas, you lose your life, then so be it.*

He was charged, but was found unfit to stand trial on the grounds of insanity and detained at Lake Alice Psychiatric Hospital. He died not long after. Jones fully recovered. He was a practicing lawyer in West Auckland.

He continued to serve as a Member of Parliament.

The point of all this is that just because a case may seem to be trivial to the judge or lawyers, it is very important to the individual concerned. Important, even life changing.

---

[1] I cannot find the name of the JP. The way things went with, Tindall he probably changed his name, sold up everything and emigrated to outback West Australia.

[2] Justice Speight was a greatly admired judge. He retired in 1998 after 32 years on the bench. He was knighted in 1982. He died in 2008 at age 86. Sir Graham was chancellor of Auckland University in the late 1970's.

Te Ringa Mangu Nathan (Dun) Mihaka

Dick Kearney told me he was presiding over the Mayor Island Protest case for the third week, when his blood ran cold. He looked up and saw the muscular figure of Te Ringa Mangu Nathan (Dun) Mihaka walk into his court. Dun, who was a Māori activist from way back, with many convictions and notable cases under his belt, was a real pain in the butt he loved to display to the world. His hobby was taking up other Māori's protests as his own and baring his backside to royalty as the ultimate insult.

I sent him off to periodic detention a few years earlier after a defended hearing in which he raved on in a disturbingly illogical fashion.

He called us all "Mr Judge". He was intelligent but irrational. I believed him to be a dangerous man. He had well over 20 convictions for assault, and his demeanour was always aggressive and arrogant.

In 1989, he published a book *Whakapohane*[1], telling of his defended hearing when charged with baring his buttocks to the Prince and Princess of Wales in 1983. I haven't read it. I don't know anyone who did. The concept behind whakapohane (baring the bottom) was to show contempt for the enemy. It is not historically or geographically just a Māori insult. In England, the USA and even with some Pakeha sports team members in the back of busses, it is called "mooning." At the battle of Crécy in 1346, the French army bared their bums to the English archers. King Edward III of England was not amused. He ordered his longbow archers to aim at these irresistible targets. The battle was won, and the much larger French army was badly defeated and routed.

But even in the present day, such baring of the posterior parts is still employed as a powerful tool of protest. President George W. Bush was confronted by 1000 naked behinds during a state visit in Sweden in 2001. The youthful protesters were angered at America's rejection of the Kyoto protocol on global warming.

Dick said there was some incident in the foyer as he walked past with his clerk. Mihaka had been arrested. That would cause more trouble than it was worth, but what do we do with such radicals? He says he is protesting for his people. But it was people like Professor Ranginui Walker and Sir Tipene O'Regan, both well-educated and balanced leaders with Māori heritage who made great progress for Māori with intelligence and compromise. Mihaka is just a pain in the posterior parts.

I first came across him after his arrest for trespass in the Bastion Point land dispute in 1978. He appeared before me again over later years mainly for offences of violence.

---

[1] By Te Ringa Mangu (Dun) Mihaka & Diane Patricia Prince , Auckland, Ruatara Publications, 1984.

He hated community-based sentences and always preferred prison sentences. As with many activists he did not lack intelligence. He was just single-minded, narcissistic, intolerant of others, and lashed out when challenged.

Without surprise, I read that in 2010 he was sentenced to 28 days imprisonment for contempt of court. Nothing much has changed over many years. On a busy Whangarei court day, he appeared before my colleague Judge John McDonald, a local judge and earlier the Crown Solicitor in Rotorua during the days I presided over jury trials in that city. John and the other Northland judges earned their pay. They faced frequent abusive behaviour by Māori activists. John had convicted several for contempt in the face of the court and sentenced them to prison. I applauded his stance. Showing weakness in a public courtroom only leads to further future problems.

What happened was that Mihaka had referred to cases he had before another local judge, Keith de Ridder. He bluntly referred to him as "De Ridder". Judge McDonald corrected Mihaka and told him to refer to the judge properly as "Judge de Ridder". Mihaka, never one to back down, persisted in omitting the title. He was warned and then finally held in contempt.

It was then that he called Judge McDonald "an arsehole". It seems that, with his predilection for exposing that part of his anatomy, he has an undue fascination with backside broadsides. The notes of evidence showed he repeated the "arsehole' epithet several times. He was sent to the cells but when he appeared back before the judge later in the day, he apologised to the judge but refused to apologise for not properly referring to Judge de Ridder.

He appealed the 28-day sentence but the High Court judge, Justice Rodney Hansen (a sensible judge very supportive of our bench), refused his appeal, saying Mihaka's outburst was a "flagrant and provocative challenge to the authority of the court". He said the sentence was severe but not excessive.

As an example of illogical thinking, Mihaka told Justice Hansen that because Mihaka's name had been misspelled on the court list, he could see no reason to refer to Judge de Ridder by his correct title. He said that the word "arsehole" had "escaped his lips" on just one occasion. Justice Hansen did not accept such patent nonsense and declined the appeal.

To give him his due, Mihaka had a valid argument about demanding recognition of the use of the Māori language in court. He appealed this issue to the Court of Appeal in 1979. Partly because of this, in 1986 the Waitangi Tribunal recommended that Māori be confirmed as an official language of New Zealand. Parliament agreed, and in 1987 the Māori Language Act became law. Māori was affirmed as an official language of New Zealand.

No racist

Jack Waerenga testified before a jury and me, and a remarkable experience it was. He was very intelligent, used English with considerable skill and vocabulary, but did not know when to shut up. His lawyer lost control of him and over about 20 minutes his paranoia was there for all to see. The Crown prosecutor quizzed him about why he had used a bottle to assault the complainant in a Wanganui Hotel, and the suggestion that there was a racist background to their disagreement.

"Rubbish", he said. "I am proud of my Scottish genealogy. Pure Sutherland. Tartan, seal, Black Watch, clans and all. Through my grandmother. I'm no racist."

Racist he may not be. But "bottler" in the Glaswegian dockland tradition he certainly was. The jury, after a two-hour retirement, found him guilty. Having protested his innocence so vehemently before them for so long, he found it hard to comprehend that they had found him to be a liar. And with several Māori jurors finding against him to boot! He threw his file over the side of the dock in disgust.

He had a very long list of previous convictions. Surprisingly, having regard to the recent Armed Offender callout to his home (he regaled us with this during his testimony – "they are out to get me"), he had only one minor conviction for violence, many years ago. Given the serious violence, and injuries to the victim, I sentenced him to 18 months imprisonment.

Long Trials

I expressed concern to the lawyers that I was worried about how long the Mayor Island case might take, as the preliminary hearing had taken three weeks and I didn't want the trial to drag on ad infinitum. I was assured that if the accused behaved themselves, the case could be kept within a reasonable timeframe. I returned to the Court and expressed my concern to Gordon Woodcock our chief bailiff. He asked me how long my longest jury trial had been, and I told him it was a fraud trial of seven weeks.

He then asked me how, historically, the longest trials have taken. I mentioned one or two NZ examples and then told him about the famous trial of "the Tichborne Claimant" in England last century, which is reputed to be the longest case ever heard in that country. I have just now checked my books. The trial, which started as a civil case and ended as a criminal trial, started on the 11th May 1871 and ended on the 28th April 1874 – a total of 1025 days.

Arthur Orton

It was an extraordinary case of a Victoria con-man. A crude, 27 stone (378 lbs) scoundrel named Arthur Orton, who had been a traveling butcher in Wagga Wagga, Australia, arrived back in England claiming to be Sir Roger Tichborne, the long lost and shipwrecked heir to the Tichborne family fortune.

Despite his lower-class accent, his semi-literacy, and his inability to answer many material questions, he ended up with many ardent supporters for his claim. For every oddball, there are always gullible devotees.

The criminal aspect of the case arose after he lost the civil claim for the estates and was then charged with perjury. In Victorian England, they dealt with perjurers in a fairly robust way: He was sentenced to 14 years imprisonment! Yoww!

The case is intriguing because, in hindsight, it is remarkable that anyone could have ever supported Orton in his false claim. But Orton had prepared his case well, even hiring two former guardsmen as his servants so he could learn all he could about the regiment in which the missing Sir Roger had served 12 years earlier. He studied the facts so well he was able to produce 30 officers from the regiment who all swore he was the real Roger; more corpulent, of course, but nonetheless Sir Roger. He had even convinced the real Sir Roger's mother that he was her son. She was desperate. She obviously jumped at the faintest likenesses when she declared him to be genuine. But she had died by the time the trial commenced. At the trial, Orton was cross-examined for 22 days and by then it clearly emerged that Orton was a conman.

He did not know his mother's Christian names. He could not speak French (Sir Roger had been fluent). He thought Caesar and Virgil were Greek writers (Sir Roger had enjoyed a first-rate public school education in the classics at Stonyhurst). But the crunch came when a former schoolmate, Lord Bellow, testified for the prosecution that Tichborne had a tattoo on his left forearm. And Fat Arthur couldn't replicate the same! So down the plughole went this incredibly shameless pretender.

King of Con Men

New Zealand's most notorious conman was Murray Beresford Roberts who died in 1974, age 55. I have a copy of his autobiography, *A King of Con Men*[1], published after his death in 1975.

A very succinct biography of him appears in the Dictionary of New Zealand Biography.[2]

---

[1] London, Hodder & Stoughton, 1975

[2] Volume 5, 2000

Born in Wellington in 1919, he was raised in an upper middle-class family in Auckland as a spoiled only child. He went to King's Preparatory School and Auckland Grammar School, both regarded as top schools. At Grammar, he was in the 'A' stream and school reports say he was modest, unruffled and charming, with a soft and persuasive voice. He went to the Otago Medical School, but he enjoyed alcohol more than medical texts and was expelled in his second year for cheating in an examination.

His career path changed: he became a conman instead of a doctor. His fleeting studies at medical school, good looks, educated voice, and great charm often led him to impersonate doctors. In 1944, he was arrested for posing as a doctor, and sentenced to 2½ years imprisonment for forging a death certificate and indecent assault. He had enlisted in the army but was discharged after six weeks because of "psychological abnormality". He moved to New South Wales, married under an assumed name, and divorced in 1955. He had one son. After several more prison sentences, he remarried, again fleetingly.

He gained notoriety in the press. He posed, at various times, as the Brigadier-General assistant medical director of the 3rd New Zealand Division, a naval surgeon commander, numerous medical practitioners, a Governor General designate, a Professor of neuropsychiatry, the manager of Barclays Bank Limited, a Major-General, an atomic scientist, a High Court judge, a Privy Counsellor, Baron Alfred von Krupp (the infamous German industrialist), a well-known author, and a Professor of classics. His list of criminal convictions was impressive. He had convictions and terms of imprisonment, for fraud, impersonation, theft, and obtaining money by false pretences. He often targeted wealthy women who fell for his doctor impersonations and charm. Although money, and the need to keep up appearances and a well-stocked liquor cabinet, was part of it, many of his deceits seem to have been just for the excitement of it all. He died in 1974 of alcoholism, choking on his own vomit in a Papakura hotel room.

The Last Englishman

At the top of my list of people I would have most liked to have dinner with, was Lieutenant-Colonel Alfred Daniel "Freddie" Wintle, MC, the quintessential eccentric monocled Englishman whose life makes fiction look tame. He served as an officer in both World Wars, went to prison three times, and is the only layman to win a lawsuit in the House of Lords.

He spent 12 weeks in the Tower of London at the beginning of the Second World War, awaiting trial for assaulting an Air Commodore with a revolver, feigning infirmity, and breaching discipline.

He recorded in his diary:

"My cell became the most popular meeting place in the garrison and I was as well cared for as if I had been at the Ritz... Visitors dropped in at intervals, usually bringing along bottles which were uncorked on the spot. I don't recall that any of them contained any tea... After a few days of settling in, I was surprised to find that – as a way of life- being a prisoner in the Tower of London had its points.

At his trial, audacious Wintle read a list of prominent army and air force senior officers who he considered should be shot for cowardice and dereliction of duty.

He was about to give his reasons, when a quick plea bargain was arranged. The charges of breaching discipline and feigning disability (he was nearly blind in one eye from serious injuries received in the First World War) were hastily dropped. Some say Churchill intervened to avoid damaging publicity. He pleaded guilty to the assault on the Air Commodore and was severely reprimanded.

In 1947, an eccentric and mentally handicapped cousin of Wintle's died leaving a £115,000 estate (£4,414,000 or NZ $8,915,000 in 2019 currency), Mr Frederick Nye, the solicitor who drew up her will was to receive £44,000. (£1,690,000 in 2019).

Wintle was understandably outraged. He wrote to Nye protesting that he and his sister were not prepared "to tolerate that you should acquire for your own use the bulk of my cousin's estate by means of a will drawn up by yourself in your own office in your own favour." He called the lawyer "a cad, a liar and thief and embezzler".

In 1955, he lured Nye to a flat where Wintle seized him and forced him to give him a cheque in the sum of £1,000 payable to Wintle's sister, and to sign a confession of his guilt. He then photographed the distraught solicitor with no trousers and wearing a newspaper hat and pushed him out onto the street. Wintle then took the man's trousers and displayed them in the trophy room of his London Club.

Wintle was arrested and went to trial. After three days, Wintle pleaded guilty to assaulting Nye and the judge acquitted him of a charge of intention to defraud. He was sentenced to 6 months' imprisonment. His appeal was dismissed. He served his sentence with stoicism and emerged ready for the next battle.

He sued Nye in the civil jurisdiction. At the jury trial, he was represented by two eminent barristers.[1] He lost, and was ordered to pay the costs. He appealed the jury's verdict to the Court of Appeal. He represented himself, lost, but with one Lord Justice agreeing with him. Leave was granted to Wintle to appeal to the House of Lords. Again, he was ordered to pay heavy costs. Again, with no lawyers, a large mortgage, but with the help of a former army trooper Cedric May, he went on the House of Lords.

He later wrote that "it was not until I got to the Lords was I dealing with my intellectual equals". His intellectual equals unanimously granted his appeal, thought to

---

[1] Phillimore QC (later Sir Henry Phillimore, Lord Justice of Appeal and Scarman QC (later Lord Scarman, Lord of Appeal in Ordinary). Later, Wintle was to describe these lawyers in equestrian terms as "*unreliable outriders spilling at the first ditch.*"

be the first such win by a man without legal training. The House of Lords ordered Wintle to have his costs from the estate but, accepting Wintle's submissions, made Nye pay his own costs.

The Times of London headline read Cavalry Officer Jumps Last Hurdle to Win.

In 1959, he was the subject of a BBC *This is your Life* programme. In 1960, the indomitable colonel had Nye struck off the roll of Solicitors. In 1995, Jim Broadbent played Wintle in a TV biopic called *The Last Englishman.*[1]

At Wintle's funeral at Canterbury Cathedral, his friend Cedric Mays, his grief assuaged by a bottle of Glenfiddich, tearfully sang the Cavalry Last Post and Cavalry Reveille to some astonished worshippers. I cherish my now rare copy of Wintle's autobiography *The Last Englishman*[2].

Dean Wickliffe

Dean Hugh Tekahu William Wickliffe[3] is one of the few prisoners to have escaped from the maximum-security prison at Paremoremo, now called Auckland Maximum Security Prison. Wickliffe was imprisoned for the murder of a Wellington Jeweller, Paul Miet, in 1972. There was a massive manhunt down on the Maketu peninsula where he had family. The media and politicians were beating drums about the absence of sentries at the prison. This undoubtedly helped Wickliffe to make his escape. The sentry towers had not been manned for some time as the result of staff cuts.

But how he escaped from the maximum-security prison one Saturday morning I found hard to comprehend. On one of my visits to Paremoremo, the Superintendent showed me how Wickliffe had made his first, nearly successful escape in 1976. He was recaptured within 100 metres of the perimeter fence.

When he managed to get over the walls in 1976, he was the first prisoner there ever to do so. In order to escape from 'D' Block (for maximum security prisoners) it required:

(a) making and concealing a sheet rope some twelve metres long.

(b) avoiding the watch of prison officers.

(c) scaling a four-metre masonry wall (one-metre-thick) surrounding the exercise yard.

(d) avoiding a single wire strand alarm system.

(e) running along the top of the masonry wall and leaping a two-metre gap over a walkway to the outer concrete wall.

(f) dropping the four metres to the ground without breaking a limb.

---

[1] 1995, directed by John Henderson, written by Anthony Horowitz.

[2] London, Joseph Publishing, 1968

[3]Possibly a descendant of the great 14th century, philosopher, theologian and religious reformer John Wycliffe?

(e) running 30 metres across bare ground over an in-ground alarm to a four-metre wire fence

(f) scaling the fence, with another single strand wire alarm at the top.

(g) dropping the four metres to the ground without breaking a limb!

(h) running a further ten metres to the last wire fence, of the same height, and positioned parallel to the first wire fence.

(i) scaling the fence – topped with several strands of barbed wire.

(j) running across open ground to the boiler-house where he took a hostage and forced him to drive him to Mangere.

An amazing feat! Few Olympians could match that athleticism. I was told he spent much of each day exercising in his tiny cell. This is why such stories stir the public imagination and, quite improperly, stimulate support for the escaper.

Years ago, we had George Wilder – a burglar not a murderer – who was so admired by the average Kiwi during his 65 days on the run that a ballad was written and sung about him.

But Wickliffe was not a man to be admired. I believed he must be a psychopath. The extracts from a letter he wrote to Mike Bungay (who acted for him at his murder trial), and referred to in Mike's *book Bungay on Murder*[1], indicated that. In an interview on television, sociologist Dr. Greg Newbold, himself once a long-term prisoner in Paremoremo for drug offending, also suggested that the 20 years Wickliffe spent in prison had turned him into someone totally incapable of living in the community.

Controversially, Wickliffe's murder conviction was overturned by the Court of Appeal in 1986 and reduced to manslaughter on what I (and many other inferior jury trial judges) thought to be somewhat tenuous grounds. Wickliffe based his appeal on the basis that he had no intention of hurting the jeweller. But recklessly committing a robbery and killing a man with a loaded semi-automatic pistol seemed to many of us to make that claim a nonsense. I was later to read that retired judge Sir Trevor Henry[2] agreed with us.

He was then granted parole, only to receive a seven-year sentence for the armed robbery of a Mt Smart video shop the following year.

Two men appeared before me charged with assisting Wickliffe avoid arrest. They were both Mongrel Mob members, and both had appeared before me in the past: Petera James Marsden and Oscar Rua Paki, aged 30 and 28, respectively. Police objected to bail and I agreed with them. I remanded them in custody. I pointed out that:

> *It is of the utmost importance that the persons who are allegedly assisting the escaper realise that, if they are found to have done so, their own situation is in jeopardy.*

---

[1] By Mike Bungay and Brian Edwards (Author): Auckland, Whitcoulls, 1983

[2] Sir Trevor died in 2007 aged 105. He was a much admired Supreme Court judge from 1955 to 1974.

I also expressed my concern that the Mongrel Mob gang was assisting Wickliffe. There was a great flurry of reporters exiting the court after I had concluded this case.

Wickliffe, now in his 70s is back in prison for breaching parole.[1] He has spent over 40 years in prison for various offences. He is not without a sense of humour. He is reported as having joked about his Irish, Scottish and Māori ancestry by saying "my Celtic blood leads my Māori blood astray".

[1] 2019

Keeping Up Appearances

Bare foot

Are bare feet a sign of the times? I kept seeing them in court more frequently.

I have already mentioned how some judges refused to hear lawyers who were not properly dressed in court regalia. Similarly, many judges get angry at the inappropriate clothing members of the public wear in court as witnesses or members of the public gallery.

When I was a young lawyer, men were expected to wear a jacket and tie in court. Women were required to wear a hat and gloves. Today this sounds ridiculous. In those ancient times, lawyers and court registrars kept a closet of clothing (albeit old, inelegant and sometimes smelly) to dress witnesses if they had come to court unprepared.

I draw the line at bare feet and deliberately outlandish clothes, but apart from that, provided people are clean and tidy, I am prepared to let people wear what they like. Judges should not be arbiters of fashion.

My wife's Hat

In the late 1980s, we still held a Saturday morning court. This was because public drunkenness was then an offence. On Friday nights, the police would arrest drunks and put them in the cells overnight. Rather than have them remain at the police station all weekend, the practice was to have a Saturday morning court so the judge could clear out the cells and the police could prepare for a Saturday night repeat of drunken revelries.

One Saturday morning, my wife Suzanne came with me to the court. After the court concluded, we were going on a rare visit to the Ellerslie horse-races. She was seated in the back of the court where I could clearly see her. As always, she was beautiful, elegant, well-dressed and wearing a hat.

Much to my surprise, I saw the well-known lawyer Christopher Harder[1] approach her at the back of the court. I saw him talking to her but could not hear what was said. She looked upset. She stood up and left the courtroom. She never returned. When the court closed for the day, I found her in my chambers

"You never told me it was wrong to wear a hat in court!" she remonstrated

"Whoever told you that?" I queried

[1] A talented, flamboyant, and impetuous criminal lawyer who in 2006 was struck off for inappropriate and sometimes intoxicated behaviour.

"Christopher Harder came up to me and told me to take off my hat: that it was improper and disrespectful to wear a hat in court."

I was astonished. It seems that Mr Harder was unaware that quite the opposite had been true when I was a young barrister. Just as in church, hats were then obligatory for women. I told Suzanne not to worry about the incident. I said that Mr Harder was quite wrong in admonishing her. However, she was sufficiently upset that for many years she never returned to Court with me.

Head Gear

Some visitors to the courthouse wear headdress of unusual types. Rastafarians, like other religionists, believe that God gets very testy about hair covering. Frankly, I think God should turn his omnipotent mind to more important things. Surely wars, genocide, massacres, starvation and man's inhumanity to man deserve his greater attention than whether a Sikh wears his dastar turban, a Jew his yarmulke, a Muslim woman her hijab, or a Rastafarian his tam? Is hair more important than holocausts?

One young fellow appeared in the Hawera District Court before Judge John Dalmer. He was wearing a bright blue tee-shirt with a large inscription across the front:

I like fugby 'cos it's a rucking good game.

I have often wondered just what the public thinks of the pomp and panoply of the courts. The pomp was relatively minimal in the Magistrate's Court. The beaks wore lounge suits and both language and procedure were relatively simple. With the advent of the District Court in 1981, we emulated the California Courts and adopted our present simple black stuff gown[1] with centre zip. The Court of Appeal judges followed suit several years later. They abandoned wigs, bibs and gowns.

Bewigged Bothered & Bewildered

The use of wigs and gowns, while still used on special State occasions, was abandoned in 1996, again at the urging of Chief Justice Sir Thomas Eichelbaum. Since then, judges wear simple black gowns. Robert Lithgow, a Wellington QC, argued that gowns, scarlet robes, wigs and white gloves belonged 'in the dress-up box' and had no place in an egalitarian society such as New Zealand.

At a special dinner celebrating the elevation of Judge Ron Young to the High Court bench, my friend and colleague, Judge Jeremy Doogue, teased his former partner by referring to the formal costume of that court as a most unusual get-up, with a wig that

[1] Ordinary barristers have for centuries worn a "stuff" gown. That is a gown made of relatively coarse woven fabric as opposed to the much better silk gown worn by Queen's Counsel – hence them being termed "silks".

looks like "a toupee on steroids" and an "ermine-edged frock" making them "look like unemployed butlers from the 18th-century still looking for work". He thought his friend should only wear this outfit at home with the curtains drawn and never wear it outdoors for fear of being attacked by dogs or stoned by small boys.

In 2006, the United Kingdom followed suit. British judges abandoned the 300-year-old tradition of wearing horsehair wigs. The judges also adopted a modern form of gown. Some critics said the judges now look like Star Trek officers. The simple black gowns are decorated with gold, red or lilac bands, depending on their status. No more fraudulent ermine, which for a century had been rabbit.

The Guardian fashion correspondent, Hadley Freeman, wrote at the time:

"Lord Phillips[1] now just looks like the man who sells you tickets for the Star Trek Experience at Caesars Palace in Las Vegas."

It is a good thing that wigs and the old form of robing has gone. It was an anachronism at best and comedic nonsense at worst. There was a high degree of the ridiculous in having judges perched on the bench wearing a horsehair wig.

My experience in the District Court has been that jury trials proceed just as properly, expeditiously, and fairly in the less formal environment our courts provide. I believe that the search for the truth is more likely to be found when everyone involved is less stressed and better able to concentrate on the issues at hand than to worry whether their wig has slipped, or their pants are the wrong colour.

Pure Theatre

People love dressing up. There is an element of the ham in all human beings – and men are just as much enchanted by adornments as is the fairer sex. It is part theatre, part vanity, part sexual attraction. The latter may seem an overstatement in terms of court dress, but psychologically and socio-culturally I believe it to be true.

In his chapter on the "Bench and Bar" in *Portrait of a Profession - the Centennial history of the New Zealand Law Society*, Lord Cooke[2] refers to Sir Michael Myers' penchant for exotic court dress. When Sir Michael was Chief Justice, he was the first to import the full ceremonial scarlet robes and full-bottomed spaniel wig[3] of the English High Court

---

[1] Lord Phillips (Nicholas Phillips, Baron Phillips of Worth Matravers) was the inaugural President of the UK Supreme Court, holding that office from 2009 until he retired in 2012. He was the Master of the Rolls from 2000 to 2005.

[2] Robin Cook QC, Wellington, Reed Publishing, 1969. See p.51.

[3] Called "spaniel wigs" because they hung over the ears like a cocker spaniel. Before 1820 wigs were made of black rather than white horsehair. The fashion was: the bigger the wig (Bigwig) the higher you were in the judicial hierarchy.

judges.[1] Sir Michael wore court dress complete with "velvet suit with lace and ruffles, knee breeches, shoes with a buckle, and dress sword".

Sir David Smith[2] caught the fever and couldn't resist a good fancy-dress party either. He says that when he wore his court dress to a gubernatorial function in Auckland, he was "almost mobbed by fashionable ladies".

British Lord Chancellors still dress up for special events. It is pure theatre: fancy dress ball. The Lord Chancellor, on formal state occasions such as the State Opening of Parliament, wears formal court dress consisting of a black silk velvet cutaway tailcoat with cloth-covered buttons, waistcoat and breeches worn with white shirt, lace stock and cuffs, black silk stockings and cut-steel buckled patent court shoes. Over this is worn a black silk damask robe of state with a long train, trimmed with gold lace and frogging, with a black silk "wig bag" attached to the flap collar at the back. A full-bottomed wig is worn and, in the past, a black tricorne hat. In formal procession, he is preceded by a mace bearer, a purse bearer (who carries the magnificently embroidered bag that used to hold the Great Seal of England), and is followed by a train bearer.

There is a story that Lord Hailsham,[3] when Chancellor, was parading through Westminster, when he saw a friend in the crowd. He called out to him by his Christian name, "Neil!"

Several American tourists are said to have fallen to their knees in veneration.

I Cannot See You

As a young barrister, I was always nervous about my clothes when I appeared before Justice Alec (later Sir Alec) Haslam.[4] He was disturbingly obsessed with counsel wearing proper clothes. He would instantly pounce if a wig was tilted crooked on the cranium, a bib dirty or untied, and, quelle horreur, if your trousers were anything other than black or dark grey. Sometimes he used the starchy euphemism, "I cannot see you, Mr Smith", which he had seemingly adopted from some anal-compulsive Victorian judicial predecessor.[5] What the code really meant was: "Mr Smith, you may not appear in my court improperly dressed."

---

[1] This wig alone costs about $5000.

[2] A Supreme Court Judge from 1928 to 1948, he died at age 94.

[3] Douglas McGarel Hogg, 1st Viscount Hailsham, PC.

[4] See p.48.

[5] Such as 19th century judge Mr Justice Sir John Barnard Byles (author of *Byles on Bills* – a riveting textbook on bills of exchange that makes perfect bedtime reading!), who said he "always listened with little pleasure to the arguments of counsel whose legs are encased in light grey trousers".

In his excellent book, *Reform: A Memoir,*[1] Sir Geoffrey Palmer says he saw Haslam rebuke barrister Denis Blundell[2] for appearing in court with a dirty wing collar.

Bungay's Trousers

During a jury trial in Wellington Justice Haslam tried this nonsense on Michael Bungay, a pugnacious, naughty and irreverent leader of the criminal bar. Mike was wearing some light brown trousers under his gown. Like a predator eagle, high on his roost, Mr Justice Haslam instantly spotted the offending trousers and became greatly stressed. He twitched and twisted. His cheeks coloured. The jury must have anticipated a coronary arrest!

"I cannot see you, Mr Bungay", he spluttered.

"I am sorry, sir. You cannot see me?"

Mike grinned impishly at the jury but understandably they had no idea what the judge or Bungay were on about.

"I repeat, Mr Bungay. I cannot see you."

"I'm sorry, Your Honour, perhaps if I stand closer to your bench."

"No, no! Mr Bungay. You know perfectly well what I am alluding to. It is your trousers, Mr Bungay. Your brown trousers."

"Yes, sir?"

"Your trousers are an unacceptable colour, counsel. They are totally inappropriate and deplorable in my court."

"You wish me to remove them, your Honour."

"Most certainly, Mr Bungay."

"As your Honour pleases", Bungay responded with a certain glee. He turned to the jury, opened his gown, reached down and started unbolting his trousers.

"That is quite enough!" protested the judge, undoubtedly appalled at the discourtesy of counsel.

"The court will now adjourn."

With that the judge angrily rose and stormed out of the courtroom. But I am told he never censured Bungay again. Perhaps he was too fearful of Mike's response!

Jandals and Shorts

Some other judges were pedantic and cranky about dress codes. They would expel members of the public from the court if their dress was considered inappropriate. I was

---

[1] Wellington, Victoria University Press, 2013

[2] Later, Sir Edward Denis Blundell, GCMG, GCVO, KBE, QSO lawyer, cricketer, diplomat, Governor-General of New Zealand from 1972 to 1977.

always fairly casual about such matters, but I did become irritated at the empanelling of a jury when one of the prospective jurors appeared in jandals and what looked like swimming trunks. Fortunately, I did not need to make comment. The prosecutor challenged the man, and he returned to the beach!

No White Jacket

It is probably sensible for doctors to look like doctors. There is a story, perhaps apocryphal, about a judge visiting Carrington Hospital to make compulsory treatment orders for the mentally ill. Carrington psychiatrists had recently given up the old practice of wearing collars, ties and white clinical coats. They wore any old thing, as I can testify having been there many times to do the same task.

The story is that the judge, the patient, and the psychiatrist were in an interview room. The well-groomed patient calmly pointed to the psychiatrist and said:

"Well what do you want to say?"

The doctor immediately started describing the patient's symptoms of schizophrenia. The patient leant over, patted the doctor on the knee, and said:

> *Well said. You know the symptoms well. Do you understand what a compulsory treatment order means? It means that legal rights are abandoned and a doctor can treat you against your will.*

The doctor looked flummoxed. He agreed with what had been said.

The judge asked the doctor's name and wrote it on the printed form. He then signed the papers. He had committed the doctor to inpatient treatment thinking that the rather unkempt fellow was the patient! It took some time for other hospital staff to convince the judge that he had committed the wrong man!

Tattooed Porn

A young bull-necked, barrel chested forestry worker from Ruatoki was covered with the most extraordinary collection of tattoos. All over his visible extremities. Not traditional Māori tā moko

but a fresco of ugliness. I knew that police files record tattoos for identification purposes, so I checked it out on his computer printout. In that sometimes-indecipherable blending of police/computer jargon and officialise, it described his tats as being:

> *Animal related L cheek; Animal related R cheek, dots spots lines nose, Animal & related FR neck; animal & related Chest; copulating figures R shoulder, animal & related back, gang name back, Name D to I back.*

The mind boggles at such living pornography! Epidermal self-mutilation with grotesque ill-drawn graphics so frequently flaunted by defendants, their associates, and witnesses are most irritating. It is distracting for a judge to gaze for hours at incomprehensible and often misspelt words or skin art so badly drawn that it is ugliness personified. When a man can't even successfully spell four letter Anglo-Saxon words, it makes me worry either about the standards of teaching in our schools, or the intelligence quotient of some of our more delinquent citizens.

One witness was asked to identify an accused by describing the man's tattoos. I applauded his response.

"I can't really describe his tattoos. They were a load of rubbish. They looked like the graffiti on a public dunny wall."

Samoan Interlude

Hot Wigged

I wore full judicial regalia twice while I was in Western Samoa; for two openings of the Fono.[1] The attire was the same as worn by English judges in England, but the climate was not. An afternoon in the tropics, dressed in such unsuitably Britannic and temperate garb, was almost enough to bring my judicial career to a premature and rather sweaty demise.

The Samoans said they thought I looked very much the image of an English judge and were impressed by the full bottomed wig, scarlet robes with grey silk facings, and lacy jabot. But they were probably greatly amused at the permanent misting of my spectacles and the unending spectacle of the drops of perspiration dripping from my nose as I roasted in the tropical sun. I have little doubt that after I had left, they rolled around the ground with side-splitting merriment at my extraordinary and climatically ludicrous appearance. I literally had to wring out the faux ermine at the end of the day!

Wigs were worn on a daily basis in the Supreme Court of Western Samoa. They weren't so bad when the air-conditioning worked. But the air conditioner – a noisy, rattling, obsolete monstrosity – did not work very often or very well, and I thought both then and since that it was nonsense in such relaxed and beautiful islands to foist upon such a different culture such ludicrous English customs.

The barristers looked as silly as I did, particularly counsel like Semi Epati. He had a head of very fuzzy hair that spoke more of the Melanesian than the Polynesian. He certainly didn't need the adornment of a grey horse-hair wig carefully handmade with 300 years of skill by Messrs Ede & Ravenscroft of London. It contrasted poorly, I thought, with the lava-lava and sandals that Semi and others wore to complete their exuberant barristerial finery.

I must confess that once or twice I wore shorts under my silk gown, and never wore a jacket. Because the high bench hid me from the waist down, no one was any the wiser. Frequently, I took off my shoes and wiggled my liberated toes during the course of a case without anyone ever suspecting. I never made the mistake of a New Zealand magistrate who left his socks under the bench in a small rural courthouse and wrote a letter to the Registrar asking that they be retrieved and returned to him by mail. I would have left them there and sneaked back to recover them under cover of darkness!

[1] The Parliament of Western Samoa.

Volcanic Anger

Volcanic anger may erupt to trigger murder or grievous injury. I had a disturbing murder trial that was solely the result of explosive anger, and confirmed the observation of Horace 2000 years ago "*Ira furor brevis est*".[1]

It was breakfast time in the Samoan family fale.[2] The three children were outside sitting on the steps waiting for the school bus. A male guest had stayed the night. He was talking to the accused. The accused's wife, busy preparing the breakfast, called to her husband to make himself useful by preparing the hot cocoa drink for breakfast. The husband flew into a rage at having his status as father, husband, and chief denigrated by such a blunt domestic demand. He seized a machete and with one violent swing severed his wife's head from her body. It rolled down the steps past the children. The jury and I were appalled at what happened. We could not imagine the trauma caused to the three children.

We heard testimony from the guest. He told us that within seconds of the horrific decapitation the husband was totally bereft at what he had done. He screamed his frenzied regret. He wailed his abject remorse. A few seconds of uncontrolled anger had changed his family forever and made him a murderer. I sentenced him to death by hanging, a sentence always commuted by the Head of State to life imprisonment.

The only pathologist in Western Samoa, whom I knew quite well, testified at the trial that it was actually very hard to sever a head with one blow. It takes great strength. Even professional executioners in mediaeval England frequently had to use more than one blow to complete their terrible task. It took three blows to remove Mary Queen of Scots' head at Fotheringhay Castle in 1587.

Toppling the Government

I had gone to Apia in 1982, at the invitation of the Government of Western Samoa[3] to be Chief Justice for a term of six months. The main purpose of my appointment was to hear election petitions following a parliamentary election earlier that year. Most of the petitioners claimed that members of parliament had been elected as the result of bribery, treating, or personation. I heard these cases over several months and found 12 members of parliament guilty of such corrupt practices. I gave certificates of indemnity from prosecution because they gave voluntary self-incriminating evidence.

---

[1] Anger is a brief madness.

[2] Traditional thatched Samoan house.

[3] In 1997, the name of the country was changed from 'Western Samoa' to 'Samoa'. This angered the citizens of American Samoa, which lies about 160 km to the south-east.

In Samoa, at that time, only chiefs (matai) voted. The electorate was therefore very small in number, only a few hundred voters in each. As a result, the effect of corrupt practices was significant. In the early history of colonial New Zealand, there were similar cases of petitions against election results based on bribery and treating. Those practices become inconsequential when the population is large and there are sizeable numbers of potential voters. In 1991, the introduction of universal suffrage in Samoa transformed the electoral system. It was not universal suffrage in a Western sense. While everyone over 21 could vote, in 45 of the 47 electorates they could only vote for matai. Untitled citizens could not stand for Parliament. This was done to preserve the ancient traditional matai culture.

The most noteworthy of the cases were those that involved 'personation'. Personation is a fraudulent vote in an election where someone deceitfully votes in someone else's name – pretending to the person described the voter roll. In a number of instances, the registered voter had been dead for some years, in one case for twenty years. The scrutineers did not know the identity of all the voters on the electoral roll. Many voters lived overseas, mainly in New Zealand. Many were New Zealand citizens but had the right to vote in both countries. This confounded the situation. The rolls had not been effectively purged before the election.

The most significant case was a petition against the election of the Prime Minister Va'ai Kolone. One of his sons, a son-in-law, and other supporters were alleged to have carefully organised a scheme whereby untitled persons were used to cast votes in place of dead matais or matais living abroad. The hearing occupied 16 days. I gave my decision on a Saturday morning. A large and anxious crowd flowed onto the street. The decision was urgent because everyone realised the Government would fall if Prime Minister Kolone lost his seat. His party only had a one seat majority in Parliament. At the election, Mr Kolone had polled 195 votes against 173 for his opponent, Tufuga Pule: a majority of 22.

I found much dishonesty and perjury. Some witnesses were blatant liars.

> *...So much so, I fear, that, having heard from the 35 witnesses, I had grave doubts as to the reliability of many of them, at least as to aspects of their evidence, and with consequent serious concern that the true facts may forever be hidden.*
>
> *...In earlier election petitions heard by me this year I have expressed anxiety that, unless the oath is taken seriously, then not only will the proper administration of justice become an impossibility, but democracy in this land may become so distorted as to become unrecognisable. In a land that so zealously and totally professes Christianity, such perversions of the truth can only be considered extremely serious. Here the face of truth has not been merely clouded: it has at times been darkly lost in impenetrable fog.*

Many of the personation allegations against the Prime Minister were not answered by any evidence from him. I was troubled that on one day in July 1982, 104 new matai titles were created in his home village Vaisala. The new matai were all either members of, or allied to, the Va'ai family. In my view, this was an attempt to stack the pack in favour of Mr Va'ai. He disclaimed any participation in these conferments of title. He says he knew the 104 titles had been conferred, but had been sick on the day. However, he was one of the three chiefs whose approval was obligatory.

I was made aware that the Prime Minister had a history of mass-producing chiefs. He was had been a participant in what had been called the "matai race" preceding the General Election in 1967, when Chief Justice Spring had chastised him and Tupuola Efi[1] for "indiscriminately creating or permitting to be created matais ostensibly for the sole purpose of obtaining additional votes".

I found ten instances of personation proved: those votes were disallowed, giving Va'ai a reduced majority of 12. I had the special power to physically open and examine the voting papers. Of the 14 personated or allegedly personated ballots, 13 were votes for Va'ai. The remaining voter in fact made his peace with both camps: at Asau he voted for Va'ai, at Vaisala he voted for Tufuga! He swayed like a palm in a storm.

I held that corrupt practices committed in relation to the election, for the purposes of promoting or procuring the election for Va'ai Kolone, had so extensively prevailed that they might reasonably have affected the result.

I granted the petition, the Prime Minister's election was voided, and his government fell. Tupuola Efi, then leader of the opposition, became the new Prime Minister.

Quite predictably, my decision caused an uproar. The opposition hailed my wisdom and legal acumen. The fallen government politicians, suddenly out of office and power, damned me as a scoundrel and legal hack. I received a note, on official letterhead from an unnamed cabinet minister (whom the police could or would not identify) threatening me with death.[2] The police provided me with armed protection. Nothing happened, but as a precaution I sent my family back to New Zealand. I stayed on as Chief Justice for four more months and then resigned "for personal reasons".

---

[1] A long-term politician, Prime Minister, and Head of State from 2007 to 2017, Tupua Tamasese Tupuola Tufuga Efi. Previously he was Prime Minister of Samoa from 1976 to 1982 and again later in 1982.

[2] Not to be taken lightly. In 1999 two former cabinet ministers ordered the assassination of Luagalau Levaula Kamu then Minister of Public Works. They were later convicted of the murder and sentenced to death. Kamu, a lawyer and popular politician, was shot by the son of the former Minister of Public Works who had been sacked amid accusations of embezzlement of public funds. According to the London Guardian newspaper Kamu "was trying to clean up the incestuous and often corrupt nature of Samoan public life."

Sex

Insatiable Teen

At a parole hearing we were astonished to read a psychological profile of a sex offender. It reported that the man had his first girlfriend at age nine and had intercourse a year later. He kept a notebook of his sexual conquests. By the age of 15, he had 300 "marks" in his book but stopped keeping a record soon after. We were unsure whether it was bravado or fact, but his sex crimes had sent him to prison three times.

Loving a Bad Boy

It is commonplace and fascinating that some women are irresistibly attracted to bad boys. I had a case on the Parole Board where an intelligent and well-respected lawyer fell madly in love with the president of a Mongrel Mob gang. When he sought parole, she offered her own home to him. I was the convenor of the Parole Board Panel. We thought she was totally obsessed by the man. He had a disturbing, almost psychopathic profile, and a long and frightening criminal history. She was clearly blind to his criminality and ardent about her feelings for him. Not long after his release on parole, as we predicted, he speedily ditched her.

Why do women love these criminal, often violent men? Mainly, I believe, because they find them compellingly sexy. They are never boring. They are primitive. They are cavemen. Intellectually, women know it is safer and more acceptable to settle down with a sensible, hard-working, predictable, decent man who will care for them and their children. But they crave the sexual excitement of the wild man, the criminal, the predator, a man known to have committed an outrage, cheating, lying, known infidelities or crime, such as rape, murder, or armed robbery.

Some women, I believe, are emotionally overpowered by the notion that they can nurture and change the ugly duckling into a Prince Charming. Some psychologists say it is an evolutionary, primitive, genetic imperative based on the concept that the dominant alpha male is best able to protect their offspring; hence some women have "affairs with the strongest, smartest, best-looking man available, while being married to the nicest and most reliable man available". They see the gangster as stronger, tougher, impulsive, healthier and more exciting. They see him as being tough on others but tender to them. It is, of course, nonsense, because these women are often abused, beaten and even killed by their caveman. But we human beings are remarkably capable of believing in nonsense.

My wife Suzanne periodically arranged film evenings for the Auckland judges. We would go to a movie and enjoy a meal afterwards. In 1984, we saw a compelling and well directed movie, *Mrs. Soffel*[1] which was based on a similar psychology.

A true story, a prison warden's wife, Katie Soffel, mother of four, falls in love with Ed Biddle a handsome and charismatic murderer, condemned to death. She helps Biddle and his brother escape. She smuggles metal files and guns into the prison during her Bible reading sessions. They all get away, but not for long. The men are caught by a posse. The brother is shot dead. Ed, badly wounded, commits suicide. Katie tries to do the same, but only wounds herself. She ends up divorced, imprisoned, penniless and ostracised by society.

Abused Daughter

Sentencing offenders for sexual offending against children is one of the most worrying responsibilities facing any judge. I had a man charged with "feeling" the private parts of his 12-year-old daughter. The offender was an intelligent, professional man working in one of the caring professions. His wife was similarly employed. He knew full well that what he was doing was wrong but was compulsively drawn to repeat his acts on four separate occasions over several years. The little girl reported it to a teacher.

The defendant was charged with sexual assault and then absconded overseas. While there, however, he received advice, re-thought his situation, and returned to New Zealand to "face the music". It was clear he did so out of love for the daughter and because he was intelligent enough to realise that the girl was tearing herself apart at the thought that she was responsible not only for his plight but for breaking up the hitherto sound marriage between her parents.

He immediately pleaded guilty, was genuinely remorseful, and sought immediate counselling. His offending was not extensive and involved none of the more serious forms of sexual activity or penetration. He had done all possible to minimise the effect on his daughter and accepted full responsibility in all respects.

The Court of Appeal pronounced some very heavy edicts as to the tariff for sentencing those who sexually offend against children. The court directed virtually the doubling of the prison terms currently being imposed. It said four years' imprisonment was to be the benchmark for serious offending where trust is abused. The innocence of children – the right to be a child – must be protected. Society must denounce those who commit such crimes.

[1] Directed by Gillian Armstrong, starring Diane Keaton and Mel Gibson

But since then several High Court judges – particularly Justice Allan Holland in Christchurch and Justice David Tompkins in Auckland – had expressed the view that many of us at the cliff-face of the District Court Bench had held for years - that such cases cannot be seen in a vacuum, and that consideration must be given to rehabilitating sex offenders.

When I started on the Bench in 1978, I read the report of an English committee that recommended prison sentences be as short as is consistent with attaining the ends of justice. Our Criminal Justice Act now says much the same thing. What a judge must ask is: What term of imprisonment is appropriate? Will a shorter term achieve the same ends?

In other words, in sentencing a schoolteacher who has indecently touched a 10-year-old girl, will the impact or effect of punishment be any different if the prisoner gets 18 months instead of 4 years?

His life is virtually ruined anyway. His career has gone. His marriage has usually ended. He suffers the shame, the "slings and arrows", the "whips and scorns of time". By the time the judge sentences him it is really all over. The shock of a prison sentence is the "clang of the prison gate." Can one say the shock of hearing the judge say "12 months' imprisonment" is any greater than hearing "two years"?[1]

And the corollary question is: unless he gets treatment, will anything change? The answer for those who have offended against their own children will often be in the affirmative because I know from my years on the Parole Board that men may offend against their own children, but they never would with the children of neighbours or strangers.

His counsel argued the matter sincerely and covered all the important considerations. I did not send the father to prison. I released him on probationary supervision for 12 months with counselling. I hope the family survives. Unlike many, they had the intelligence and support to work through the trauma and hopefully emerge at the other end in one piece.

My First Case

When I started work as a Stipendiary Magistrate in February 1978, my first defended case involved a young apprentice mechanic having intercourse with his girlfriend. He was charged with "performing an indecent act in a public place, namely Queen Street, Auckland". The constable realised something was amiss when he saw a small crowd gathered on the footpath watching something happening in an elderly motor car parked

---

[1] It didn't worry a young Canadian burglar sentenced to 2 months prison on 10 charges. *"How much did I get?"* he asked the jailer. *"20 months"* came the reply. The young fellow smiled and *said "Oh, well, it coulda been worse. I coulda got a year!"*

against the kerb. As he approached, he saw a pair of legs protruding from the rear seat out onto the pavement. Although the crowd was not clapping in two/four time, when he saw the smirks on the onlookers' faces, and the rhythmical movement of the legs, he immediately, as they say, put one and one together. He arrested and charged the young man.

The defence was that the act had been in the privacy of the car, and not in a public place. That was nonsense. I found the charge proved. I delayed sentencing until I had the chance to speak to other magistrates over morning tea. They were astonished at my lack of sophistication when I indicated that I thought a short prison term was appropriate. I argued that if such a dreadful event had happened in the main street of my hometown it would have resulted in such a sentence. The others laughed in a kindly way and suggested that a fine of about $200 would make him think before the next time.

This case took place in those balmy days when gender roles were viewed differently, and only the male partner was ever prosecuted for offences of that sort. I did not even ask the young woman to contribute to her boyfriend's fine!

Castration

A squad of hefty over-nourished women in the first row of seats in the court public gallery didn't take kindly to the weak-looking, pale young man slumped against the side of the dock charged with indecently assaulting a four-year-old boy. He lured the boy into a caravan with the intention of having sex with him. Fortunately for all concerned, he had second thoughts, desisted, and then later confessed to the boy's parents. I remanded him for pre-sentence and psychiatric reports. I saw one of the matrons, put down her knitting[1], and call out: "He needs the knife!"

I was tempted to explain that I was a judge, not a veterinarian, but then thought it best to hold my tongue. Remaining silent, especially when emotions are running high, is often the best option. Saying something without thought can make a courtroom situation grow ugly.

I later sentenced him to probationary supervision and rehabilitation programmes for 12 months.

Child sex abuser

A disturbing case involved a youth who indecently assaulted an 8-year-old girl. The defendant was 16 years old when the indecencies happened. He removed his pants and

[1] Reminiscent of Dicken's bitter knitter, Madame Defarge, watching the Guillotine do its ugly work.

hers. He lay on top of her and simulated sex. Fortunately, there was no actual sexual violation.

His explanation was that she had offered no protest and that he would have stopped if she told him to! Offered no protest? An eight-year-old child?

The revulsion of it all is that the probation report indicated that this young man was one of many males who had perpetrated indecencies or had intercourse with the same little girl during the course of the drunken parties frequently thrown by her family. Some of the offenders were her blood relatives. It is hard to comprehend the sexual mores of such people. The little girl had seemingly grown up believing such behaviour was normal and to be expected. It was for that reason she has apparently not suffered any trauma. But who knows what effect it will have on her in the future. One shudders to think.

Professionals working with sexually abused children – psychologists, psychiatrists, social workers, counsellors, and lawyers - tell us that such abuse is much more prevalent than our society is prepared to acknowledge.

New Zealand studies suggest that one out of three girls, and one in seven boys may be sexually abused before they turn 16. A recent Auckland study reported that more than 23% of women had been sexually abused as children. Most of the abuse was perpetrated by male family members. 50% of the women, had been abused multiple times. The consequences are often "depression, anxiety, impaired interpersonal relationships, parenting difficulties, eating difficulties, and/or drugs and alcohol misuse to cope with strong feelings." Add to this an increased likelihood of suicide, an increased likelihood of conviction for crimes of violence, and prostitution.

Roughly ten out of 100 sexual abuse crimes are reported and only three of those get to court. Only about one of those is likely result in a conviction.

You would be wrong if you thought the main perpetrators of child abuse were priests, pastors and teachers. They are not. By far and away the main offenders are male family members or friends: Daddy, Uncle Pete, Brother Bert. But it isn't always men. In a small number of cases it can be Mommy, Aunty Anne and Sister Sue.

Peeping & Peering

Jock is a morbidly obese 40-year-old alcoholic, with a face and body ravaged by booze, who lives at a Motor Camp. He sated his boredom by peeping and peering into women's bedroom windows at night. He was before me for sentence on four separate charges of doing just that. There was an excellent psychologist's report including the results of a battery of psychological tests undergone by the man. They resulted in an interesting, although somewhat sad personality profile:

His I.Q. was 87. Making matters worse was the alcohol problem – the report said he would drink "anything alcohol". There was no suggestion that he was dangerous. He is just an obese, artless drunk, unable to grasp the reality either of his offending or his life problems. I put him under probationary supervision and gave the Probation Officer the power to place him in an institution or a rehabilitation programme.

Panty Pincher

A 52-year-old helicopter pilot nearly landed in prison. He was a pleasant, distinguished man who looked more like a Remuera gynaecologist than a panty fetishist. He had driven down to Whakatane, crowbarred open the door of La Femme Lingerie shop, and returned to Tauranga with lingerie worth $3,750. He was arrested at his home a few hours later as someone had spotted his car registration number. He immediately accepted his guilt and conceded that he had a fascination with women's lingerie and, following some drinking at a restaurant, had been carried away by the urge to steal the underwear.

A report from a psychiatrist showed he was a typical fetishist who had struggled since adolescence with his dark secret but been unable to break the habit. The doctor pointed out that fetishism is almost exclusively a male sexual deviation, is more common than is generally realised, and is usually a life-long deviancy. It is not a mental illness, and is not associated with homosexuality. The condition is fairly readily treatable.

The main concern of both the psychiatrist and the man's lawyer was the question of suppression of name. I granted it because it was clear that publication could well cause grave psychological damage or suicide, particularly as the man's de facto partner was presently overseas and knew nothing of his problem! Wouldn't she have been shocked if she had arrived home early to see her jam-packed panty drawer?

After some excellent submissions from his lawyer, I fined the chopper pilot $1,500.00 and ordered him to pay for the damaged shop doors. All the lingerie had earlier been returned, unstained, to La Femme. I suppressed publication of his identifying details.

The poor man looked as if he could have hidden under the carpet.

Fetishists

Over the years, I have had to deal with several fetishists. Most were "panty pinchers", but at least one was a "foot fetishist" who had a morbid fascination with women's shoes. He only achieved sexual stimulation while fondling elegant shoes.

When I was in law practice, I acted for a clever engineer whose wife finally sought a divorce because she became weary of her husband wearing her bras and panties, not only during lovemaking but at other times as well. It was a case of first up, best dressed!

Sandy

A tall, blonde, long-haired man, appeared before me charged with doing an indecent act in a public place, namely the sand dunes on the beach at Mount Maunganui. On the 29th January, at 5.30 p.m., to the delight of some, and the consternation or disgust of others, he allowed his hormones full sway and engaged in somewhat lusty and vigorous copulation with a 16-year-old hitchhiker he had met earlier in the day. It is clear that friendships readily blossom in the summer bliss of a holiday resort, but it cost him $500 and a public vow of chastity – at least in public places. His drinking mates would probably chip in and pat him on the back. And he would seldom lack a certain variety of notoriety. The 16-year-old girl later appeared in the Youth Court, but I was not told the outcome.

I was reminded of my mother's often repeated ditty:

Sand between the fingers!
Sand between the toes!
How it ever gets there
Goodness only knows!

Therefore, somewhat uncouthly, I noted on my bench blotter, a sequel:

Sand between his buttocks!
Sand within his crotch!
He enjoys some sand dune loving,
But grits his teeth too much!

Our Registrar, Kevin Nally, heard about this jotting and recorded it for his annual Court Christmas party awards. I won a booby prize!

At the morning adjournment, salacious minds being what they are, there was some jocularity in the tea-room. Wayne Moultrie, lawyer, and Karen Maule, my clerk, told me there had been a case earlier in the year of a young woman who denied a similar offence on vacant land next to a line of tents in a camping ground at Papamoa. When she viewed certain pre-trial prosecution evidence, she rapidly blushed and changed her plea to guilty. Several campers had indulged their voyeurism by not just watching young Minnehaha and her Hiawatha behind the tents, but by video-taping the highlights of the performance.

Apparently, the resulting movie would hardly have made the Cannes Festival, but it totally dispelled any possible defence argument that the witnesses had dirty minds or that the two lovers were merely playing leapfrog. I had wrongly believed that surfing had become the most popular summer sport in the Bay of Plenty.

Rex Reed the American film critic said: "Cannes is where you lie on the beach and look at the stars – or vice versa."

Adultery

Adultery often leads to prosecutions for violent crimes, even murder. The prohibition against adultery is ancient – number seven of the ten commandments. An old joke describes Moses coming down Mt Sinai with the tablets, saying to the Israelites:

"The good news is: I brought Him down from 15 to 10. The bad news is: adultery is still in."

To the ancient Hebrews it was very bad news indeed. Deuteronomy 2:22 prescribes:

> *"If a man is found sleeping with another man's wife, both the man who slept with her and the woman must die. You must purge the evil from Israel."*

A Hundred Lashes

The Qur'an was much kinder. It prescribes a mere hundred lashes for both the man and the woman (Qur'an 24:2). Stoning is out; lashing is in. But only rarely, because Islamic law required four eyewitnesses to prove adultery by giving identical corroborative testimony. And with adultery usually being furtive and secret, it would have been rare to have four eyewitnesses peeking into the tent, boudoir or bedroom. And if the accuser didn't come up with the four witnesses, or failed in some way to prove the intercourse, then he or she copped the 100 lashes instead.

Although being found in flagrante delicto[1] no longer has such a fatal outcome, adultery in our world still has awful consequences: domestic violence, trauma and divorce. It strikes at the very heart of a marriage relationship. Of all the commandments, it is the most often breached. Accurate bedroom statistics are impossible, but social scientists guess that 60% of men and 40% of women will have an extra-marital affair at some point in their lives. It shatters trust and affection.

Infidelity is a betrayal. The partner who lusts into an affair justifies the adultery by rationalising that the marriage lacked sexual excitement, intimacy, love and friendship. Often that is true. But are the consequences of adultery worth it? Abiding loss of trust, divorce, anger, suicide, violence, negativity, hurt to children, and family disintegration.

---

[1] This Latin phrase does not mean "in fragrant delight". It means "in blazing offence" or "caught in the act" – red-handed.

Even if the couple decide to stay together, it will never be the same again. Forgiven, perhaps, but never forgotten. The pain may wane, but the wounds remain.

Nyet

A very unhappy, thin, fair, Russian seaman had been caught stealing three pairs of panties from the Deka store. He was not a fetishist. I gained the impression that they were probably for his girlfriend back in Mother Russia where such delights are probably not readily available, except to the favoured apparatchiks in the Moscow *Gosudarstvennyi Universalnyi Magazin.*[1] Fishermen probably do not qualify! His ship's captain, a handsome man with good English, acted as interpreter. He told me the man had $120 in cash and the ship was sailing in two hours. With a few winks and nods, da and nyet, I got the message, fined the romantic seaman $50 plus costs of $65 and directed 24 hours' imprisonment if the fine was not paid forthwith. It was paid very forthwith and he was off to Vladivostok!

Dirty Old Neighbour

A 73-year-old handyman (I am often worried by the sexual promiscuity of some handymen) defended two charges of indecent assault on two girls aged 10 and 12, respectively. The parents of the girls knew him as a friendly old neighbour. He offered to babysit from time to time. That was a mistake. He seized the opportunity to fondle them in their beds and then had sex with them. He had, on the evidence, complete sexual intercourse with one girl seven or eight times. The sad fact was that she seemed to be strangely attracted to him because she kept returning to his flat knowing that she would be subjected to further sexual intercourse. More than once.

The hearing went on all day and I gave my decision at 5.30 p.m. after the defendant had given evidence. He calmly and sincerely told me that a kaumatua of his age and seniority would never perpetrate such terrible offences against his own people.

The little girls had impressed me as being honest and their stories were perfectly plausible. One made errors and exaggerated. She seemed to have some anatomical factors somewhat askew. The penis seemed to make its entry soft and its exit hard, and the vigour of this 73-year-old man seemed to make Casanova wilt somewhat in comparison. But, even given the tendency to tint the tale, I had no doubt that both little girls were telling very essential truths. One young witness, a girl of ten, was not a victim

---

[1] GUM – Main Universal Store.

but she had observed events from under the bedclothes as her young friends were being molested.

"I was angry", she said, "that he was so rude."

She was totally unshaken by cross-examination. She clearly saw what was happening to her friend and was totally reliable. Then came the moment of decision. I had the vibe that the girls, young as they might be, were telling me the truth. But then, the defendant was old, calm and of pleasant appearance. What a terrible injustice would be perpetrated if my instincts about the witnesses were wrong! He looked so pleasant. He sounded so truthful. But the youngsters had the very honesty of youth about them – especially when the details came out.

I found the charges both proved. My stomach was in my mouth as I asked (as I have many times asked with similar concern), "Anything known about him, Sergeant?"

"Oh yes, sir!" came the response.

The thin sheet of computer paper was passed up to me: Nine previous convictions for sexual offending against young girls! He had been to prison on three previous occasions and the last time, some judge, mindful of rehabilitation, had given him community care – no doubt because he didn't want to send the then 70-year-old to prison. I had no such qualms when it came to sending the now 73-year-old to prison. Men who sexually prey on unsuspecting innocent children should not be treated with leniency. A month later, I gave him five years' imprisonment.

Paedophiles

Sexual molestation and assaults by stepparents are not uncommon. Over the years, I have dealt with many cases of stepfathers who have sexually offended against their stepdaughters. One overseas study indicates that a child living with a stepparent is 100 times more likely to suffer assault than one living with natural parents.

In New Zealand, sexual offending against children is of such concern that there are two special prison units designed solely to rehabilitate child sex offenders. Offenders normally stay in such a facility for at least 12 months. The Kia Marama[1] Special Treatment Unit in Rolleston Prison has a 60-bed unit and has treated over 1000 men since it opened in 1989. The Te Piriti[2] Special Treatment Unit opened at Auckland Prison five years later. It is a similar model but with a more significant focus on Māori offenders. Māori offenders respond well to the mix of Tikanga Māori and western psychology than they do at Kia Marama, with its predominantly western psychological approach.

---

[1] In English: "Let there be Light".

[2] In English: "The Crossing". My friend and long-time Parole Board colleague Lavinia Nathan was the first manager of the unit.

Treated paedophiles have only a 5% rate of reoffending, contrasted with 20% for untreated offenders. Psychologists and counsellors, through group and individual therapy sessions, try to re-wire the offender so that he is unlikely to reoffend when released back into the community. The statistics on reoffending clearly show that such intensive therapy significantly reduces the likelihood of reoffending.

As a Parole Board convenor, I have read many psychological assessments of child sex offenders. One common theme is that the offender was himself the victim of sexual offending while a child.

This suggests that much sexual offending is learned behaviour and that it can thus be unlearned through expert psychological rehabilitation techniques.

The abuse of children is a universal phenomenon. This is surprising, as nearly all cultures abhor abuse of children and condemn incest. Child sex offenders face great hostility, not only within the prison population, but also when they are finally released into the community. Many struggle to get jobs and there is often a hostility toward them living in a given community.

The arrest and conviction of a stepfather presents traumatic consequences for the child involved. Many sexually abused children have a great affection for the abuser and are appalled that their complaint has the direct result of the family breaking up and the father going to prison.

I have seen many extended families split down the middle by allegations of sexual abuse. Often, and usually unfairly, the child is believed to have fabricated the complaint. Some family members will side with the adult, others with the child. The family conflict becomes much worse where there is a defended criminal prosecution requiring family members to testify in public.

At Parole Board hearings, I have heard many men, who have fully defended a case at a jury trial, recant and make a full and frank confession of their offending to a prison psychologist or prison officer. It is appalling that they first deny the offending and force a child or children through the trauma of a full-scale defended trial by jury.

Often supporters of the offender are dumfounded to subsequently learn that the man they ardently championed now acknowledges guilt, because for many months or years they had steadfastly believed their family member was innocent of any offending.

Expert psychologists tell us paedophilia involves the exploitation and misuse of the power relationship within the family. Often, we see the criminal as being an immature man, rigid in his views, and often in denial for many years. Unlike the public perception, these offenders do not present as being "sickos", grubby old perverts, or mentally disturbed. More likely they are narcissistic, selfish men who criminally use children as the targets of the sexual desires. Sometimes this sexual abuse goes on for many years. The offender urges secrecy on the part of the child and sometimes threatens the child if there is disclosure to a third person.

"If you tell Mummy about this she will leave me and I will go to jail."

Or even worse:

"If you tell anyone I will kill myself and you will be sent away to live in a home for naughty children."

Often some members of the family group close ranks and refuse to discuss matters with police. They see protection of the offender, and family honour, as being of more importance than the trauma that has occurred to the young abused child. They see the police as a hostile enemy and believe matters can be sorted out within the family. They are often fearful of community reaction. The accused and potential family witnesses exercise their right to silence and refuse to cooperate.

Frequently, the mother of the abused child presents as a weak and immature person who is very dependent upon her partner. She feels guilty about not having protected the child and she denies having any knowledge of what was happening, often even in circumstances where it is clear to judges and juries she must have known that sexual offending was taking place under her roof. There is blindness to what has happened.

Sometimes we see the mother taking sides with the father and blaming the daughter for what has happened. Often the dependent mother is more anxious about living without her spouse than she is about the consequences to the unfortunate child.

Traumatising Children

Certain guilty paedophiles selfishly elect trial by jury on serious charges of sexual violation of children. They force innocent children to testify about traumatic and sensitive sexual issues in the usually futile hope a jury will acquit. They deny their offending. They lie through their fangs. And then, after being sentenced to imprisonment, they confess all to a prison psychologist and ask for a rehabilitation programme and the earliest possible release date. On the off chance of fooling the jury into an acquittal, they selfishly aggravate the pain of their young victims.

Granddad

Some years ago, I presided over a jury trial where an arrogant and controlling man had sexually abused several members of the same family over two generations. The father was well-known in the community, having served on local organisations and on the local city council. The case was brought to the attention of the police when a 12-year-old granddaughter disclosed to her mother that "granddad has been doing bad things to me".

The mother of the child was horrified. She immediately telephoned her two sisters, the aunts of the child concerned. In the telephone conversation, she simply said:

"We've got to do something. Dad is now doing the same to his granddaughters as he did to us."

At the jury trial, the three daughters all testified that their father had not just sexually assaulted them, but had raped them over extended periods during their childhood. One daughter was now the principal of a large secondary school for girls. Another was a successful chartered accountant. Two of the granddaughters also testified that the grandfather had sexually abused them.

To my surprise, and the distress of the jury, the only witness for the defence (apart from the accused himself) was his wife, the mother and grandmother of the prosecution witnesses. She testified that she believed in her husband's innocence, and that he never had the opportunity to do any of the awful crimes with which he was charged. She said all five family members were lying to the jury. The prosecutor asked:

"Are you saying that your three daughters and granddaughters are all lying to this jury?"

The old lady looked pale and distraught and in a quavering voice she answered:

"Yes, I am."

The intense silence in the courtroom was profound.

After a short retirement, the jury found the man guilty of all counts in the indictment.

A month later he appeared before me for sentencing. Apart from court personnel and the two lawyers, the only other person in the courtroom was the accused's wife. None of her daughters or granddaughters attended. I sentenced the man to a long term of imprisonment for rape and serious sexual assaults. He was taken from the dock out to the cells. The frail, elderly wife stood there alone, bewildered, tearful, and distraught. She looked around for support. There was none.

I sometimes wondered whether the daughters or granddaughters later reconciled with the old lady. Her behaviour was not unusual. But she had made Sophie's choice[1] by labelling her intelligent, mature daughters liars, and that was inexcusable. She saw her security, status and future with her dominating husband. As the French so aptly interject "Quelle horreur!"

Over the years, I have seen several examples of mothers turning a blind eye to sexual abuse or incest. In my third year studying psychology at university I was taught about "defence mechanisms". Denial of even obvious evidence of abuse is such a mechanism. The mother shuts her eyes and ears so as to block out what is happening. The denial hides the pain of acknowledging the reality of knowing that the child is being abused

---

[1] William Styron, *Sophie's Choice,* New York, Penguin Random House, 1979, and later a well-received movie starring Meryl Streep, includes an unforgettable scene in which Sophie arrives at Auschwitz death camp with her young son and daughter. A sadistic camp doctor at the selection says she can only take one child with her. The other must die. She makes her dreadful choice and the little girl is taken to the gas chamber.

by a man and not providing protection. Sometimes they even blame their daughter for what has happened.

Consequences

What happens to the child victims? The experts tell us that the offending traumatises most victims. They experience depression, confusion, are sometimes sexually precocious, and often feel a sense of shame and guilt. Many have difficulty in adult relationships, and some experience physical and mental ill health. Often the greatest trauma is not the actual physical abuse, but anger or disbelief that the mother has refused to believe them.

However, some young victims show no overt evidence of trauma. With appropriate counselling, and love and support from other caring family and friends, they seem to adjust to life and move on.

Public indecency

Masturbation featured in two of my cases in one court day. In one, a lonely 24-year-old kept driving his car to where a pretty 14-year-old papergirl could see him masturbating. He told the police he would never have approached her. He would only do this in order to say "hello" and would have had to be drunk to build up the courage to do so. He said he had fallen in love with her because she was so beautiful.

It reminded me of the probably apocryphal story of the teenage schoolgirl who was cross-examined by defence counsel as to whether she had actually seen the defendant expose himself to her.

"You couldn't see anything from where you were standing, could you?"

"Yes, I could see very clearly."

"But you couldn't see anything through the gap in his overcoat?"

"Yes, I could."

"Well describe what you could see."

"It looked like a penis, only smaller."

The second case was a telephone masturbator named Bert. Aged 35, Bert's specialty over the last six years had been making random dirty phone calls. If the voice on the other end of the line sounded like that of a young woman, he then said he was conducting a survey about the sexual behaviour of young women. He asked details about sex education, underwear preferences, menstruation and how often they masturbated.

He masturbated himself while conducting his "survey". Both men were sick and needed help. I requested psychological reports on both men, and a month later placed them both on 12 months' probationary supervision with counselling and treatment.

Lolita

A stepfather had a passionate affair with his 15-year-old stepdaughter. She reciprocated his passion until she got a hugely negative response after confiding in her best friend at school. They then told a teacher. It was a Lolita tale. When interviewed by a detective, Humbert could not see that he had done wrong. His wife very strenuously disagreed with him. I gave him credit for his guilty plea, the fact that the girl had seemingly suffered no emotional harm, and that he was remorseful. His counsel foolishly submitted that there was not a great difference in their ages and that thus the offending was more understandable!

"He is 29! Twice her age", I exclaimed with surprise, wondering how much older one must be to be a "dirty old man"!

I sentenced him to 8 months' periodic detention and 12 months supervision. He was lucky it wasn't jail time.

Shock Acquittal

I had a whisky in the judges' common room with Haddon Gilbert and Gerry Monaghan. Gerry had retired from the Rotorua bench 18 months previously, but was still retained on a temporary basis to fill in when necessary when local judges were on leave or when we couldn't cope with the pressure of court business. He told us a delightful tale about his first and only Supreme Court jury trial. He practiced law in New Plymouth. He did a lot of Magistrates Court work but passed the Supreme Court work to his partner, Arthur Middleton (also now a District Court judge, although specialising in Accident Compensation). He said it was the last trial held in the old Supreme Court building in New Plymouth before it was demolished to make way for a modern replacement.

His client was charged with incest. Gerry said the evidence against the accused was substantial, and he was astonished when the jury returned a verdict of not guilty. The accused was even more astonished. When the judge told the man that he was free to leave the courtroom he promptly collapsed on the floor of the dock with a massive coronary arrest and was ill for many months after. Lady Justice works in mysterious ways.

Crying Rape

A false allegation of sexual violation may be made as attention-seeking, out of anger or revenge, or to cover up behaviour deemed socially or culturally unacceptable.

When I was presiding over trials in Samoa, I had two cases which illustrate the problem. In both cases, teenage girls were caught by younger siblings on a beach or under the coconut palms having sex with their young man.

Premarital sex was in the eyes of most Christian Samoans a grave sin against God. Consequently, when caught in the act by younger siblings the young woman would normally cry out that the boy had raped her. She did this rather than acknowledge that she was no longer virginal and was a "naughty" sinful girl.

Fortunately, most of the sensible old matai jurors recalled their own youthful tropical trysts under the palms. They would usually (as they did in both my cases) have the good sense to acquit the accused youth.

As I write this, I see that in the USA there have been 314 prisoners exonerated, with many of those released from prison, as the result of DNA profiling establishing that they could not have committed the crime for which they were imprisoned. Misidentification, improper or negligent forensic examination, inept defence counsel, poverty, and overzealous police and prosecutors all contributed to juries erroneously finding the accused guilty.

Excessive Appetite

I also sat on a preliminary hearing of a middle-aged man on eight counts of indecently assaulting young girls. The offences were historic. There were two other charges admitted by him of indecencies with the 15-year-old daughter of his de facto wife. He had a penchant for standing where she could see him masturbating. He then started the practice of placing bananas and carrots in her bed at night. Just what this was intended to do I have no idea. Either he thought she suffered from night starvation, or he thought the sight of such phallic fruit and veges would send her into a paroxysm of sexual abandon. It seems, thank goodness, that she suffered from neither form of excessive appetite.

He went to trial at the High Court and ended up in prison for four years.

Harry or Larry?

I presided over a preliminary hearing for rape. It only took 15 minutes because counsel agreed that there was a prima facie case[1] against the accused and agreed to all the evidence coming in by written statement. All I had to do was initial the exhibits and commit the accused to the Hamilton High Court for trial.

[1] Enough apparent evidence to proceed to a hearing.

The facts of the case looked very interesting. The accused and the complainant had known each other for over 20 years as they have lived in the same small rural community. It seemed everyone had drunk Bacchanalian quantities of booze at the local tavern. He says he and the complainant exchanged "bottom rubs" when the opportunity arose and, in the intoxicated and illogical thinking of both drunks and Romeos, he wrongly formed the conclusion that this was an invitation for a deeper and more intimate relationship.

Consequently, after the tavern had closed, he waited for a while, drinking more to calm his excitement, and then in true Chaucerian style climbed through the good lady's bedchamber window. Both the lady and her husband were snoring stertorously and drunkenly together in the matrimonial four-poster. Undeterred either by snores or spouse, our gallant slipped on top of the lady and had his way with her until she roused somewhat and loudly cried out the name of a third man – the next-door neighbour.

At this point, hubby surfaced to consciousness, and thinking it was the neighbour, pushed the accused to the floor and whacked him a few times. Then the lights came on and he realised the ardent suitor was not his neighbour but his mate from the tavern. He swore at him, and advised him that to avoid imminent death he might like to emigrate urgently to Australia.

Meanwhile, however, the complainant lady, upset that she had been treated in such an insensitive way, and had not been able to differentiate Harry from Larry, had raced across the road to a different neighbour. The neighbour wisely recommended that she phone the police.

Hence this prosecution. The accused was in deep trouble, as rape is intercourse without consent, and a sleeping woman is not consenting. There need not be any resistance. It will be hard for the jury to believe that her minor teasing frolic with him at the hotel may have reasonably led him to believe that she had consented to him visiting her later in the evening for sex in the presence of her husband.

Four months later I was told the accused was found guilty at trial. He was convicted and sentenced to six years imprisonment.

Swindlers, Cheats & Benefit Bludgers

Cheating and Bludging

Benefit bludgers and tax cheats are seldom caught. Tax evasion is an ancient art form[1] but benefit bludging is new – because until social welfare legislation materialised last century there was no such thing as a benefit from the state. Your family or tribe looked after you, or you starved to death or died of some malignant disease with benefit of clergy but with nothing else.

When people improperly take benefits, they steal from the State – from the rest of us who obediently, albeit reluctantly, pay our taxes. I have seen people working in well-paid jobs who for years have illegally supplemented their pay with unemployment benefits totalling thousands of dollars – in one case nearly $100,000. And often they have the cheek to look very disgruntled when they are caught, convicted and order to pay it all back. And then, adding insult to injury, they smile sweetly and offer to pay it back at $15.00 per week over the next 128 years! Naturally, without interest.

As mentioned, resistance to tax is as old as mankind, and somewhat more understandable. Historically, some taxes have been manifestly unfair, but when they are sensibly imposed, we all have a duty to play fair and pay our way. Hospitals, schools, roads and other services must be paid for. I was once told by my lifelong friend Kevin

---

[1] In 3000 BC, evading tax did not amuse the Pharaoh. Offenders were punished with 100 strokes of the cane or, for very serious cases, "five bleeding cuts."

Greer, a chartered accountant, that if every New Zealander properly paid their taxes, and didn't cheat or hide behind trusts, the general tax rate for everyone could be halved.

False Car Claim

Some young men make false claims under their car insurance policies. Usually they have a friend "steal" the car and they pocket the insurance money. Sometimes they claim on the insurance to escape prosecution for driving while disqualified or drink-driving – that is, they say someone else had stolen their car and used their name.

One young man changed his plea to guilty of attempted false pretences and making a false declaration to the State Insurance Office. He and friends drove their cars into a private forestry road one night. They then started doing wheelies and 180 degree turns on the gravel road. They were not quite as competent in driving as their macho mentality had them believe, because two of the cars collided and damage was caused. The defendant's car cost just under $3000 to repair. He told the insurance office a cock and bull story and also omitted to disclose that he had consumed beer before the accident.

The insurance company became suspicious, and its investigators checked and found the story to be false. Foolish fellow. I learned that he had lost a leg in a previous car accident and was now on an invalid's benefit. I later sentenced him to home detention and ordered him to pay a modest weekly sum in reparation.

Inside Job

Two enterprising prisoners from Tongariro Prison continued their fraudulent criminal activities in prison with the use of modern technology! Their scam involved an attempt to obtain $100,000 worth of computer equipment on credit with fake Government order forms. They seem to have used a mobile telephone and computer to carry out their scheme. Apparently, one of the prisoners was quite a genius in the use of computer technology, and while still serving his sentence, had been advising Turangi businesses on setting up computer programmes. The computer equipment had been delivered to a Mangere address, but detectives intercepted a courier who had been employed by the prisoners to collect it. With our economy in such sad shape we need such entrepreneurial skills! But not employed so as to cheat the innocent.

Ticket to Tina

In December 1985, pop star Tina Turner, the "Queen of Rock 'n Roll"[1] performed in New Zealand with her *Private Dancer* tour. She was welcomed onto the Orakei Marae

[1] Who has sold 200 million records and won 12 Grammy Awards.

in Auckland with a traditional Māori greeting ceremony. She was photographed with some of the Māori performers. One happy press photo showed her shoulder to shoulder with Rangiora Te Maari. He was a confidence trickster and rogue, with all the charming lies and bullshit such rascals display.

Rangi appeared before a jury and me in Hamilton a few years later, charged with obtaining a pecuniary advantage by false pretences. It was a clever but inevitably doomed scam. He had cheated his own Māori people and they were angry and unforgiving. Two of the jurors were Māori. The evidence was so compelling that his blatant lies to the jury fell on deaf ears. I gave him two years in prison and an order for reparation I knew would never be paid.

Using the press photo as a hook, he went to a marae committee and told them he was a personal friend of both Tina Turner and Patti LaBelle[1] and had just returned from the USA where he had been hosted by them. He said they both adored Māori culture and wanted to fly to New Zealand to give a concert just for Māori. He needed a back-up group. He approached four young Māori musicians from Gisborne who were elated to be asked to appear supporting the two megastars.

A country hall was hired, advertising was printed rather crudely by Rangi, and invitations were sent to several hundred Māori. They all responded with speed and enthusiasm, and Rangi collected the substantial ticket price from everyone. Tina and Patti were appearing at no cost but the ticket price was to cover airfares, hotels and a donation to a Māori Charity.

Ten days before the concert he phoned the four eager musicians in Gisborne.

"Hey, bros", he asked, "are you all members of the NZAFM?"

"The what?"

"The New Zealand Branch of the American Federation of Musicians?"

"What's that, Rangi?"

"Musicians Equity – affiliated to the American Federation of Labour and Congress of Industrial Organisations. Tina and Patti will be blacklisted by all musicians if they sing with a band that isn't a paid-up member of that union. Hell, I should have told you that when I arranged the gig."

"Gee!" said the guitarist. "What do we do now? Is there time to join up?"

"Yeah!" said Rangi. "I've got a great mate in the Union who can do it for you quickly. But it will cost you. For the union joining fee, annual fee and his cut, $750 each."

"Jeez, that's steep, Rangi"

"I know, but it's that or nothing. Luckily, I will be in Gisborne on Monday on business. You can pay me cash."

---

[1] The "Godmother of Soul" who has sold 50 million records.

He met them outside the best motel in Gisborne and took them to the pub in the latest Subaru WRX STi.

"Wow", said the drummer, "some car, Rangi. Must have cost a fortune?"

"Nah, it's a hire car – see the sticker – I get them at mate's rates because I own half the shares in Hertz NZ."

Rangi pocketed the $3000, returned the car to Hertz, and hitch-hiked back to Hamilton. He collected the proceeds from the ticket sales off the marae secretary and disappeared. At the venue, a big crowd, excited young musicians, but empty hall. No Tina. No Patti. No Rangi.

Some years later, I was crossing a yard at Rangipo Prison when my name was called. It was Rangi. Grinning.

"Kia Ora! How are you, Judge? I'm back inside again", he laughed. "Want to buy a cheap ticket for Michael Jackson at Ericsson Stadium in November?"

He was a rogue with a sense of humour.

Rangi died not long after.

Genuine Remorse

A tall, sad-eyed, fragile-looking woman was charged with defrauding the Social Welfare Department of $12,000. The pre-sentence report was very sad: her personal relationships with family and de facto partner had been terrible. She had a serious cancer. With great difficulty, she had raised the $12,000 and had it with her to pay into court. She was too ill to perform community service or periodic detention. Prison was not indicated by reason of her genuine remorse and the re-payment. Her de facto husband had virtually forced her to keep taking the benefit while she was working. She was now unemployed and could not pay a fine.

What to do? All I could think of was to order her to pay the agreed reparation and to come up for sentence if called upon within 12 months.

With Cheque & Child

Nanette Bellamy, a big, wary woman of 48, with sly eyes and shy smile, had a penchant for passing dud cheques. She had five convictions for similar offending over the last three years. She was given two months' jail for six offences. She emerged from prison and the first thing she did was steal a chequebook and do a further $2000 worth of damage. She knew she was looking at more imprisonment and she told me as much. She also told me she was pregnant and had a drug problem. I knew of the latter but not the former. She said prison would make it difficult for her to resolve both these problems.

I disagreed. I remember Judge Augusta Wallace's stern feminine injunction against treating pregnant women in any way different from other offenders. She pointed out that many young women with troubled backgrounds and difficult financial circumstances were better off in prison than they were on the outside. As the defendant had a major drug problem, I could only agree with Gussie's philosophy. I gave Nanette 12 months' imprisonment. I hoped all went well for her, and, particularly, the baby.

Quick Withdrawal

The defended case before me was a waste of time. The brainless young man stole some cheque forms from his neighbour. He then opened a new bank account with Trustbank and paid in a forged cheque for $750. Using an automatic teller machine, he withdrew $500 a half hour later. There were some flawless photos of him in the bank opening the account. His defence was that, although he admitted to opening the account, he didn't pay in the $750 or make the withdrawals. That was done by Fred and Charley – men he didn't know well. He did not give evidence. He did not call witnesses. No Fred. No Charley.

He was clearly guilty as I am sure his counsel, Mr Kit Clews, knew well enough. I remanded him for a reparation and pre-sentence report. Later, I gave him community work.

Probability

The local judge's library holds an interesting book by the famous American advocate Louis Nizer.[1] He gives details of such famous cases as the libel case in which he acted for Quentin Reynolds against Westbrook Pegler. In his preface, he describes what he believes to be the all-important factor in any court case. It is what he calls "the rule of probability".

He says: "What was probable, probably happened."

To test the credibility of evidence, he says that the lawyer must evaluate both prosecution and defence versions of the facts in the light of the lawyer's own life experience and common sense. The "rule" also applies to documentary evidence. If the evidence is inconsistent with the other evidence in the case, or is not what a reasonable person in those circumstances would expect, it is suspicious and must be very carefully examined.

Nizer was counsel in a dispute over a huge oil discovery. The plaintiff claimed a finder's share in the oil wells and produced a letter from the Minister of Petroleum Affairs of a foreign government supporting his claim. The letter was too perfect. It

---

[1] *My Life in Court*, London, William Heinemann Ltd,1961

referred to matters that the writer would be most unlikely to know. Nizer's team, sensing the improbability, had the letter examined, and proved that the letter was typed on an Olivetti typewriter that had not been manufactured until two years after the date of the letter. The letter was a fake, a fiction designed to pervert the course of justice. One plaintiff, kaput. One defendant, pleased. Preparation, observation, memory, and knowledge of the law are all important, but not as valuable as the rule of probability.

Easy Money

In June 2013, I convened a parole board hearing where fake letters also failed Louis Nizer's probability test and resulted in us declining parole for a very serious con-man, Wayne Thomas Patterson. He was serving a sentence of 8 years 9 months' imprisonment for multiple fraud and forgery convictions.

Using forged identities for 123 fictional people, he obtained $3,417,800 in benefits from the Ministry of Social Development. He had earlier served prison sentences in the USA and Australia for similar fraud offences. We noted that he had earlier created 43 identities in Australia during his similar offending there. We declined his parole. I wrote:

> *Our belief is that he is so ingrained in his fraudulent beliefs, and greed for easy money, that he is unlikely to stop. Two solid imprisonment sentences overseas failed to deter his later offending here. He cannot seem to control his urge to cheat the system. Despite what he tells us, he has an unhealthy sense of entitlement and an arrogant, egocentric inability to feel remorse for what he has done. As a reclusive man, with only a modicum of family support, there is no-one to say him nay.*

Before the hearing, we were worried about a letter from the Carterton District Council purporting to offer him the possibility of employment in Carterton with its Horticulture Department. Our administrator wrote to the Carterton District Council. The Council immediately responded saying it was unaware of any letter from Patterson, that they had no employee of the name on the letter, and that the Carterton Council had no horticulture department.

Another letter of support purported to come from Patterson's sister in New Zealand when, we were told, she had lived in Australia for some time. One of our concerns was that the typewriter seemed to have been very similar in each case, and we thought the letters were fraudulent.

We questioned Patterson at length. One of our board members, Glenda Hughes, a former police officer, astutely cross-examined him. He was cunning, but obviously lying. Given his extraordinary history of fraudulent dishonesty and the nature of his very grave offending, we asked our Chair to refer the matter to the police.

As we suspected, the letters had been typed by Patterson on the same typewriter and were shown to be bogus. He was charged with two charges of using forged documents, and one charge of attempting to pervert the course of justice. He initially defended the charges but in August 2015 pleaded guilty and on conviction was sentenced to an additional two years imprisonment. As Shakespeare has Lancelot Gobbo, Shylock's servant, say in the Merchant of Venice: "at length the truth will out."

Māoridom

No Jet Boating

We had the television cameras outside court one day. I had to fix dates of hearing for six local Māori who tried to disrupt a Jet Boat Race on the Whakatane River over the holidays. They rode horses into the water in protest at the river being used for such purposes.

As tangata whenua[1] they said they had control over the river and it should not be used in such a way. They festooned the front of the court with banners (which were not there when I went out at 1.30 p.m. for lunch) proclaiming their sovereignty under the Treaty. Apart from their leader, Tame Iti, they were reasonably well-behaved. He kept interrupting me. Despite a warning, he persisted so I had him placed in the cells while I dealt with the setting of the dates of hearing.

Judge Peter Graham was designated as the trial judge. For two sound reasons, it was an excellent administrative decision to put the case before him:

(1) because it was him, not me!

(2) because he is an excellent judge at controlling potentially disruptive hearings.

But I was not to escape the fervour of Māori land protesters.

Race and Racism

How sad it is that mankind tears itself apart over puerile territorial and cultural nonsense. The reality is that most animals manage their tribal and territorial impulses in a more sensible way than man.

Can you be tangata whenua if you are just the descendant of an earlier immigrant? Does the earlier arrival give you greater rights? Can you be tangata whenua if three quarters of your ancestors are not Māori? As a direct, albeit genetically tarnished, descendant of ancient Celtic Picts, can I make claim to the Royal Mile in Edinburgh or a share of the North Sea oil and gas fields?

Race and racism has been a very major sludge on the pond of our society and will continue to be so until we have the intelligence and universality to realise that it is all a lot of nonsense. Religion and race are the two bogeymen of mankind's history.[2] Or can we stop eyeing alien neighbours with contempt, and start to be rational, reasonable, and

---

[1] People of the land, or more specifically, the people of the district.

[2] Beatle John Lennon (1940-1980) got it right:
"Imagine there's no countries, It isn't hard to do, Nothing to kill or die for, No religion too, Imagine all the people, Living life in peace."

caring human beings no matter what the colour of skin, the shape of nose, or the cultural saga of stunted historical deceits.

Today, sociologists tell us that there is no scientific reality in the concept of a distinct race. There are multifarious physical and genetic variations among all peoples. Studies show that less than 0.1% of all the DNA in we humans accounts for the physical differences among people that we associate with racial differences. Biology tells us of just one race – the human race. It is just that, as with our canine friends[1], we just look different.

At the 88th annual general meeting of the American Association of Physical Anthropologists in March 2019 there was a unanimous resolution supporting this scientific truth. Our (Western) concept of race has no basis in biology, but is a nevertheless a social reality. As the AAPA emphasised, race and racism are real. The organisation summarised the dilemma of race and racism:

> *The groupings of people that exist in our species are socially-defined, dynamic, and continually evolving — amalgamations of socially- and biologically-interacting individuals with constantly-shifting boundaries, reflecting the myriad ways that individuals, families, and other clusters of people create ties, move, trade, mate, reproduce, and shift their social identities and affiliations through time. Race does not capture these histories or the patterns of human biological variation that have emerged as a result. Nor does it provide a clear picture of genetic ancestry. It does, however, reflect the legacy of racist ideologies, as well as the socio-political considerations, cultural identities, and social experiences prevalent in the eras during and since the start of European settler colonialism. Race should therefore be seen as a paradigm for sorting individuals and populations into units based on historical contexts and social, cultural, and political motives.*

Jet Boat Trial

Judge Peter Graham[2] was sitting cheerfully in the main Judges Chambers when I arrived at court at 8.45 a.m. to prepare for the civil list that lay ahead. He was just concluding the second day of hearing the case of the Māori defendants who had tried to stop the Jet Boat Rally on the Whakatane River. They were the defendants I told to "shut up" when they appeared before me last month, with the consequential headline in the Whakatane Beacon

"Judge tells protestors to 'Shut Up'".

---

[1] Genetic variations in mix-breed dogs (mongrels) are simple. If a Labrador is bred with a Rottweiler, and the offspring bred with an Irish terrier, those progeny are just dogs.

[2] Judge Peter William Graham was appointed a judge in 1980 and served in the Auckland region until retirement when he moved to live at Ohope Beach. He continued as an acting judge in the Bay of Plenty. Formerly Crown counsel in Wellington, he was the author of *Graham's Law of Transportation,* published in 1975, which became the holy writ of transportation law. I gave the eulogy at his funeral in 1994.

I had become very angry at the exchange between the prosecutor and the protestors who were acrimoniously arguing with one-another in the courtroom. While I later felt that I had overstepped the mark somewhat by using such a sergeant-majorly and judicially inappropriate directive, it certainly worked. There was a deathly silence from everyone in Court – especially when I added the magic words "or I will have you locked up!"

Peter told me a bit about the case. He said it was really another instance of prosecutorial overkill. He told me during the morning break that he had discharged all but one of them without conviction on the main charge of obstructing the police. What they kept doing was wading out into the river to impede the jet boat races. They were protesting that the river was "theirs" – at least spiritually as Tainui tangata whenua – and yet they had not been consulted as to whether the races should be held.

However, the evidence showed that the Race organisers had actually written to the Tainui Trust Board in Rotorua to ask permission for the races but had not been given the courtesy of a reply. They also wrote to the local Council, the Harbour authority, and the Department of Conservation and got the thumbs up from all three.

While Māori certainly have some justification in being upset about the matter, they certainly overreacted and could easily have communicated their displeasure in a less antagonistic way by writing to the authorities to ensure there was no repeat performance without them being notified.

The leader of the activists, a well-known middle-aged but very angry man named Tame Iti, was not discharged because he had only recently been found guilty by a jury of disrupting the same race the previous year by throwing rocks off the Whakatane Bridge as the jet boats passed underneath. Dick Kearney was to sentence him shortly on that matter so Peter had remanded him to see what Dick did on the more serious matter. I am not sure just what his Rotorua Jury conviction was for, but it was obviously fairly serious, as a rock on the head could prove to be a very serious, mind-boggling, or fatal experience!

Mayor Island Occupation

I was not to escape the current smouldering of fringe Māori anger. I was requested to preside over the jury trial of the Mayor Island Māori who are charged with trespass and demanding with menace. Dick Kearney said I had been allocated the case because I handled the bail hearing so effectively before Christmas. Flatterer! As Adlai Stevenson said, "Flattery is all right so long as you don't inhale." Dick just didn't want to do the case himself!

The pre-Christmas case he referred to was a fairly torrid session where the accused asked me to lift the bail condition I had earlier imposed on them forbidding them to set foot on the Island until after the trial.

They were very angry, but finally calmed down once I had threatened old Matiu Tarawa, arch-agitator and chief fomenter, with contempt if he continued to belabour me with irrelevancies. He was not an accused. He was a McKenzie friend only. I told him he could pass notes and give advice, but was not to act as counsel. He behaved himself very well once I told him that I expected a chief of high rank to act like one, and not be discourteous or disruptive.

The Māori leader of the Island stand-off, Isobel Birkett, addressed me interminably and it seems the dispute had nothing to do with the Treaty or with the Pakeha. It was a dispute between two separate iwi[1] factions seeking control of the island. Mrs. Birkett's group were Coromandel people. The trust board currently administering the island was apparently dominated by Māori from a Taranaki tribe which "took" the island by force shortly before the missionaries arrived. The island was important to Māori as a source of black obsidian, a volcanic and very sharp glass created by the rapid cooling of silica-rich lava. The obsidian was called Tuhua by Māori who called the island by the same name. Captain James Cook called it Mayor Island when he sighted it on 3 November 1769, in recognition of the Lord Mayor's Day to be held in London a few days later.

Mark Moynihan, who leases what was formerly the lodge operated by the Deep-Sea Fishing Club, was not as Irish as his name implied. He had, it seemed, some Māori heritage as a descendant of Māori from the Taranaki iwi and his being given the lease had inflamed the Birkett group.

I confused Mrs. Birkett somewhat by asking her to explain her whakapapa.[2] She did not seem to know what it was. I then asked the defendants how often they had visited the Mayor before the invasion. Only one middle-aged man was a regular visitor. I lifted the bail condition on him and said he could be their eyes and ears over the holiday period as I was assured that he would act maturely, lawfully, and with decorum during that time.

The whole group then said their thanks and left quite happily, despite the fact that there is a Māori Land Court injunction and a Trust Board trespass notice extant against the man I allowed to visit. I explained that he might still not be permitted to visit. I don't know whether he did. Peace has since prevailed, but for how long?

Activism and protest movements are part of humanity. Protesting about human rights is important, but the method used can be disruptive or even criminal. Terrorists

---

[1] Tribal

[2] Lineage, genealogy. Maori culture reveres the ancestor. Maori imbued with the tikanga (customs and traditions) are generally familiar with this.

who blow up innocent bystanders see themselves as legitimate protestors: one group's terrorist is another groups' freedom fighter.

Gross, violent, stupid and unreasonable protest must be curtailed in the best interests of most citizens. On a considered analysis of a given issue, it is often seen that the large crowds of banner-waving and angry people have simply not paused to think carefully about the issue and resolve the problem by quiet dialogue and intelligent assessment.[1]

Abducting Grandson

The jury and I heard an intriguing saga of a 62-year-old Māori grandfather, Matiu, charged with abducting his five-year-old grandson from the home of his daughter. Talk about over-kill! It was a case that should never have gone this far – especially not before a jury of staunch and true citizens of Rotorua.

Firstly, the police should never have charged him with abduction, a very serious crime.

Secondly, having seen and investigated the charge, his counsel should not have elected trial by jury.

Competent counsel would have advised him to plead guilty and make the obvious mitigatory plea. I would then have told him he was a naughty kaumatua[2] and that if he did it again within the next 12 months he would be punished. But no! Everyone wants to proclaim from the roof of the grandstand!

What happened was very simple. Matiu, a lean, wiry, steel-haired grandfather was worried that his daughter, Whetu, wasn't properly caring for her four children. He told us she smoked lots of dope, and she drank too much as well. As did her husband, although he hadn't been seen around much over the last few years.

Granddad Matiu also thought Whetu was uncaring: too selfish to give the five-year-old boy permanently to her sister, his only other daughter, Hine. Hine had only one kidney, was single, and could not have children. In the Māori way, he said, Whetu should have done the decent thing and let Hine raise young Eru. Apparently, she had done more for the boy than Whetu. Whetu acknowledged that her son Eru calls Hine "Mum!".

Everyone who testified at the trial had been raised in the Māori way – mainly by grandparents or by some relative other than their birth parents. *Whangai* is the ancient and accepted customary Māori practice whereby a child lives with and is raised by a

---

[1] Ireland is a grim example. In the 20th century about 11,000 people were killed or injured as a result of political violence there. Eventually an agreement (Belfast Agreement 1998) was reached. It is contentious as to whether the killings achieved much.

[2] Maori Elder.

family member, and not by the birth parents. A parent who takes on a child is called a *matua whāngai,* and the child is a *tamaiti whāngai.* All the extended whanau know about the relationship and play their part.

"Nothing wrong with that", said the accused. "That is the Māori way."

The problem was that whenever the money from the social welfare benefits had been spent, the kids were sent back to the real mum and dad who then became angry at having to resume parental responsibility for a few days until they could send the kids back to grandfather.

There is no doubt that Māori grandparents do a wonderful job with their mokopuna.[1] The problem is that some birth parents abdicate responsibility. Historically, grandparents were often primary caregivers, freeing up the young parents so they could be warriors, farmers, or the preparers of food. But those days are long past, and the arrangement is not intended to enable the natural parents to laze around living off the dole, smoking dope, and guzzling vast quantities of alcohol.

In saying this, I am not being racist. I have spoken to several Māori elders who tell me that in their own upbringing they resented what they saw as being parental indifference, and begrudged being raised in a modern world by old people constrained not by a one-generation gap but by a two-generation gap!

I have also seen such resentment expressed by young Māori in pre-sentence and parole reports, where they tell the probation officer they blame many of their problems on the fact that they hardly knew their birth parents and that dear old grandmother, as kind and caring as she may have been, let them have free rein with no discipline. Many older Māori overdo the aroha[2] and underdo the whakaraupapa.[3]

Granddad Matiu was a delightful character. Without asking me, he exited the witness box and waltzed around the front of the court as if it was his home marae, gesticulating at the jurors and me with his carved kauri walking stick. He had been genuinely concerned for young five-year-old Eru. That was why he angrily stormed around to Whetu's home and left with Eru, Hine, and Jenny's older daughter, Ngaire. A week later, two sturdy policemen with white faces arrived on his doorstep. Whetu had complained to her lawyer. The lawyer had complained to the senior sergeant about kidnapping. The senior sergeant had studiously thumbed through the Crimes Act.

"Not kidnapping," he said, "abduction".

He sent a sergeant to uplift the child. Old Matiu was most exasperated. He wanted to handle things in the Māori way, and did not want European police and European courts to stick their nose in.

---

[1] Grandchildren

[2] Love, affection.

[3] Discipline and control.

Whetu had thoughts to the contrary. She had wanted her child back – in the European way. And sad as it may be for old Matiu, he too is subject to the law. Instead he became enraged. He verbally abused the sergeant and the constable. He demanded to see a Māori constable so he could communicate better. Why, I don't know; he was communicating very effectively to the jury and me in court, in fluent and convincing English. Better, in fact, than many lawyers!

In any event, it went from bad to worse. He struggled with the two officers, resisted, was arrested, and was handcuffed. All in the name of family! He really spat the dummy. He had not understood King Lear:

> *"O! Let me not be mad, not mad, sweet heaven; keep me in temper; I would not be mad!"*

He complained bitterly that when he had looked after Eru in the past, Whetu had never given him any part of the Child Allowance. And for a pensioner that was understandable. But cross-examination revealed that he had thrown another mokopuna out of the house because she accidentally broke a window.

> *"I don't mind looking after the grandchildren, provided I am compensated. After all," he told the jury with some solemnity, "my pension is only $150 per week. That," he added sagely "is only $300 a fortnight!*

Ten jurors gave little smiles. The remaining two of them, wrestling with the difficult arithmetic but understanding the poverty expressed in such a sad observation, nodded back at him without smiling.

The jury trial should never have started. I felt sorry for the old boy, the little boy, and everyone else involved. The accused has a ton of character and strength. Essentially, he cares very much for his children and grandchildren, and will probably have more say as "an elder" than I will at the same age.

We heard testimony from an expert in Māori custom. It was interesting. He did not push kaumatuatanga[1] too far, because what may have been appropriate before 1840 in a structured, disciplined, tribal society may have little relevance to the urban modern Māori of today, who know all about abduction and grandfathers from watching *Days of Our Lives, Dallas, and Falconcrest.*

The jury found him not guilty.

Parenting

There has been great change in the way Māori now parent children. Social and economic change has significantly altered the part kaumatua now play. Māori still adopt out (whangai) children to other family members but the rapid changes presented by

---

[1] The concept of old age.

today's society have modified and reduced the incidence of that traditional Māori custom. The impact of unemployment, inadequate education, poverty, early pregnancy, and the economic advantage of keeping one's own children to preserve income from State benefits, all erode the customary practice. Māori women have babies earlier in life than non-Māori. Māori teens have the highest fertility rate.[1] Because of their youthfulness, they are less likely to engage in further education and more likely to depend on state benefits, live in single-parent or multi-family households, and have lower incomes and less assets. Poverty, drugs and alcohol abuse, and domestic violence often result. Judges are gravely concerned that the Māori child-homicide rate is more than double that of non-Māori.

There have been a number of initiatives designed to improve these ugly statistics, but socio-economic deprivation, which affects many underprivileged groups worldwide, is a hard problem to successfully tackle. The anger shown by the old grandfather, and directed physically at the two police officers, is not unusual. Often such anger is fired by alcohol or drugs. Not so with old Matiu. He lost his temper because he did not get his own way and felt aggrieved.

Te Reo[2]

As far as I know, during my term of office, there was no-one on our bench fluent in Māori – and that included the judges who have Māori ancestry.

That was not the case with Justice Rodney Gallen of the High Court, who was completely fluent in Te Reo, having been raised in rural Māori areas where his Dad was a postmaster. A slim, fine-featured, somewhat frail pakeha man he was one of the last people I would ever expect to be a fluent speaker in Māori.

I am told that several years ago, he was chairing a session of a conference held in New Zealand by an international group of persons concerned with the rights of ethnic minorities. Some Māori activists entered the room and one of them became loud, aggressive and challenging.

Justice Gallen waited for the appropriate moment and then sternly reprimanded him in fluent Māori, reminding the man of his chiefly blood, and reminding him that his ancestors would be most disturbed to see his lack of respect and courtesy to the many distinguished members of minority groups from over the world. That, I am told, put a speedy end to the disturbance.[3]

---

[1] Almost three times the European birth rate.

[2] The Maori language.

[3] A compassionate, sensible, witty judge, he was knighted in 2000. He died in 2012, age 79.

Sir Rodney Gallen, as he later became, was very special. Throughout his life, he used his deep understanding of Māori culture to urge compromise and reconciliation between the races. Notably, he said:

> *The comment about "all being New Zealanders" does have some significance... We all live in this country and for most of us we have no other, not any relationship with any other. Our relationship with the land is one which binds us all together, although we need to bear in mind that not all people who live here relate in the same way to the land as such. Nevertheless, because for most if not all of us the land gives us our first identity we start from a unifying factor and can reasonably build on that. There is no doubt Māori have a special attachment to the land and to particular places, for many reasons, but it is also true that Pakeha hold such attachments as well.*

One of my astute Māori friends on the Parole Board reminded us that all Kiwis are immigrants to this country, or descendants of those who were. Māori were the earliest immigrants, it seems between 1250 and 1300 A.D., according to radiocarbon dating, D.N.A. studies, and Māori oral history. At that time, the Seventh Crusade had ended, Marco Polo was off to China, Kublai Khan, the grandson of Genghis Khan, founded the Yuan dynasty in China, and the Scots unsuccessfully rebelled against the English at the Battle of Falkirk.

New Zealand is unique in having a remarkably short period of human occupation. This was not so with our Australian Aboriginal neighbours who, over a timeframe of 50,000 years, developed 250 distinct languages. Until 1642[1], no one in Europe knew New Zealand existed.

Activists

Much court time is expended by Māori activists who profess that Māori sovereignty renders them somehow immune to the laws of New Zealand. No-one minds legitimate protest about cultural concerns or land confiscation. In a democracy that is fine. But to waste hundreds of hours of jury and judge time dealing with repetitive and often illogical and unreasonable tirades about things that have for years been rejected by the appeal courts, is worthy of thunderous judicial rebuke.

As I have jotted elsewhere, forget the racial elements: let us march together into the future with a prospect of hope and unity. Let us be responsible, innovative, caring and sensitive to the wants of humanity. There is not a human being on the face of this puckered planet who has "pure" blood. What on earth is "pure blood?". Purity in terms

---

[1] With the arrival of the Dutch explorer Abel Janszoon Tasman (1603-1659)

of what? What criteria? Of Adam and Eve? People take great pride in their bloodline, but humans being humans, sexuality being sexuality, warfare being warfare, and economics being economics, what comes out of the modern washing machine could not, in any way, be called "pure". We are all out of Africa.

Civil Squabbles

The Boat

I heard a dispute about a boat. It all started with a matrimonial squabble. The husband separated from the wife and went to Auckland with all he then needed: a 16-year-old girl and a large General Motors Holden Statesman car.

The wife was more concerned about the car than the teenager. She didn't want her husband back: she wanted the Statesman back. She felt it gave her a superior status in life. Instead of applying to the Family Court to resolve the question, she hired her son and his friend to go to Auckland to pose and act as repossession agents. The agreement was that she would pay them $500 each if their mission was completed.

They returned with the car the next day. It had been a breeze. Dad, no doubt preoccupied with matters of more carnal interest than the Holden Statesman, never even looked out the window as they seized the car and headed back to Tauranga. But mother welched on the deal. She didn't pay the boys the agreed $1000. They protested. She said she did not have the money. They continued to protest. To pacify them, she finally gave them an elderly 18-foot runabout which her husband had purchased several years before from a local farmer for $1500, complete with inboard motor and trailer. It was by then barely seaworthy with rot holes in the bow.

The two young men, keen fishermen, agreed to take the boat in lieu of payment. They then spent a lot of money and time completely rebuilding the old boat from the hull up until it was unrecognizable. Although the valuation figures varied, I finally fixed its present value at $4000.

Not long after that, the son sold out his half share in the boat to his friend, and the plot thickened. Husband and wife reconciled. He had sorely missed both the Statesman and the boat and was exhausted. The wife, in an odd sort of way, missed him.

But the boat… Alas! Alack! was not to be seen. But when wifey told hubby what had happened, he rubbed his hands like Shylock at the thought of his old tub having been restored to pristine order. The two of them snuck round to the young man's house while he was at work and uplifted boat and trailer. They refused to return it.

The young man became the plaintiff with Mr Gerald McArthur, counsel, as helmsman. Mum became the defendant with Mr Tony Fitzgerald as bosun.

It became a naval battle royal. Even after I gave my decision in favour of the plaintiff for $4000 damages (but not the boat), the argument raged in the court foyer after I had disembarked. The boat was really just the catalyst for a great deal of family angst. I heard from several other family members who had much hearsay evidence for me to hear and then forget. The son testified against his mother and stepfather. The 16-year-old nymphet was even mentioned in despatches.

I even heard from an honest but flamboyant middle-aged woman who responded to the oath with the impressive cry of American witnesses, "So help me God!". The defendant was her mother-in-law's sister!

Mother was less than frank, although I did feel sorry for her. She was a sad little woman with a tired, lined face, and dull, bottle-black shoulder length hair which might have looked better on the 16-year-old. On the evidence, I was forced to find that Mother had no right to give away Dad's boat as it was jointly owned property, but at least the young fellow will receive some compensation for Mother's breach of contract.

This case illustrates how family dysfunction can get out of hand. I do not envy Family Court judges their task.

Not Steering Clear

I had a "running down" case. A battle between O'Neil v O'Neil. They were the lawyers, not the parties! It could have been a real donnybrook with such resolute counsel of Irish stock. But it proved to be quiet and orderly.

Five years earlier, a farmer's wife parked her car on the roadside near the Golf Course at Piopio. A keen golfer, she was checking the condition of the greens. A car driven by the defendant along 100 metres of straight, sealed, wide road with unobstructed vision, hit the rear of her car. The woman, by way of her insurer, sued for the repair bill. The defendant said it was her fault for parking where she did. "Why?" I asked myself.

Why did he hit the parked car? Answer: he failed to exercise the standard of care expected of the reasonable and prudent motorist in those circumstances: he was, in short, negligent in failing to keep a proper lookout, steer clear, or stop. His solicitor, I fear, poorly advised him.

Hey! Hey!

I always believe in the "Hey! Hey!" principle. If someone overcharges or does a shoddy job, I think it a normal reaction to say "Hey! Hey! I'm not paying that!".

In one case, an architectural draftsman prepared house plans, delivered them to the defendant and heard nothing more. Two months later, his boss sent out a bill for just over $3000. Silence. Three months later the defendant was asked by telephone whether there were any problems as to payment. He replied by saying he would get his lawyer to write a letter, as there was a problem about the bill. Nothing more was heard from either the defendant or the lawyer. There was complete silence until a summons was served 15 months after the plans were delivered. Only then was there a belated "Hey! Hey!" from the lawyer.

I always feel, that to be credible, the aggrieved party must protest as soon as reasonably possible. In such circumstances, silence may be far from golden as a response is clearly called for. I gave judgement for the draftsman.

No Tackle

Another mistake I commonly find (in all cases – not just civil) is a failure to tackle. If an opposing player has the ball and is running to the line, a good attempt must be made to tackle him. You can't simply put hand to hips and let him sprint past.

"Mr Smith, why did you not write or telephone Mr Brown and tell him you were unhappy about his fees and the plans he had drawn for you?"

"I was too angry. I was furious that he had charged me twice his original estimate and that his plans were so useless."

"But you never complained or told him that for 15 months. Surely you owed him an explanation?"

"Why did I? The plans were defective and were too late getting to me."

"You say the plans were defective in six different respects. Mr Brown has only heard of four of them for the first time today. Why did you only mention two of the six in your statement of defence?"

"That was my lawyer's job."

"But you have never mentioned them at any time."

"Well they were there to be seen in the plans."

"Even your own expert architect witness was not asked about those four alleged defects when he testified on your behalf this morning."

"Well that wasn't my fault."

"And neither Mr Brown nor his draftsman were asked about them when they gave their evidence on Monday."

"Well I am raising them now."

The alleged defects were quite unsubstantiated. If they were relevant or material, they should have been raised as soon as they were recognised, and the plaintiff should have been tackled about them:

(1) in the pleadings,

(2) under cross-examination, and

(3) by calling expert evidence to prove them.

Nothing of the sort happened. And even on the topics mentioned in the pleadings and by cross-examination, the defendant's architect gave no supporting evidence. This is not the way to convince a judge "upon a preponderance of probabilities"!

Charlie's Will

Joan Catherine Keeble was the audacious widow of a very wealthy farmer, Charles Thomas Keeble (who died 1971, aged 95 years), and whose two large, well-managed farms at Fitzherbert West, neighboured Massey University.

Charlie, a bachelor until he was 92, had a lifelong passionate interest in breeding thoroughbred racehorses. As did Joan Catherine. In her case, it was probably more a passion for stallions of the equine species than a passion for 92-year-old Charlie. She was a single woman 45 years his junior.

He made a fresh will in contemplation of his marriage to her. One of the earlier partners of my law firm, Martyn Abraham,[1] prepared the will. Charlie gave Joan Catherine a modest interest in his estate commensurate with the predictably short duration of the marriage. Martyn Abraham, then in his 70s, was astounded that Charlie was getting married at such an advanced age. After the honeymoon, he spoke to Charlie in the street. He enquired as to how well the honeymoon had progressed. Charlie grinned and simply said, "I ended up in hospital with back problems".

Charlie died. Joan Keeble was not happy with her legacy. Like Oliver, she wanted more. She wanted the thoroughbreds. She sued. In the lengthy court saga arising from her application for further provision from the estate, I acted for the trustees of Charles Keeble's estate, the Guardian Trust & Executors Co. Ltd.

Joan Catherine was very difficult. She was cantankerous, neurotic and demanding. She would not listen to legal advice. She had several lawyers during the course of her court proceedings. One, Barry O'Regan,[2] failed to appear as her counsel at a hearing to determine some preliminary issues. The reason for his absence, we learned from the presiding judge, was that very morning he had been appointed a High Court judge. She therefore had to find a fresh lawyer. She chose Mike Bungay.

The case went to trial in Wellington before Justice Quilliam. Joan Catherine testified. She did not perform well. She was revealed to be the money-grubbing harridan that Charlie's nephews said she was. It was clear that Justice Peter Quilliam[3] was not impressed with her demeanour, her testimony, or the answers she gave to my cross-examination and that of counsel representing the beneficiaries.

His Honour directed that there be a brief adjournment. Bungay retreated out into a corridor and spoke to her. He returned 15 minutes later and asked to speak to me and

---

[1] Lionel Martyn Abraham, partner of Fitzherbert Abraham, Palmerston North Solicitors, was one of the four lawyers who inaugurated the annual Devil's Own legal golf tournament in 1932. He had retired before I joined the firm. Born in Palmerston North, he studied law at Cambridge and served in the King Edwards Horse Regiment and later as a Lieutenant in the Royal Artillery during the First World War. He died in 1986, aged 93.

[2] Justice John Barry O'Regan, knighted in 1984. He died in 1995, aged 80.

[3] Sir Peter was a judge of the High Court from 1969 until 1988. He was the inaugural Chair of the Independent Police Conduct Authority 1989-1992.

the other lawyers. Mike told us she would settle for $100,000, forgoing her claim to the racehorses. After consultation with our respective clients, we all agreed. We returned to court and asked the judge to make a consent order to that effect. He did so, and we all went home, relieved that the protracted and challenging litigation was over.

A month later, we received a surprising motion from her next lawyer, John Desmond 'Des' Dalgety, an eminent Wellington barrister.[1] Joan Catherine sought to have the consent order set aside.

She said she had never agreed to the settlement. She said Mike had forced her into it by using both physical and verbal aggression and duress. She said he had pushed her against the wall of the court corridor and told her she was "a stupid bitch if she did not agree to settle the case."

So back to court we went. Mike, now her ex-lawyer, naturally had to give evidence to clear his name. Half the Wellington bar were in court, delighted at the prospect of seeing Mike Bungay on the receiving end of a cross-examination instead of being the interrogator. Des Dalgety gleefully and capably cross-examined Mike, who did not do well as a witness. He was quite disconcerted and, to the joy of the assembled lawyers, fumbled his words, struggled to remember facts, and was not very convincing when he denied any inappropriate actions on his part.

Most of us who knew Michael well were quite convinced that he probably did, as she said, call her a "quite stupid bitch" and tell her to "take $100,000 now before you lose the case completely".

We thought that his advice was very realistic and the description of his client justified, appropriate, and far from defamatory! In the event, His Honour Justice John White[2] dismissed her application, making it clear that it was a very difficult task to overturn a consent judgement and that he did not accept her testimony.

Lucky

How could the plaintiff in a civil case ever lose? His name: McLuckie!

---

[1] He was counsel for Sir Robert Muldoon, NZ President of the Society for the Protection of the Unborn Child (SPUC) and Deputy Chair of Air New Zealand at the time of the Erebus plane crash disaster.

2 Sir John Charles White MBE, 1911 – 2007, a considerate and competent judge who was aid-de-camp to Lieutenant General (Later Baron) Bernard Freyberg, VC, GCMG, KCB, KBE, DSO & Three Bars for most of WWII.

Lawyers

Wrong Letters

William "Budge" Fitzherbert was not the first partner of my old law firm, although the name Fitzherbert Abraham Crossley & Evans (later shortened to Fitzherbert Abraham & Co) gives a contrary impression. John Herbert Hankins[1] had founded the firm in 1881. He had a brief partnership with a solicitor named Loughnan and then Budge Fitzherbert married Hankins daughter, May, and later joined Hankins in the law partnership.

My senior partner, Graham Crossley,[2] told a delightful story on himself. J.H. Hankins died in 1928 and Mrs. Hankins survived him. She was hospitalised with severe dementia for about the last 8 years of her life. An earlier partnership agreement between the partners Fitzherbert, Abraham, & Crossley contained an ongoing stipulation that the firm would pay an annuity for the support of the old widow. Crossley hardly even knew the old lady and yet, as junior partner, he had contributed to her support for some years.

Crossley was overseas on war service as ADC to Major General Sir John Duigan, KBE, CB, DSO, who was Chief of the General Staff of the New Zealand Military Forces from 1937 to 1941. He received a letter from his partner, Martyn Abraham, telling him that Mrs. Hankins had passed on at age 98. Crossley dashed off two letters. One to the son-in-law, Fitzherbert, as per:

> *Dear Budge, I was very sorry to hear that your mother-in-law has finally passed on. You have my deepest sympathy at this difficult time. All my love to May etc. etc.*

The second letter was to his other partner Martyn Abraham in this vein:

> *Dear Martyn, thank God the old girl has finally shuffled off after all this time. We can now spend the surplus income on a better-quality gin! Cheers! etc. etc.*

About two months later a letter arrived through the Army post from Fitzherbert. It read something like:

> *My Dear Major Crossley,*
> *Thank you for your letter expressing your condolences at the death of my mother-in-law.*
> *It seems that I got the letter intended for Abraham.*

---

[1] He was the inaugural President of the Palmerston North Law Society and a president of the Manawatu rugby club. in 1896, he presented the Hankins Shield (known as "the Hank" or "the Bertie"), which is still contested annually. It goes to the winner of the Manawatu rugby senior club championship and is considered to be the oldest New Zealand rugby trophy at senior level.

[2] He was appointed to the rank of Queen's Counsel in 1970.

May I say I agree entirely with your sentiments. I trust you are enjoying the better-quality gin and that the trauma of war will not affect your ability henceforth to post the correct letter in the correct envelope.
Warmest regards,
Budge Fitzherbert.

If Your Majesty Pleases

In 1976, Jack Horn was on the bench when Mick Cleary, a solicitor from Foxton, made a rare appearance in the Police Court in Palmerston North. Mick had been a partner of Joe Bergin before the latter became a magistrate. The previous night he had been watching the excellent British TV production Elizabeth I. He began his submissions to His Worship with the deferential:

"If your Majesty pleases".

Jack Horn smiled down from his throne.

"No, Mr Cleary. I'm not Royalty. Please just 'worship' me!"

Loco

When I had just arrived in Palmerston North as a Law Clerk, an elderly solicitor from the Wairarapa was heading home from a Manawatu Law Society Bar Dinner. In those days, no one seemed to be too worried about drinking and driving and he was very much "over the eight" when he slowly approached the main trunk railway line at Pahiatua. The crossing lights were red and flashing, the barrier arm was down, and the bell was sounding. The lawyer sat there for a while. He noticed the train slowly shunting 50 metres up the track. Annoyed, he got out, lifted the arm, and drove onto the track. The train driver moved the train towards him and remonstrated.

The lawyer roundly criticised the train driver for his inconsiderate use of the locomotive, turned off his car, and emerged onto the verge. The car was left straddling the railway line. The train driver became angry with the stubborn old fool, and very soon realised he was dealing with a drunken "gent" in a monkey suit.

The "gent" kept arguing the law to the rugged driver. The latter finally sent his guard off to the local constable, who arrived (no doubt in carpet slippers and police greatcoat), to say, "Hello Hello" to the elderly lawyer he knew so well.

But pressed charges are charges pressed, and the poor fellow pleaded guilty before DG Sinclair Esq., S.M. (who had been tippling at the same function), who scowled, grimaced, and hit the poor practitioner with a fine and disqualification that adversely impacted Bar Dinners for the next decade!

I used the expression "over the eight". I realise that is now a linguistic archaism that the younger generations don't use. The phrase was a military one. Apparently, a soldier could safely quaff eight pints of beer (then of lower alcohol content than today) and remain acceptably sober. But if he had "over the eight" he was a problem drinker! Now we say "over the limit" – the limit being clearly, legally and scientifically defined.

Bad Neighbours

There have been TV series based on bad neighbourhood disputes. Sometimes people fight over fence-lines, overhanging trees, or pets. Sometimes it is loud music or kids. Sometimes the neighbour is a drunk or mentally ill. Often such disputes end up in court.

I have had two cases where lawyers fell out with their neighbours. One lawyer disputed the positioning of a letter box. He said it was unlawfully on his property. The other involved a senior Auckland tree-hugging barrister who refused to have his boundary trees trimmed to let some winter sun warm his neighbour's shaded house. The lawyer was acting for himself (and the old rule for lawyers is that if you act for yourself you have a fool for a client). I called him and counsel for the neighbour into my chambers and the conversation went something like this:

"Surely you can agree to at least a judicious trimming of the trees if only in the interests of neighbourliness," I asked.

"No, your Honour, the trees were there when the Plaintiff came to live next door. He is assumed to have accepted that situation. I will not agree to them being touched in any way."

"But just to be a good neighbour...?'"

"I don't want to be a good neighbour. Has your Honour not heard the ancient proverb: 'a good lawyer is a bad neighbour'?"

Neither lawyer proved to be a good lawyer: both lost their case.

Alcohol Specialists

Judges, both at first instance and on appeal, hate excess breath/blood alcohol cases because over the years the lawyers have microscopically examined and exhaustively argued about every word of the relevant legislation, and have interpreted them in many ways. I can't think of any other area of the law that has received such an intense scrutiny. That is understandable because for most people a disqualification is a grave hindrance to their business or personal lives. In Auckland and Wellington there are lawyers whose entire legal practice consists of defending motorists charged with excess breath/blood alcohol offences.

Bar Dinners

Bar dinners have an ancient origin. They are not called that after a drinking bar such as the counters we have at restaurants and hotels today. The legal word "bar" has a quite different meaning. We lawyers still refer to the "bar of the court". Young lawyers are "called to the bar" after they have completed their exams and have "passed the bar". Courtroom advocates are called bar-risters. The "bar" is the physical rail or barrier that stretches across the courtroom. The only people allowed inside the area past the bar on the side of the judge's bench, are the judge, court officers, the barristers (attorneys), a witness giving testimony and the accused. The "bar" performed a practical purpose of preventing angry members of the public from attacking or abusing the judge, jurors or parties. In modern courtrooms where extreme violence might happen, the old wooden rail is sometimes replaced by a bullet-proof glass wall.

Bar dinners were conventional over the centuries in London, when lawyers of all rank, station and age, wined and dined together in the Inns of Court. Artisans of other trades and callings had similar dinners in their guilds. Bar dinners in New Zealand are but a shallow and now almost defunct reflection of the dinners still held in London at the four Inns of Court.

The customary dinners held at the Inner Temple, Middle Temple, Lincoln's Inn and Gray's Inn had their origins in the Middle Ages. In those times, the Inns were where lawyers learned their trade. Young students would come from all over England, take lodgings at the Inns of Court, receive legal education, take part in mock courts, and all eat and drink together in the main hall. The Inns no longer provide legal education. Law schools now do that. But it is still compulsory, before admission to the bar, for graduates to attend at least twelve formal dinners at their Inn.

At these dinners, there is great tradition. The senior barristers ("Benchers") all dressed in their barristers' gowns, enter the dining hall in a procession and, at the end of the night, leave the same way, although with less steady gait! There are toasts to the Queen, the Church, and "this Honourable Society". There is no handshaking at these occasions. It is an ancient rule that barristers never shake hands. They bow to one another. Historically, shaking hands evolved as a way of showing you were not concealing a weapon. Barristers all knew each other and as collegial professionals of honour and good repute considered it unnecessary and insulting to demonstrate the lack of weapon.

A four-course meal is provided, and as much wine and port as they can drink. The cheap booze has always been a great attraction to many of the youthful attendees, although in these cosmopolitan days, those of Muslim and other abstemious persuasions are no doubt unimpressed at the degree of intoxication.

Kiwi Bar Dinners

New Zealand bar dinners are not held often – now perhaps once every 18 months or so – and usually to celebrate an important event. When I first joined the profession, we held an annual bar dinner irrespective of any specific event. We invited the visiting Supreme Court Judge to be the after-dinner speaker. There were toasts to "the Sovereign", "the Bench", and "the Bar". To allow for a good degree of uncensored intoxication, spouses were not invited. The dinners were formal black-tie affairs and, as in those days there were few women practising as barristers or solicitors (at least in the Manawatu), the nights tended to become fairly boozy – at least after the judge had withdrawn to his hotel.

Ignoring Advice

John Pierpont Morgan, the American billionaire banker, said: "I don't know as I want a lawyer to tell me what I cannot do. I hire him to tell how to do what I want to do."

I had three clients who completely and deliberately ignored my advice!

I acted for a private hospital in Palmerston North where surgery was performed on the wife of a well-known New Zealand politician. She suffered complications and weeks later it was discovered that a swab had been left inside her: a clear case of medical negligence. I was consulted and was asked two questions: (1) Do we tell her of our mistake? (2) Do we charge her for the surgical and hospital fees required to remove the swab?

I said they must fully acknowledge and apologise for their negligence, and not charge her anything for the reparative surgery or further hospitalisation.

I learned later from a doctor spy that they lied to her, and charged normal fees to avoid adverse publicity. The hospital no longer exists. Perhaps just as well.

I also acted as honorary solicitor for the Board of Governors of my old high school. I was called to an emergency meeting to discuss how to resolve the accusations made by several boys at the boarding house that a teacher had sexually assaulted them.

Questions: (1) Do we tell the parents and make the facts known? (2) Do we lay a complaint with the police? I said yes to both.

As was common in those days, but morally and legally indefensible, they quietly asked the teacher to move to other employment in another province, and a cone of silence descended. My advice was ignored.

As we now know, Roman Catholic priests sexually molested boys over many decades.[1] Investigations showed that Catholic bishops did what my high school board did: they kept the crimes secret to avoid public anger, and transferred the offenders to other parishes. As I have already noted in these jottings, "truth will out" and some bishops have been forced to retire or resign. Hundreds of millions of dollars have been paid by that church to victims.

The local freezing works at Longburn had serious trade-union issues for some years. One issue was that prime export fillet steak was being stolen by some workers in large quantities. The workers put it in their clothing lockers and later smuggled it out of the factory. The question asked of me by Mr Tom Hastie, the manager: "Can we open the lockers and remove the stolen meat with or without police assistance?"

I said it was clearly criminal behaviour, the lockers were the property of the company and could be opened, but it would be best to lay a complaint of theft and let the police effect a search under warrant.

Mr Hastie smiled, paid my fee, and ignored my advice. Later, he explained that a search would cause a major strike by all workers and potentially cost the company millions in lost production.

In 1986, Longburn's owners imposed a lock-out of all workers when workers led by Roger Middlemass, the local Meatworkers' Union secretary, refused to accept a severe wage cut. The result was that the factory was mothballed. It is unfortunate that strident union angst, and ego-driven leadership, did nothing for workers but lose all their jobs. The freezing works, just on a century old, closed down in 1989, and the desolate ruins of the plant still scar the small community.

Laid Out

A likeable family law practitioner from Levin was famed for his customary behaviour at bar dinners. It consisted of becoming insensible with alcohol and, after regaining consciousness, taking off his trousers, and staggering back into the PDC[2] dining area with the glazed expression that "spirituous liquors" tend to imprint upon the human face!

---

[1] Clergy and churchpersons from many other religions have committed similar crimes. For example, as at 2019 nearly 400 pastors and leaders of the Southern Baptist Convention (which has 15 million members and 47,000 churches in the USA) have pleaded guilty to or been convicted of sexual offending against 700 victims since 1998. This was exposed by journalists from The Houston Chronicle and The San Antonio Express-News.

[2] The PDC was, until the building was demolished in 1990, the leading department store in Palmerston North. The four-story Premier Drapery Company shop was erected in 1929. As was common in those times, the top floor was used for restrooms and a large dining room. It was a popular venue for weddings and 21st birthday parties, including mine in 1961.

There was a large ornate carved oak table in the foyer against the wall directly opposite the lift doors. On at least two occasions, I remember this practitioner, whose name must forever remain unspoken, "laid out" on the oak table as if at a wake. Intoxication hit him early in the evening because it was the practice of the Levin contingent to hire a bus to transport them on the 45-minute drive to the Palmerston North venue. This enabled them to imbibe on the way up and, for those of stalwart constitution, to do the same on the way home. His compassionate companions always handled his comatose and somewhat portly body with tender care, so that his tuxedo was tidy, his arms crossed and his hands clasped over his chest. He would lie like that for an hour or so, usually missing the meal completely.

At one celebrated bar dinner, His Honour Justice Haslam[1] a man of almost obsessively fastidious habits and curiously eccentric and unreasonable concern for protocol and propriety, was in the course of concluding his erudite and carefully constructed after-dinner address.

Suddenly, much to the irritation of His Honour, the half sozzled audience were resuscitated from their boredom by the late entry of our Levin colleague, arisen from the dead. Although by the look of him, only just. He had drunkenly clambered off the hall table, taken off his trousers and folded them carefully over his arm. He then tottered up to the head table where with much alcoholic solemnity he scrutinised the esteemed guest speaker. Garters held up his black socks. His shirttails were in disarray. His elderly underpants were of the boxer variety. His bow tie was awry.

We were enthralled at his lack of concern for the "martinet of the bench". He showed no sign of fear. He just stood there, swaying slightly, with the same serious and inscrutable look on his pale face as he had on entering the room.

The judge glowered at the intruder: he was grossly and intolerably offended at such indescribable discourtesy to one of Her Majesty's judges. But he said nothing. The Levin conveyancer (who had never ventured into a courtroom for decades) said nothing. He just burped mildly, wobbled his portly frame, puckered his lips, and for no discernible reason turned and toddled off to the bathroom from whence he was later extracted and poured onto the bus for home.

All Harte

Some lawyers who defended drunk drivers– like Michael Harte in Auckland – were very good. When the law is on his side, he argues the law. When the facts are on his side, he argues the facts. But when neither the facts nor the law are on his side, unlike

---

[1] See p.48.

foolish lawyers who then attack the police officer or even the judge[1], he simply concedes that the prosecution has properly proved its case.

Watching Michael in Court was edifying. He never wasted time with irrelevant questions. He always prepared well. The police are required to disclose all relevant documentation to defence counsel before trial. Michael had always studied the briefs of police witnesses and another documentation with great skill and care. Often, as the critical police witness was testifying, Michael would sit with his eyes shut, absorbing all the officer said. Then he would ask a few important questions and sit down. At the conclusion of the police case he would address the court. If he had spotted a flaw in the case, he would immediately identify it, and make a submission that the mistake was fatal to the prosecution case. He had the relevant High Court and Court of Appeal decisions at his fingertips. He did not use a scattergun approach in the vain hope that one pellet would strike the target. He would often just fire one shot and frequently that was fatal.

He told me that he explained when advising potential clients that a defended alcohol case was much like betting on the racetrack. He said to the client:

> *You are betting $1000 (his fee at that time) on one horse. But there are seven other horses in the race. You only have one in eight chances of success. Are you prepared to bet $1000 on those odds?*

Obviously, many were. Mike prospered, with many clients, many wins, and many good fees. Like Winston Churchill he got more out of alcohol than alcohol took out of him.

In nearly all cases the motorist is obviously guilty. The lawyer's job is to try and find a critical defect in the prosecution case that gets their guilty client off the hook. They emphasise the old saying that it is better that 100 guilty men go free than one innocent person be convicted!

Michael Bungay

I had an unexpected lunch with Michael Bungay one day. He moved to Rotorua from Wellington in 1990. He was much more relaxed, looked healthy, and was much more fun. He was currently appearing before Justice Penlington in the courtroom next

---

[1] A very old legal chestnut:
"If the facts are against you, hammer the law. If the law is against you, hammer the facts. If the fact and the law are against you, hammer opposing counsel."

to mine for the Patterson brothers and others from Matatata charged with kidnapping. I had the same men before me in Whakatane when they were first arrested.

Mike appeared before me at 9.30 a.m. to seek an adjournment of another jury trial that was meant to start that morning before me. He said the kidnapping case was already in its 8th day and only three of the 40 Crown witnesses had been heard! He grinned and said he had even been required to appear in court last Saturday – all day – to argue legal points before the new judge and had been concerned that he might not have been able to watch *Praise Be* on Sunday! He was worried that the case might be long-running like *Dynasty* or *Neighbours* and was worrying whether, given his health issues, he would survive long enough to appear in the last episodes. Rogue of a man.

He introduced me to his third wife, Ronda, a delightful, intelligent and personable woman. He told her I had done a stint in Samoa. He almost had me in hysterics with a story of an appeal he did up there appearing on behalf of several Samoan policemen who had been convicted of some serious crime. The Samoans, being economically poor, cannot afford to assemble a Court of Appeal very often, and the appeal Mike was involved with had been pending for over three years.

The first problem was getting him admitted to the bar of Samoa. The Government wanted $800 for the admission fee and proof of good character. The Government was, in short, trying to make it difficult for Bungay Q.C.to appear for the appellants. But Mike paid up and announced in his inimitable way that if the Queen of England thought he was of sufficiently good character to give him a warrant to act on her behalf, then who were the Samoans to question his character? They gave in.

He won the appeal in 20 minutes on a preliminary technicality, got his clients on the next plane to New Zealand, and then settled back to enjoy a few pleasant days working through the limited choice of liquor at Aggie Greys' famous hotel.

That was not to be. The Attorney General, later Acting Chief Justice and other things, knocked on Mike's fale door a few hours later.

"Mr Bungay", he perspired. "What about the re-trial?"

"The re-trial?" queried Michael.

"We want to set a date for the re-trial and set bail for your clients but we have learned they left Faleolo Airport yesterday for New Zealand."

"True!" grunted Mike.

"Well what about the re-trial?"

"What about it?"

"Why didn't you ask for one?"

"I am counsel for the successful appellants. It is not for me to ask for a re-trial. They don't want another trial. That was for you to seek."

"Well then", said the A-G looking flustered, "we shall have to seek extradition of your clients back from New Zealand."

"That's up to you", said Mike, no doubt lighting a cheroot and taking another sip. "But you took over three years to get the appeal off the ground. I don't know any judge in New Zealand who would allow extradition in such circumstances."

The A-G retreated, having lost the battle.

But Mike lost the war. As sometimes happens with childlike spoilsports, especially when they hold the power, they win the war. Samoans, thank goodness, always react benignly. An impressive car, albeit in need of a re-bore, arrived at Aggie's Hotel a few hours later to transport Mike to the airport and off on the next plane to New Zealand. The Prime Minister – or some other senior spoil-sport – had cancelled his visa and declared him *persona non-grata.*

Michael told me he was working at a reduced pace. He had heart problems and Ronda, he says with a smile, was watching him like a Hawk.

He died of a heart attack two years later (1993). As his friend, colleague and eulogist Gary Turkington said, he had "gone down to the tongueless silence of the dreamless dust".

Mike was a nuggety rascal, rogue, and hard case. While in law practice, I did several trials with him. We became friends. That was not difficult as he was such a gregarious, fun-loving, alcohol imbibing scallywag.

One afternoon in 1984, he left a message for me while I was doing a jury trial in Auckland.

"You look thirsty. Meet me at 5:30 after work for a drink at O'Connors."

I did so. I never got home that night! I ended up accompanying Mike in a taxi to the airport at 8:00 a.m. the following day. He had a scheduled radio interview in Wellington that morning. We had slept the night at the North Shore home of his former wife, who despite all, was still very fond of him.

He was electioneering for Parliament as a candidate for Bob Jones' N.Z. Party and wanted some media coverage. We had only slept for two hours. We were both still well over the limit. I struggled that day in court. But I was sure Mike finished his interview with his usual ebullience.

In 1986, despite several convictions for alcohol-related offending, he was granted silk to become Queens counsel. The criminal bar cheered but some of the fustier old civil lawyers and judges looked askance. Mike was no legal genius. Of course, he knew his criminal evidence backwards, and if pressed could make solid legal submissions. But his remarkable ability was his gift of connecting with the ordinary person on the street or the farm.

I would sit in court fascinated by his consummate skill. He kept everything simple. He treated jurors as though he was drinking with them as friends in a bar, He talked to them with respect, not at them. He humanised his client and avoided the theatrical. He won many cases others thought unwinnable.

Mike had many of the notable attributes of the famous US criminal lawyer Earl Rogers, who died of alcoholism in 1922 aged 52. While Rogers is not remembered the way Darrow and Nizer are, he won more murder trials than either of them, and is remembered because he won. And he won a lot. Out of 77 homicide cases, he won full acquittals in 74 of them.

Rogers was noted as a great cross-examiner. Francis Wellman, who wrote the famous *The Art of Cross-Examination*[1], said Rogers invented the modern art of cross-examination. Rogers was known to disappear for days at a time, to fight cops, and to frequently go to jail himself for his drunken antics. Rogers boozed all his considerable wealth and died penniless in a cheap hotel. It is said that Erle Stanley Gardner modelled his character, Perry Mason, on Rogers.

Horace Rumpole

While Sir John Mortimer achieved notable success as a London barrister and Q.C., he became famous as a writer, dramatist and screen-writer. The BBC TV series "*Rumpole*", played by Australian actor Leo McKern, became a huge success throughout the English-speaking world. We all empathised with Horace Rumpole when, suitably fortified, he trained off home to Hilda, "she who must be obeyed".[2]

I had a delightful conversation with Sir John at a national Law Society Conference in Christchurch, where he was a guest speaker. He told me, as he often said, that he preferred writing to Law. And he preferred criminal law to matrimonial law.

> *I found criminal clients easy and matrimonial clients hard. Matrimonial clients hate each other so much and use their children to hurt each other in beastly ways. Murderers have usually killed the one person in the world that was bugging them and they're usually quite peaceful and agreeable... People will go to endless trouble to divorce one person and then marry someone who is exactly the same, except probably a bit poorer and a bit nastier. I don't think anybody learns anything... Knowing the law is not much help for an advocate, in fact it is a bit of a disadvantage. Cramps your style.*

But there was another side to John Mortimer. His biographer, Graham Lord, saw him as a "clever, witty, mischievous, naughty, jolly, charming and funny; an immensely lovable man who was irresistible to women and inspired affection in almost everyone who met him". But, Lord added, he was a "compulsive liar, alcoholic, and sensualist almost completely devoid of morals". Perhaps he was just human. Mortimer wrote:

---

[1] New York, MacMillan Publishers, 1903, with many later editions, and still read today.

[2] Rumpole was never a prosecutor. He only defended accused persons. When asked why, he said he disliked the concept of people being imprisoned. "I'm not going to use my skills, such as they are, to force some poor devil into a condemned Victorian slum where he can be banged up with a couple of psychopaths and his own chamber pot." See *The Second Rumpole Omnibus* London, Viking 1987.

Are people naturally destructive, immoral, predatory and self-seeking, only to be kept in order by harsh laws and fiercely deterrent mandatory sentences? Or are men and women naturally orderly, merciful, humane and bred with a need for justice and mutual aid? Of course, these qualities, or defects, are not evenly distributed, and undoubtedly there is much of each in all of us, but when it comes to the law some sort of distinction can be drawn.

The Baddies' Buddy

Like Rumpole, Trevor de Cleene [1] mainly acted as defence counsel. He was known in our city as "the Baddies' Buddy". Trevor and I were both born and schooled in Palmerston North. He was seven years older and a hundred years smarter. He became the best criminal defence counsel our city ever had, hence his nickname, and had remarkable success in civil claims for damages. Both varieties of case were decided by juries, and Trevor had an outstanding gift of persuading them to acquit his accused clients or award generous sums to his plaintiffs. His skills were not just those of advocacy. He was an individualist, extremely clever, tough-minded, colourful, hard-working, controversial, and he knew his law.

The retired Dean of the Victoria University Law School, Professor Ian Campbell, was asked at a special dinner to mark his 80th birthday:

"Professor, in all your 40 years lecturing law students, who was the brightest of them all?"

He pondered briefly, and said "it comes down to two. One is now our Governor-General – Sir Michael Hardie-Boys. The other is Trevor de Cleene, the revenue and customs minister. But, all-up the brightest was Trevor de Cleene".

Trevor had won the Law Moot Prize, and was Senior Scholar in Law in 1955. An almost eidetic memory helped.

I was still at University when Trevor achieved an outstanding acquittal in a murder trial. A brutish, cruel and violent farmer near Pahiatua was shot dead while in a drunken sleep. His long-suffering wife and a female farm worker, both the targets of his coarse sexual brutality, had reached the point of no return, and put a bullet in his head.

They were tried together at the Palmerston North Supreme Court. The jurors were horrified at how brutal the monster had been. They acquitted both women of both murder and manslaughter, and they walked free. This was a rare result, the first time any lawyer in our community had seen a jury nullify the law.

---

[1] He was also a City Councillor, Member of Parliament and Cabinet Minister. In 1991 he was awarded the OBE. As a young man he was a liberal socialist. As an old man he was a conservative. This proved the adage wrongly attributed to Churchill: "If you're not a liberal when you're 25, you have no heart. If you're not a conservative by the time you're 35, you have no brain."

Jury nullification is unique but important. Our legal system is based on statutory rules and case law. Those rules and laws delineate whether a crime has been committed. Evidence that does not comply with those restrictions is not allowed. Sometimes, though, the twelve good jurors may see the law as unfair, immoral, unduly punitive, or obsolete. If so, they have the right to ignore the law ('nullify' or ignore it) and acquit the accused even if he/she does not have a legally recognised defence. It is not something we tell the jury about, because it could lead to juries all ignoring the law and deciding on a sympathy vote! I was once handed a note from a deliberating a jury. It read:

"Judge, can we just ignore the evidence and decide on our intuition and sense of fair play?"

While I could see some merit in the idea, I had to say nay.

Meagre skills

The case of the missing guitar droned on discordant and cacophonous! If I had heard it without a jury, it would have been done and dusted within two hours. With a jury, and inexperienced counsel, it became a full two-day trial!

I sometimes wonder whether it is proper that the law should allow for jury trials in such relatively minor matters. It costs the state a frightening sum when a judge alone hearing would be cheaper, quicker, and hopefully just as fair. And the expense is even worse in a case like this where the accused, for some rather inexplicable reason, was granted legal aid. Normally, legal aid is only granted if imprisonment is a real possibility. The statute says so. That is certainly not a likelihood for someone who steals a guitar and a small sum of cash.

I had a very junior lawyer attempting to hone her very meagre advocacy skills at the expense of the taxpayer – and transforming a simple police prosecution into a Perry Mason TV epic. I wondered what the jurors thought of all this?

The cross-examination took an eternity, with the young barrister asking her questions with an expectant omniscient jauntiness indicating that she expected the next succeeding question to force a dramatic confession of guilt from the witness or to bring the witness to breaking point.

But the witness, honest as day, and only giving formal evidence anyway, kept on calmly. And when the witness refused to go along with the imaginative and irrelevant suggestions put to her by young Portia, and said so with force, counsel, chin squared and indomitable in spirit, lamely, but with a strong voice, simply replied:

"Thank you, Mrs. Smith".

This was said as though counsel had somehow achieved a forensic triumph. But we all knew that was not true, and awaited the next line of dramatic if irrelevant questions. And some further "Thank you, witness" responses, with Mussolini chin.

Ho! Hum! At one point, the youthful prosecutor (who had only been doing the job for the last ten days) interrupted this totally ineffective cross-examination with the objection:

"Excuse me sir, but I can't see the relevance of this line of questioning?"

He said this with the polish of a Kiwi Matlock,[1] with the same studied facial expression (half smile, with knowing look), and larger than life body language.

I was impressed. I had been thinking the same thing myself but had for the last 30 minutes been slumped in my chair wearily waiting for the punchline. I was suddenly galvanised into action.

"You are correct" I responded with judicial solemnity and looked sternly at defence counsel, whose eyebrows were knitted together in consternation.

"Just what ***is*** the relevance of all this?"

Defence counsel just stood there. She said nothing for several very long seconds. She boldly maintained her self-assured composure. And then she blew it by saying:

"I don't really know!"

There was rustling, rumbling, and sighing from the jury box. They agreed with the prosecutor. They had wondered about where the cross-examination was heading, if anywhere. For 30 minutes, they had been planning their evening meal, worrying about being late for the pub or deciding on which T.V. programme to view that evening.

Inexperienced barristers never give the court reporter time to record an answer before they ask the next question. It drives typists and judges to acute frustration. Some never learn. Over many years, they persist with the same behaviour, despite judges constantly and crustily telling them to "Pause", "Please Wait" and "Please, Counsel, let the answer be recorded before you ask the next question!".

Both counsel had so confounded the jury that I had to get up an hour early the next morning to get my own brain together so that I could sensibly instruct the jury on the facts.

The facts were simple enough. Or at least they were until the young lawyers were let loose to spend another day of taxpayers' hard earned money on such a trivial case!

We heard testimony from the manager of the Music Shop and then from the Detective Sergeant. He was at least a breath of fresh air: Detective Sergeant Scott. He had a delightful, matter of fact, down to earth, and colloquial way of putting his evidence across. I liked him and so did the jury.

In contrast, the accused, who spent much of the afternoon testifying, was pettifogging, pedantic, and painful. We all gained the distinct impression that he and his lady counsel didn't like one another anymore. He seemed to think he was not

---

[1] Ben Matlock, the star of the TV series, played by Andy Griffith, is a winning but expensive criminal defence lawyer who charges $100,000 a case. But he and his team always win by exposing the real killer!

getting his money's worth. Which was puzzling when you remember that he wasn't paying anything for his lawyer, and that we were!

There was a major dust-up when the accused started criticising the typed statement he had signed in the presence of the detective sergeant. He said he only signed it because the police swore at him and told him he would be arrested unless he did so. This was somewhat remarkable for three reasons:

(1) He had actually gone to the police to make a voluntary statement. They hadn't apprehended him first;

(2) There was nothing of any importance in his criticism because his statement contained nothing that incriminated him anyway;

(3) His counsel had not challenged the detective sergeant about any of these criticisms.

The young prosecutor stood to his feet and objected. At least he had learned something valuable in Law School. I agreed with him entirely. I asked defence counsel why she had not challenged the sergeant's evidence. She said she had instructions from her client to that effect.

The client, in a very angry and loud exclamation, made it clear that he disagreed with what she had just told me. I formed the impression that that the client was right, and the lawyer was dissembling.

Then there was a real dust-up. I intervened and said I would re-call the detective-sergeant if he could be located. He had left the courthouse and, no doubt believing he had fully performed his duty to God, Queen and Country, had retired to the police canteen for a beer.

I managed to get him back. He was re-sworn. He denied the allegations with a bland, laconic professionalism. I believe he did not intimidate the accused in any way.

We then heard counsel's addresses to the jury. They were just like mine when I was a fledgling lawyer: a sprig of Perry Mason, a dash of Marshall Hall, a drop of Clarence Darrow, a shot of Atticus Finch, and a pinch of Horace Rumpole. All this combined to produce an omelette of inedible and indigestible legal confusion that ultimately lead to the jury acquitting the astonished accused.

Extraordinary, really, because his own poor performance in the witness box should have led to his conviction.

"Oh! What does it matter in the scheme of things?" as Mick Brown used to say. "It's all just a game!"

Female lawyers

Since 1993, there have been more female law graduates than male. In 2018 there were 615 female law graduates and only 370 males. One of the females was my lovely granddaughter, Arieta Apa. In November 2017, I proudly moved her admission to the bar. As at February 2018, exactly half of all New Zealand lawyers are female. 6,922 females; 6,921 males.

Top female lawyers are more likely to be compassionate than their male counterpart. They are more likely to better understand how a witness or accused feels, and use that to advantage. I have found them to prepare their cases more thoroughly, and more creatively have the skill to analyse evidence and listen to witnesses. They are assertive rather than aggressive.

As at 2017 82 judges of our 252 active judges are women. When I started in 1978 there was only one judicial officer – Judge Augusta Wallace.[1]

Ready, Aim, Fire

I seldom listen to any radio station other than the National Programme. As I was heading in to work one morning, I heard a delightful interview by Jeff Sinclair with a Lancashire solicitor named Deering. Mr Deering was not a man to be trifled with. He was a battler in the spirit of the ancient English yeomen. He believes that an Englishman's home is still his castle and that the common law right to protect home, hearth, and hedges should not lightly be suborned.

The local council decided to lay a pipeline through his neighbourhood. Unsympathetic modern engineers, who gave no thought to the woodland at the bottom of Mr Deering's four-acre garden, designed the line of the pipe rather thoughtlessly. Neither did they pause to question the line of compacted rocks and clay that stretched across the thicket.

The rocks were part of the original Roman road extending north from Londinium. And these wretched ignorant engineers and their senseless henchmen armed with heavy bulldozers and diggers had mutilated history without so much as a how-de-do.

The battle lines were drawn. Deering and his wife told the council workers to sod off. They refused. He took other steps to keep them off. Those measures also failed. So, putting his legal and adversarial mind to work, he decided to abandon infantry skirmishes and send for the bigger guns to defend his right, title and interest. He purchased a Russian T 34 tank.

I am familiar with Russian T 34 tanks. They make most conventional vehicles look fragile and impotent. Even bulldozers and diggers were no match for the formidable 26-ton Russian juggernaut.[2]

So far, the indomitable Lancashire lawyer had not fired a shot. The big Russian armoured fighting vehicle just sat there, hull down in his thicket, its cupola and its 76mm

---

[1] See p 57.

2 By the end of WW II the Soviets had produced 60,000 T34 tanks! You can still buy them for about $200,000, but beware: they are sold without weaponry or military componentry, and can't be driven on any pubic road. Damn!

gun pointed menacingly at the enemy, and effectively preventing further excavation of the Via Romanum.

It is perfectly legal to purchase T 34 tanks, for those unusual citizens so inclined. After all, said Mr Deering, who sounded a decent sort of chap, it isn't a question of money. It is a matter of pure principle! And by Gad! We can't have these heartless bureaucrats destroying all that is historic and beautiful in the countryside, especially when proper planning permission was not first obtained.

"Up turret, 2 degrees port. Armed, sergeant. Right Oh! On target... Fire!"

Impunity of Age

Maurice Jackson was at 80 the oldest practitioner still practicing law in Tauranga. He sat next to me at a Lawyers lunch. He told me he had been in law practice for well over 50 years. He was the chief legal officer for the Royal New Zealand Air Force right through the Second War. He was still going strong despite a heart attack, a stroke, and surgery for cancer.

After the luncheon, he most politely, and with an old-world charm seldom seen today, enquired whether I would object to him lighting up his pipe. I gave my assent. Then he leaned forward to Mary Capamagian, whom I do not know (she practices law with her husband, Alan Liddell) and sought a similar consent from her. She looked at him somewhat stonily and said: "Maurice, if you start smoking I shall leave."

Jackson eyed her with a naughty, possibly chauvinistic, glint in his eye, threw both caution and courtesy to the wind, and promptly ignited his pipe. I gained the distinct impression he would have done the same even if I had said I preferred not to be enveloped in smoke. One of the few blessings of old age is that the elderly can ignore rigid social conventions without the criticism levelled at younger people.

Ms Capamagian was a woman of her word. As the first cloud of smoke erupted from his pipe across the table she stood, glowered momentarily in our direction, and prematurely left the luncheon.

When someone is over 80[1], they can ignore almost anyone with impunity: kings, bishops and, with suitable armour, even wives! They certainly may ignore judges the more so if they never appear in court and thus have even less to lose!

[1] As I am in 2020.

Jacobs and the Rabbi

There is a delightful Manawatu tale of Bert Jacobs[1], a very well-liked and capable practitioner known for his ready wit, happy smile and presidency of the both the local and national Returned Services Association.

Jacob's firm still exists as Jacobs, Florentine & Co. Jacobs had died before I returned to Palmerston North in 1963. As President of the local Manawatu branch of the Wellington Law Society (the Manawatu District Society came into existence later), he was seated at a Bar Dinner between a very dour Supreme Court Judge (former President of the Temperance Union) and an equally arid President of the Wellington District Law Society (current President of the Wellington Branch of the Temperance Union).

Bert was not a wowser. Far from it. He very much enjoyed toasting "L'Chaim" with a Scotch. Many of his fellow practitioners had a similar appreciation of the amber Scots fluid. There was much laughter and applause when he rose to address the gathering:

"Gentlemen" – at that time there were no lady practitioners in the Manawatu – "here I stand; a rose between two thorns![2]" Bert was known for his good sense of humour.

He had a very strict and appropriate rule that he was not to be disturbed when he was in conference with a. That rule extended to unscheduled visits from fellow lawyers. This irked some of them. Bill Fitzherbert, the doyen of my firm, Fitzherbert, Abraham, Crossley & Evans (he had also died before my arrival client), affectionately known as "Budge", hit on a delightful way to spring Jacobs from his lair.

In those days, it was fashionable for both ladies and gentlemen to carry printed calling cards, similar to the business cards of today, recording name, address and telephone. When visiting a home on social occasions, the card was placed in a receptacle on a stand by the front door. On a visit to a Wellington friend in the late 1920's, Fitzherbert saw a card in a dish which took his fancy. He pocketed it and returned to Palmerston North where he would use it with felonious intent.

Some weeks later, Fitzherbert was anxious to speak to Jacobs about some legal matter. He phoned first. The receptionist politely advised that Mr Jacobs was not to be disturbed as he was "in conference".

Fitzherbert then walked up Rangitikei Street from his office in Cuba Street. Up the aging wooden stairs he went, through the etched glass doorway, and into the reception area. He asked again to see Mr Jacobs. The receptionist was embarrassed. She dutifully and steadfastly told Mr Fitzherbert that her employer could not be disturbed. She knew that Fitzherbert was aware of his invariable direction.

---

[1] Bertram Joseph Jacobs OBE, was a partner of his law firm for 56 years.

[2] It is an incorrect and impossible modern rendition that he used the word "pricks". He would never have said that in public.

"Please urgently give him this envelope", requested Fitzherbert with a mild grin on his face that no doubt puzzled the clerk. "And please don't say from whom it has come."

The clerk frowned and took the envelope with some misgiving. After all, Fitzherbert was an enemy alien from another firm – and senior partner to boot!

"I bet", added Fitzherbert, "that Mr Jacobs is out here to see me like a shot!"

The clerk looked back as she headed to the green felt padded door of Jacob's office. She said nothing, but the rather jaunty angle of her chin indicated that she was absolutely positive Fitzherbert would lose his penniless wager.

It has never been common for the venerable senior partner of one firm to swear at and curse the venerable senior partner of another, especially not to make aspersions as to his parentage. And especially not in front of staff in the main reception area – with a startled client staring through a very recently opened green felt padded office door.

But then it was not common for the eminent Very Reverend Rabbi Herman Van Staveren of Wellington,[1] the senior rabbi of New Zealand's Jewish community, to visit a co-religionist in Palmerston North! And it was even more unusual for him to call unannounced and introduce his arrival by simply handing his calling card to a receptionist!

Jewish Judges and Lawyers

In New Zealand two chief justices[2], and many judges and lawyers have been Jewish. Our first woman law graduate, Ethel Benjamin had the courage to break gender tradition to enter the legal profession.

When she graduated in law in 1897 (with outstanding marks) the graduating class asked her to speak on their behalf at the ceremony. She said:

> *It was only yesterday that I was asked to undertake this pleasant task, and while deeply sensible to the compliment paid to me, I was somewhat diffident about taking so much upon myself at so short a notice. But I knew that little would be expected of me and even if I succeeded in talking nonsense, the charitable verdict would be, 'Oh well, it is all that can be expected of a woman.'*

---

[1] Wellingtonians held him is high regard. He was involved in many community activities and organisations. When he died in 1930, people lined the streets, and over 150 cars were in his funeral procession to the cemetery.

[2] Sir Michael Myers and Sir Thomas Eichelbaum.

In September that year, she was the first woman in the British Empire to appear in court as counsel.

Whether it is genetic, environmental, or something more elusive, people of Jewish heritage clearly have an affinity, talent and aptitude for legal reasoning, argument, debate, study, doubting and erudition. Jews have been properly called "the people of the book."

Several eminent American judges have been Jewish: Cardozo, Brandeis, and Felix Frankfurter. Ruth Bader Ginsburg was the first Jewish woman to be appointed to the US Supreme Court. In addition to Justice Ginsberg there are two other Jewish justices currently (2019) on the US Supreme Court: Stephen Breyer and Elena Kagan.

In the UK, between 1996 and 2008, two of Britain's three Lord Chief Justices were Jewish: Peter Taylor and Harry Woolf.

In Nazi Germany, Jewish lawyers and judges were dismissed and most were murdered. Although, before the Shoah, only 0.7% of the German population was Jewish, 16.6% of the judges and lawyers were Jewish.

Albert Einstein said "the pursuit of knowledge for its own sake, an almost fanatical love of justice, and the desire for personal independence – these are the features of the Jewish tradition which make me thank my lucky stars that I belong to it."

Several of my colleagues on the bench were Jewish. Two became admired friends: David Robinson and Ian Borrin. Both exhibited the legal gifts I have mentioned. I have enjoyed happy dining and social times with them both.

David was appointed a District Court Judge in 1983, and was a Family Court Judge from 1983 until 2006 when he became an Associate Judge of the High Court. A caring, capable and quality judge, he is currently the Honorary Consul for Israel in Auckland.

Ian died of leukaemia in 2016. In 1983, he was also appointed a Family Court judge in Wellington and also for six years was the Police Complaints Authority. He was caring, committed, humble and diligent. He retired in 2007. On his death, he bequeathed $38 million to create a Foundation in memory of his parents, Michael and Suzanne. The primary purpose of this gift is to "support legal research, education and scholarship that contributes to… New Zealand. An unsurpassed and generous philanthropic gift to the legal world of New Zealand.

Fact or Fiction

After court in Rotorua, as I was leaving the wine shop in Tutanekai Street, I ran into Michael Quirke,[1] who had a client pleading guilty before me the next day on a charge of possession of cannabis for supply.

I had known Mike for many years.

He told me that his former partner, George Israel Joseph, had died two years ago in Wellington. We reminisced for a while about George who was undoubtedly one of the most colourful legal characters of New Zealand. George was a diminutive Glasgow-born Jewish man with an expansive personality and a brilliant wit and way with words. He wrote several books and many short stories. He was imaginative to his own detriment. He was struck off the Lawyer's Roll for a time for fabricating, as I understand it, a Hawaiian divorce decree to save a client on a bigamy charge![2]

George briefed me once as junior in a trial in Palmerston North. For the life of me I cannot remember the name of the accused or what crime the client was alleged to have committed. George's ebullient personality swamped all other memories.

To thank me, he and his wife took me to dinner in Wellington for an unforgettable evening of perceptive wit and delightful anecdotes. He was a superb raconteur, although I never quite knew when fact had become fiction. (My wife says the same of me!)

George had worked in England in the late 1930's as a youthful journalist for a leading English newspaper. He was sent to Berlin as a correspondent. This was an unfortunate posting for a man so recognisably Jewish in appearance.

His tenure in Nazi Germany was short-lived. He overdid the schnapps at a foreign press party and hopped onto the stage to do his acclaimed Hitler impersonation, with black toothbrush moustache and Sieg Heil salutes. It was so good, and the laughter so loud, that the Gestapo arrived 15 minutes later just as George was sneaked out the backstage door and ultimately smuggled back to London. George Joseph: a memorable rascal.

---

[1] Michael met an untimely death through cancer not long after. He was a sound and highly respected lawyer with many fine attributes.

[2] The Oxford Companion to New Zealand Literature says George "was a prodigiously prolific writer, a flourishing but flawed lawyer and a colourful character".

Police & Law Enforcers

Hawk-eye Views

These days many of the more affluent towns and cities have closed circuit cameras installed, providing a hawk's eye view of those inner-city areas where trouble is likely. When confronted with the video record, many a mortified defendant enters an early guilty plea in the hope that his wife or Mum will not see the stark drunken reality of his nocturnal activities. Cameras in police stations are now the rule not the exception, and the astute use of mobile phone cameras by members of the public have greatly reduced the number of defended cases.

Similarly, for many years now, statements taken from suspects and witnesses have been recorded on video. They can be played to a judge or jury. The old criminal plea that "the cop beat a confession out of me" is no longer heard. The camera, as they say, does not lie.

Local Duty

In Paeroa there were two enforcement officers: Constable Hetaraka of the Police, and Traffic Officer Bloomfield of the Ministry of Transport. Both said they had Māori heritage. Constable Hetaraka, by name and features, unmistakably. T.O. Bloomfield by name and features less obviously. Both officers decided to combine their resources and conduct a traffic check point on Orchard Road, Ngatea from 6.00 p.m. one day. The hotel is in the near vicinity!

It could be asked: Why mention the fact that both officers had Māori heritage? The answer is that it was one of the primary factual issues in the case.

Constable Hetaraka testified that in eight years as a policeman he had never met a more racist or uncooperative motorist than the defendant, Otto Hofbrauhaus. T.O. Bloomfield agreed. He had been a cop for 20 years and had never seen a more racist and uncooperative motorist during that time. Hofbrauhaus was an intense, pale, croaky-voiced beneficiary. Despite an earlier police warning, he had left the hotel in his car. He was pursued by the constable and apprehended.

He had been at the hotel from 3.00 p.m. until 8.40 p.m. but, somewhat surprisingly, according to him, had only consumed one jug and two glasses of beer (plus peanuts and potato chips, mind you!). When apprehended, the defendant really became nasty. He ranted and panted.

"Are you picking on a white man?" he raved. "Why aren't you out catching rapists and murderers?"

He refused to provide a breath specimen and was warned of the consequences if he continued to refuse.

"I am not doing anything unless I have my lawyer."

He was warned again, but still refused.

The officer testified:

"This man was the most uncooperative person I have ever dealt with in the eight years I have been in the police."

"What are you saying?" asked Constable Hetaraka, "that we are picking on a white man? I am married to a European. My grandfather was Scottish. My children look more European than you do."

The confrontational man refused to give his name and address. He told Officer Bloomfield he was "a stupid Bulgarian"[1] and said he would "get him".

I completely believed the two enforcement officers, convicted the man, fined him more than the norm, and disqualified him. Next time he visits his hofbrauhaus he should drink less!

A Policeman's Lot

An irate mother abused and raved at the police. Constable Barton was walking past a parked car. He suddenly noticed the fruity odour of burning cannabis leaf emanating from the car. He approached and knocked on the driver's door. The window wound slowly down. A young woman's face was dimly visible in the haze. Constable Barton smiled more than usual as the euphoric smoke curled out of the window and enveloped him. But duty is duty. As Sir William Schwenk Gilbert proclaimed in the Pirates of Penzance:

> *"Our feelings we with difficulty smother*
> *When constabulary duty's to be done*
> *Ah! Take one consideration with another*
> *A policeman's lot is not a happy one."*

Constabulary duty is seldom a happy one. Police officers do an admirable job in situations that are often demanding, thankless and threatening.

He asked the young woman to get out of the car. She did. He quizzed her about the wonderful wafting whiffs of cannabliss. All was going well, until out of the back seat came big Momma: a very large woman with upper arms like Christmas hams and a monumental tummy. She cursed. She swore.

"How dare you suggest that my daughter is a criminal, you $#%&* #$![2]"

---

[1] Why he swapped from Māori to Bulgarian nonplussed us all!

[2] This is modern computer code for several short and meaningful ancient Anglo-Saxon expletives.

The officer, until then feeling relaxed and at peace with the world, became somewhat brusque. He told her to shut up, calm down, and get back in the car. Whereupon he was submerged by a tide of even more vitriolic and vile adjectives (and the occasional noun). She was charged with and pleaded guilty to disorderly behaviour. Was she stoned? She was certainly rocked when I imposed a $400 fine. Why should police officers have to tolerate such abuse?

Operation Vine

In July 1997, five Gisborne police officers were arrested after a raid by Hamilton Police on the Gisborne police station. It was alleged that the five had paid off Mongrel Mob informants by supplying them with cannabis seized by the police in earlier drug busts. The inquiry, called Operation Vine, cost more than $1 million and soaked up 8547 man hours. 32 charges were laid, vigorously disputed, and all dismissed by the court at a preliminary hearing.

The five officers then complained to the Independent Police Conduct Authority which oversees police actions and behaviour. They said they had been unfairly investigated and dealt with by their own. It was a tricky situation because it was *Police v. Police*.

The Chairperson of the Authority, Judge Neville Jaine, personally knowing some of the police officers involved, properly decided the Authority could not investigate and report on the case, and asked me to complete the investigation as an independent reviewer.

I found it a difficult and thankless task and regretted taking it on. There was considerable bitterness, backstabbing and conflict within the police ranks. In my final report, I found in favour of the five police officers. I believed the Hamilton police team had predetermined their guilt, failed to interview a number of potentially critical witnesses, accepted the evidence of some very dubious gang members, and had not adequately assessed the evidence.

I also recommended that the Solicitor-Generals prosecution guidelines 1992 as to when to prosecute should be expanded to include additional guidance as to the need to properly assess witness credibility.

The guidelines stated that where there was doubt as to whether a conviction is likely, the prosecution should proceed to court. I thought that was really passing the buck, and as with this case, lead to a difficult, costly and painful prosecution.

I was pleased that the *Solicitor-General's Prosecution Guidelines* were substantially improved in 2013 to give more detailed and better guidance on assessing the creditability of witnesses, namely:

It may be that a witness is plainly at risk of being so discredited that no Court could safely rely on his/her evidence. In such a case, it may be concluded that there is, having regard to all the evidence, no reasonable prospect of obtaining a conviction. If, however, it is judged that a Court in all the circumstances of the case could reasonably rely on the evidence of a witness, notwithstanding any particular difficulties, then such evidence is credible and should be taken into account.

Prosecutors may be required to make an assessment of the quality of the evidence. Where there are substantial concerns as to the creditability of essential evidence, criminal proceedings may not be appropriate as the evidential test may not be capable of being met.

Where there are credibility issues, prosecutors must look closely at the evidence when deciding if there is a reasonable prospect of conviction.

The Police Commissioner, while unhappy with my report, apologised to the men and they were paid compensation, which I understand was $200,000 between them.

That was not the end of it. The two senior Hamilton police officers criticised in my report, laid personal grievance claims with the Commissioner, claiming that they had been made scapegoats when Crown lawyers and other senior police officers had made the decision to prosecute the five Gisborne officers. They were also paid compensation, believed to be $50,000 between them.

Journalist Miriyana Alexander, currently editor of the *New Zealand Herald's Saturday and Sunday* titles and an Oxford University Reuters Foundation scholar, wrote a book on this complex saga.[1] She commences her book's forward by writing:

"This is the story about a case of alleged police corruption of the worst kind. It is also the story of how police investigations and inquiries can be flawed, with damaging consequences"—

She interviewed many of the witnesses and had extensive discussions with John Haig QC [2](who acted for two of the police officers at the preliminary hearing) and later with myself.

Taxi-Cams

Recently (March 2014), Clive McKay was caught by a camera. He received six years three months imprisonment for robbing a bank. He threatened a teller by saying he had a bomb. He took off with a trifling $150.00 in cash, hailed a taxi, took off his disguise in the back seat, and was recorded with great clarity by the closed-circuit television in the taxi. Later that day, he was identified by the synthetic DNA that had been secretly

[1] Presumed Guilty, Auckland, Howling at the Moon Publication, 1998.

[2] John appeared before me many times. He deservedly became a QC in 1993. Hardworking, capable, fearless, and with a finely honed sense of justice, he was much admired. He died suddenly in 2012, aged 65."

micro-misted on him as he left the bank. The spray turns blue under UV light and stays on skin and hair for two weeks, and on clothes (even after washing) for up to six months. He had a bad criminal history and it looks as though he had a methamphetamine habit, which may explain his stupidity in obtaining a modest benefit of 7¢ per day from his crime.

The 2010 amendment to the Land Transport Rule: Operator Licensing 2007 requires taxis operating in major towns and cities to have a mandatory in-vehicle camera system and to include 24-hour, seven-days-a week monitoring from a fixed location, and an emergency alert and response facility. This is because taxi driving can be a perilous occupation. Ten taxi-drivers have been murdered since 1943.

Parole

Jailhouse Jesus

Over my years on the parole board, I was impressed and also quizzical at how many inmates became committed Christians while serving their sentence. Do some prisoners falsely adopt Jesus to sweet-talk us into granting early parole? I believe many do. It would be interesting to monitor paroled prisoners to see how many keep attending church once they are free.

"Jailhouse Jesus" is an American term for the fact that many inmates to 'find religion' while serving their sentence. The psychology behind this is debatable. Whether it is a wish to repent or to associate with a more socially acceptable prison group is questionable.

I do not know of any New Zealand study of religious adherence in our prisons, but an intriguing recent American study showed that only .07% of prison inmates identified as having no religion.[1] This contrasts with the 26% of Americans who describe their religious identity as atheist, agnostic or "nothing in particular," up from 17% in 2009. 65% of American adults describe themselves as Christians, down 12 percentage points over the same decade.

Compassion

On the parole board, we have a process through which the victims of crime can register their details and request to be kept advised as to the progress of the offender throughout the prison sentence. Victims may also request a hearing before a board panel. These are anxious and often traumatic occasions. Most of the victims are still devastated by the loss they experienced, either as the direct victim of crime or as the parent or loved one of the victim.

In 2014, I was involved in such a hearing. It was remarkable in that the mother of a young man who'd been killed in a car crash, wished to appear before the board, not to protest against the early release of the young woman driver, but to provide support for her. She urged us to release her early. The young woman offender, believing she was being chased by dr dealers, lost control of the car, it veered off the road and the young

---

[1] USA 2013 census, completed by the United States Bureau of Justice Statistics

man was killed. The mother appeared before us and read us a letter, parts of which I recorded. It shows how perceptive and compassionate some special people can be:

> *I don't know if anyone reading this letter has lost one of their children, but I can tell you after losing my son, that this is the most horrible, indescribable situation that any parents can find themselves in. We did not know the young woman, or her family before the accident. We did not meet her until we met at a restorative justice meeting. I could feel her genuine deep remorse as I listened to the beautiful words of the letter she read out apologising for what happened. The words were so moving that my younger daughter had to leave the room temporarily, in tears of emotion....*
>
> *My son was no angel and I am a parent who is aware how our children can make some really bad choices for a multitude of different reasons... My daughters and I agreed before the restorative justice meeting that nothing anyone could do would ever bring him back so we wanted to see the best possible outcome for everyone involved. We also wanted an opportunity for healing for ourselves. One of the greatest emotional releases for us was that we were genuinely able to forgive her.*
>
> *We were devastated by the sentence the judge handed down to her. It was bad enough to lose a son and brother, but to lose a genuinely remorseful young person to prison, again threw me into bewilderment and a downward spiral of depression and disbelief at the justice system and the police.*
>
> *She is truly remorseful… She is not a criminal… I cannot ever have my son back and forever is forever, but knowing that the young woman is back with her family would go a long way towards helping us while we journey through our grieving.*
>
> *Hopefully a prison sentence will be over now for her and her family so we can all move on, we can put closure to my son's death and my son can now rest in peace. Yes, she was in the driving seat that day, but I firmly believe that she was the innocent victim in this. These mistakes cannot possibly be made again. She is not a threat to anyone. I'm certain she will make out well because she knows she is loved and supported and that we will all be helping and monitoring her continuing positive process.*

The three of us on the Parole Board were deeply moved by this letter. We granted the young woman parole and she was released from prison ten days later.

Meeting with Victims

This case highlights the outstanding value of restorative justice procedures. There is a good restorative justice system in place in New Zealand. Understandably, many people are not prepared to go through the emotional stress of meeting a perpetrator of a crime. Similarly, many offenders do not have the courage to face their victims. But for those people who are prepared to engage in a restorative justice procedure, the benefits can be invaluable. It has benefits for both offender and victim. On the one hand, the offender sees first-hand the impact the offending has had on the victim. The meetings often reduce the drama experienced by victims, especially where violence has been a contributing factor.

Some victims appear before the Parole Board annually, angrily urging us not to grant parole to the offender. Even with the passing of several years, they have not moved on. They are still bitter and angry at what happened to them. But restorative justice meetings, properly managed, and carefully and sensitively prepared, allow people to get answers to their concerns, and to move on with their lives in a positive direction.

As I have noted, following such conferences, even in the most extreme cases of murder, victims are able to forgive the offender, and proceed to have a meaningful and valuable life. Even with less serious offending, there is great value in such conferences. People who have been burgled, especially elderly victims, have mental images of huge evil gangsters re-entering their home in the dark of night, stealing their property, and assaulting them. Often, at a conference, the victim is astonished to see that the perpetrator of the burglary is an immature skinny 17-year-old, from a disadvantaged background, who is sorry for what has happened, is not an ogre, and wishes to be forgiven for what he did. I have even seen the victims of dishonesty offending give a job to the young man who has stolen from them. In this way, lives are changed in a very positive way.

Short Sweet & Simple

In 2006, I gave my shortest Parole Board Decision. The prisoner had a massive score on a drug abuse assessment and a 90% statistical likelihood of re-offending. He was serving his eighth sentence of imprisonment.

The decision:

> *Mr. H was a reluctant starter. He did not wish to appear before the Board, but he fleetingly appeared before us. It was a fleeting visit because of his Identified Drug User rating of 8/10 and his Risk of Future Conviction rating of 9/10.*
> *He knew we would not grant parole. We knew we would not grant parole.*
> *And so, he left the room happy.*

Too Big for the Prison

Before the law was changed to permit judges to impose home detention sentences, it fell on the Parole Board to do make those decisions. If suitable, the judge would allow a sentenced prisoner to apply to us for that purpose.

In a noteworthy case, we pulled the leg of the manager of the Hawkes Bay Prison at Mangaroa. The prisoner, a gang member, had been sentenced in absentia by a Gisborne judge to 18 months prison for repeatedly selling cannabis from his bed in a small Māori community near Wairoa.

He sold from his "tinny house" bed because, at a morbidly obese weight of just over 300 kg (660 lbs) he had been bedridden for over a year. He could not roll over without the help of several family members.

Before we started our hearings for the day, the manager and his deputy asked to see us. The manager explained that the offender was simply too large for the prison to cope with. He could not pass through the door of his cottage, could not fit into a prison van, and the doors of cells were too narrow. Furthermore, his obesity was such that prison nurses would find it difficult to treat his festering skin creases and rashes.

I explained to the officers that we had no legal ability to leave him at home. The legislation required that he must present himself at the prison for a hearing, and that, given his serious drug offending and length of sentence, we would be unlikely to grant him home detention.

The officers looked aghast. But I solemnly pointed out that all the alleged obstacles to his imprisonment could easily be resolved. The wall of his bedroom could be chain-sawed to get him out of his cottage, he could then be winched onto a flat-deck truck, a special temporary wooden cell with wide doors and bed could be constructed for him in the corner of the spacious prison officer's common room, and a specialist nurse could be employed to care of his many needs.

The officers no longer looked aghast; they were horror-struck. And then a woman member of our board let the dog out of the kennel and couldn't contain her laughter. Then the other member laughed. And I laughed.

The manager didn't laugh, but he did put his hands to his head and called me a bastard, which I thought was an unusual way to address a Parole Board convenor.

Not having the courage to drive to Wairoa to conduct a formal hearing in the man's bedroom, we disregarded the legislation and granted him home detention. We thought Parliament would accept that there is an exception to every rule. The prison officers were thankful that carpenters were not to begin reducing the dimensions of their common room. We later learned that the unfortunate drug dealer, a prisoner of his own morbidity, suffered a heart attack and died a few months later.

Food, Glorious Food

A middle-aged inmate declined to see us for parole consideration. On his written waiver, he simply said he: "…enjoyed being in prison and didn't want to be released because he enjoyed the food so much!"

Gangs

B.P.

I sent a 19-year-old thug to prison for 9 months on another burglary. I thought to send him off to British Petroleum Company for an interview for possible employment in their Public Relations department. He had a very ornamental advertisement tattooed across his forehead in large but somewhat crudely etched capitals. Surrounded by various Māori and Nazi motifs it simply read: "B.P."

For those of us in the know this is not an abbreviation for British Petroleum, Be Prepared, Blood Pressure, or Be Positive and certainly not Brain Power, Beatrix Potter, or Before Penicillin but for Black Power. As he was led from the dock to commence his sentence, his fellow gang-members, staunch to the end, stood in the rear of the court, and as is their custom, gave the clenched fist salute, mumbled deep throated greetings to their "Bro" and left the court for a celebratory party.

Gang Culture

One court day the numerous young men appearing in my court were all members of two hostile gangs. They are the two largest gangs in this country.

The Mongrel Mob is numerically the biggest gang, with an estimated 1000 patched members, belonging to about 30 separate chapters. Originally started by European youth, it is now mainly Maori. The chapters are loosely affiliated. Often the gangsters have facial tattoos and wear red bandannas. Strangely, the tattoos usually feature a British bulldog wearing a German army helmet, and for some inexplicable reason they shout the Nazi cry "Sieg Heil!"

Once, at the Parole Board, I asked a Mongrel member what the "Sieg Heil" cry meant. He had no idea but seemed to vaguely understand that it had something to do with Germany and that it "pissed people off."

At gang gatherings, often fuelled by alcohol and drugs, they bark like dogs. I have heard them do this outside court. It is bizarre, and incomprehensible.

I quizzed another mobster:

"Why do you do that barking?"

"Because we are mongrels – dogs."

They also have a unique mob salute, with the little finger extended.

For many years, they have been virtually at war with the Black Power gang.

The Black Power Gang was originally called the "Black Balls". Seemingly this had unacceptable genital or racial connotations, so they changed their name over 40 years ago. Mainly Maori or Polynesian, they now have chapters throughout New Zealand. The American Black Power movement inspired the New Zealand gang. Its colours are blue and black. Their comradely fraternal greeting one to the other is "Yo fuck yo!" which sounds friendly and intimate enough!

They salute with a clenched fist, and sometimes inelegantly, have such a fist tattooed on their forehead. Such graphic creativity does nothing for their job prospects, especially if the artwork is incompetent.[1]

Muldoon

Sir Robert Muldoon, the Prime Minister from 1975 to 1984, for some blurred fermented reason, believed that it was better to engage with the gangs rather than to treat them as outcasts or outlaws. He promoted a series of government subsidised work schemes to get the gang members into positive government assisted employment. As most judges and police officers predicted, the scheme rapidly failed, and was ended three years later. Why would any self-respecting gangster work on the minimum wage digging ditches for an eight-hour day when he can earn ten times that by crime in eight minutes? Members of the Black Power gang performed a haka at Sir Robert's funeral. No one else felt that urge.

---

[1] As with the 15 year old youth who appeared before me in the Youth Court with the badly lettered inscription "Fuck Cops" emblazoned on his forehead.

Stigmata

Another Black Power gang member appeared before me, very proud and resolute – staunch is the word they use. He didn't use the "BP" abbreviation but had the words Black Power stenciled across his forehead in large black letters, and, as a means of further graphic decoration, the words had been augmented by the addition of three identical drawings of the clenched fist emblem of the gang. One is in the middle of his forehead, and the others on each cheek. Irreversible stigmata of group affiliation!

Career Cartel

William Lutz, a lecturer at Rutgers University in the USA, tidily illustrates the world of "Doublespeak". In Atlantic City, he says, they don't talk of the Mafia or the Mob, just "members of a career-offender cartel"! Could the same definition apply to our New Zealand gangs?

Murder at Ruatoki

One difficult day I had a bouillabaisse of cases on my plate that resulted in real indigestion and fatigue by 6.30 p.m. when I finally completed the list and staggered out of court. I dealt with 94 people in the adult court with an additional seven young offenders in the Youth Court. Seven were for sentence; three excess breath/blood alcohol; one diversion; six warrants of arrest; nine fines defaulters.

Five young Black Power gang members were charged with murdering a member of another the Mongrel Mob at Ruatoki. Another four Black Power gang members were charged with wounding another man by shooting him in the chest.

My only concern was whether the accused should be granted bail pending the preliminary hearing. The police were vigorously opposed to bail because the incident is gang related.

The deceased and wounded man were Mongrel Mob members who had apparently visited the Ruatoki marae for a child's birthday party. During the brawl, the deceased apparently used a .22 semi-automatic rifle. It has not been found. Nor for several days was his body.

Since the fighting and killing, there have been two alleged arsons on dwellings of Mongrel Mob Members in Ruatoki. There was talk of the Blacks visiting a marae in the Ruatoki valley armed with sawn-off shotguns and other weapons, and the police say witnesses have been intimidated. A Molotov cocktail was discovered at the Black Power headquarters in Ruatoki.

The police feared unrestrained gang warfare would break out if the accused are released. Counsel for all accused argued that strict bail conditions could be imposed.

I wouldn't have a bar of it. On those facts, there was no way that I was going to release them into the community. They are the toughest-looking bunch I have seen in a long march. All had previous criminal histories although not necessarily offences of violence. Tony Fitzgerald[1] was appearing as agent of Mike Bungay. He asked permission to phone Bungay and later came back to me saying that he did not intend to pursue any application for bail. Ah! The realism of experience.

Lost Souls?

The gang problem is difficult. Members are often lost souls who band together for the support and respect they never received from their parents or family. I have looked up an old book I have on adolescent delinquency because I remembered a somewhat linguistically complex definition of an adolescent gang by a sociologist Frederick Thrasher[2]. He defined such a gang as:

> *An interstitial group originally formed spontaneously and then integrated through conflict. It is characterised by... meeting face-to-face, milling, movement through space as a unit, conflict, and planning. The result of this collective behaviour is the development of tradition, unreflective internal structure, esprit de corps, solidarity, morale, group awareness, and attachment to local territory…*
> *Isolation is common to almost every vocational, religious or cultural group of a large city. Each develops its own sentiments, attitudes, codes, even its own words, which are at best only partially intelligible to others.*

Despite its age, it is an excellent, albeit somewhat wordy definition. When I see gang members in the dock, clenching their fists and grunting and nodding to other gang members in the back of the court, I agree with every ingredient of the definition. I think, however, some additional factors could be added, such as the fact that such groups are often distinguished by race and ethnic factors, by dress and language, and by group beliefs as to status, profit, and the urge to revenge any attack, real or imagined, upon their gang.

If we think we have problems, we should look at the USA where the problem is much more serious. 2000 deaths a year are attributed to gang violence, exceeding the total rate of all homicides in almost every country in Europe.

---

[1] Tony FitzGerald was appointed a District Court Judge in May 1999, with Criminal and Family Court warrants and a Youth Court designation. In 2007 he established the Intensive Monitoring Group ("the IMG") in the Auckland Youth Court. It is a solutions-focussed court for young high risk offenders with neurodisability, mental health or drink/drug dependency. It does great work.

[2] *The Gang: A Study of 1,313 Gangs in Chicago*, Chicago, USA, University of Chicago Press,1927.

In Los Angeles over 300 homicides a year are the result of gang activity. That city is understood to have 600 different gangs with over 70,000 members – apparently far greater than the proportion found in other American cities. The activities of those gangs are much more serious than our predominantly Māori gangs. In L.A, they are the major drug distributors, and are also involved with extortion, prostitution, burglary, and murder. One social worker said:

"We're not talking about kids with zip guns. We're talking about kids with Uzis!"

A Callander Year

At Pukekohe Court, one of the clerks told me he overheard two Black Power gang members talking on the court steps. One said:

"Hey Bro! Ya know why they call him Callander?"

"Nah!"

"Cos if you give him shit, he gives you a year!"

The Killing of Two-Year-Old Jhia

Conflict between the two gangs boiled over in May 2007 in the pleasant river city of Wanganui, now after a century on local Māori insistence, spelled Whanganui. A two-year-old child was shot dead as she slept in a front room of her family home. In March 2008, I was assigned to Wellington to preside over a lengthy preliminary hearing of charges of murder and other crimes against 13 Mongrel Mob Members from Whanganui. It was a real saga because there were 13 defence counsel, all anxious to examine the various Crown witnesses.

The ongoing friction between the two gangs prompted the Mongrel Mob members to belligerently leave their headquarters and drive past the house of a prominent Black Power member, Te Tua. Quite deliberately, gun shots were fired at the house. Although the young gang prospect who fired the shots did not intend to kill the girl, he was reckless. The little girl died instantly.

The brave erstwhile warriors, mission accomplished, returned to their gang headquarters. They jauntily started drinking, boasting of their commando attack, full of bravado and excitement in the aftermath of the drive past shooting. There were many shouts of "Sieg Heil" and the bizarre barking that is the unique and most peculiar habit of Mongrel Mob members.

The mood in the club house changed dramatically when another gang member breathlessly entered the room and announced that the drive-by shooting on the house had badly backfired and that they had mistakenly shot dead two-year-old Jhia Te Tua as she slept on the couch in the front room.

Decent human emotions and reactions surface even with hardened criminals. One prospective gang member was so appalled by the child's death, the barking and the Sieg Heils that he turned Crown witness. He went to the police.

He told detectives that there was immediate silence when the news broke at gang headquarters. And then the male swagger and bluster resumed, with more alcohol and gang solidarity. While some of the members later acknowledged how upset they were, one gang member called out that the infant "... was just a Black Power Spore!"[1]

I found the evidence sufficient to put most of the men on trial, although some for manslaughter not murder, as they clearly did not intend the death of the child and were not themselves reckless. Hayden John Wallace fired the gun through the front of the house. Karl Unuka Check was the planner of the raid and Tane Forbes was the driver of the car.

Eventually, after a five-week trial before Justice Warwick Gendall[2] and a jury, those three main accused were all convicted and in February 2009 were sentenced to life imprisonment for murder. Wallace and Check received a 15-year non-parole period; Forbes a 12 year 6-month non-parole period. The two men in the back seat of the car had earlier pleaded guilty to manslaughter and received seven years' imprisonment. The lesser players received sentences running from 18 months to two years' imprisonment for participation in an organised criminal group.

---

[1] Dehumanising the enemy is a common human reaction, viz. the Nazis and the Jews, the Tutsis and the Hutus, the Turks and the Armenians, the Serbs and the Bosnian Muslims, and the Australian colonists and the Tasmanian Aborigines.

[2] Like me, now retired from the bench, but later my chief as Chair of the New Zealand Parole Board. He was a High Court Judge from 1996 to 2012, and then awarded the CNZM for services to the State and sport.

Rogues and Vagabonds

Reformed Rogue

Adrienne De La Salle first appeared in the Auckland Magistrates Court on the 6th November 1973, charged with being a rogue and vagabond by frequenting and was sentenced to 2 years probationary supervision. Since then, she has made 80 further court appearances and has been convicted of 131 further offences. 54 of those were for petty crimes of dishonesty, mainly shoplifting, and 36 were for drink or drug offending. Between 1975 and 1984 she went to prison 12 times but usually just for a week or two. Her longest sentence was 8 months for a minor burglary.

Not frightening, and with a good sense of humour, she was my old acquaintance from Auckland days. Big, tall, unmistakably masculine, but fighting the good fight to become a woman, Adi, formerly Willi, has been living in Whakatane for several years. She was charged with trespassing on the property of the Kopeopeo Service Station.

She thought it "awful" that she should be banned from a service station. She flipped her fingers at me, lowered her eyelids, and with a hint of mischief in her husky voice said:

"Why, Your Honour, I've never even heard of anyone being banned from a service station. I think it is awful they should do that to me. Mind you, your Honour (wink, wink, nudge, nudge) I had drunk a tiny bit too much!"

"Well, Adrienne", I said, "you do cause disorder when you are drunk. I remember the trouble you used to cause on K Road and in that little pub in Vulcan Lane."

"Oh!" giggled Adi. "That was in the days when I was a prostitute. I've given that up. I'm much too old for that sort of thing. That's why I am living down here in the country. I even have my own home."

Then came her plea in mitigation. No lawyer could have equalled it.

"You know me, your Honour! I have been a little naughty over the years. But you will see from my printout that I haven't been before the court for six months. And that's a real record for me. And nothing very serious even then. I promise I won't go back to the service station if you promise not to put me inside."

With her wealth of experience, she probably knew I had no intention of sending her to prison on such a minor matter. She is no fool. Highly intelligent. She just likes a little drama. She also hopes it will create some sympathy. I imposed a modest fine because what she had said about her recent good behaviour was undoubtedly true.

A Dying Breed

The term "Rogues and Vagabonds" has disappeared from the law of Godzone[1], along with "Adulterers" and "Bastards". They all disappeared with the stroke of the Governor-General's pen following legislation in Parliament.

When I started as a raw legal recruit in 1962, there were rogues and vagabonds galore, and they existed until the 1927 Police Offences Act was repealed and replaced with the present Summary Offences Act in October 1981. Under even earlier vagrancy laws, both here and in England, there was a species of rogue called the "incorrigible rogue", but he (they were seldom female) had gone by 1927.

When they referred to a "rogue and a vagabond" what did they mean? In common language, a rogue was someone who was a dishonest scoundrel and a vagabond was a tramp, vagrant or someone of no fixed address – a transient, a homeless person. But in legal terms a "rogue and a vagabond" had a much more detailed and wider description. Under the old Act, the term applied to anyone who had previous convictions for being "idle and disorderly" (another out-dated phrase!) or who begged or solicited under any false pretence. As Tom Lehrer sang: "Don't solicit for your sister. That's not nice! Unless you get a good percentage of her price!"

Roguish

Rogues also included those who cheated individuals or charities, who gambled in public places, or who were found with burglar's tools or weapons (which included "picklock-keys" and "bludgeons") with "felonious intent". It also described people found at night with blackened faces, in disguise, or "wearing felt slippers" (again with felonious intent!). Persons caught in buildings, yards, gardens, and boats without lawful excuse were also rogues and vagabonds. Finally, it applied to suspected persons or reputed thieves who were found "frequenting "ports and docks or streets and buildings adjacent to the ports with a "felonious intent".[2] It was designed to catch the whores and pickpockets – suspect people who hung around ports and public places to nick a wallet or solicit a sailor. Pickpockets seem to be a thing of the past – no doubt because modern thieves don't have a Fagin[3] to teach them, can't be bothered acquiring the dexterity, or

---

[1] New Zealand term for their country: "God's own country."

[2] Having the intention to commit a felony – a serious crime.

[3] Charles Dickens' famous receiver of stolen property, and tutor of young pickpockets – in the novel Oliver Twist. In the movie of the same name Lionel Bart has Fagin sing:
"In this life, one thing counts, In the bank, large amounts. I'm afraid these don't grow on trees, You've got to pick-a-pocket or two, You've got to pick-a-pocket or two, boys, You've got to pick-a-pocket or two."

because the age of the plastic credit card and makes most such out of pocket thefts unprofitable.

Reading Gaol

Noel O'Hare published a brief essay[1] about Oscar Fingal O'Flahertie Wills Wilde entitled *Ugly Charmer* apropos of the three-part dramatization, *Oscar*, which appeared on New Zealand television on Mobil Masterpiece theatre, written and produced by John Hawkesworth. O'Hare points out that while Wilde was "physically repulsive",[2] the moment he opened his mouth he captivated everyone with his brilliance and charm. He quotes a delightful story written by Wilde following a tour of the USA in 1883:

> *So infinitesimal did I find the knowledge of art west of the Rocky Mountains that an art patron – one who in his day had been a miner – actually sued the railroad company for damages because the plaster cast of the Venus of Milo, which he had imported from Paris, had been delivered minus the arms. And what is more surprising still, he gained his case and the damages.*

Wilde himself did not "gain" his own case. O'Hare only briefly mentions the two-year prison sentence that Wilde received for "gross indecency with men", the sentence that destroyed him both publicly and personally. The TV series deals with the trial and Wilde's ultimate destruction by both due process of law and public vilification. Wilde, who was broken by his trial, and who wrote his *Ballad of Reading Gaol*[3] while serving his prison sentence, made some memorable comments about the Law:

> *"I can resist anything but temptation."*
> *"Only Lawyers and mental defectives are automatically exempt for jury duty."*[4]
> *"I was always unlawful; I broke the law when I was born because my parents weren't married."*
> "The study of law is sublime, and its practice vulgar."

And from the ballad:

> *I know not whether Laws be right,*
> *Or whether Laws be wrong;*
> *All that we know who lie in gaol*
> *Is that the wall is strong;*

---

[1] in the *Listener* (June 3rd, 1991)

[2] A description which seems unduly harsh!

[3] The poem was published by Leonard Smithers in 1898.

[4] That is true in New Zealand, but Parliamentarians, judges, parole board members, lawyers, police, prison officers, & court staff are also exempt.

And that each day is like a year,
A year whose days are long.

Juries

"Thursday is out. I have jury duty."

Know Him Well

A jury was being empanelled before me in a Gisborne cannabis growing trial. One fresh-faced, alert young man was called. As is the custom, a person seeking to be excused from jury service, is invited to approach the Bench and quietly explain the reasons for excusal. This young man won the day, and I excused him immediately.

"I don't think I should be on this jury, your Honour", he whispered.

"Why is that?" I asked.

"I know the accused."

"OK. But the issue is whether you can be an impartial juror. How well do you know him?"

"Fairly well."

"What is your relationship with him?"

"I buy my dope off him!"

Excuses

I have heard of a few more good excuses from people reluctant to serve on juries:

"I am a methamphetamine addict and get very restless if I have to sit still for long."

"I have been watching the accused from the back of the court. He looks as guilty as hell."

"I have a very weak bladder and prostate problems. I need to pee every half hour."

"God is the only Judge. It is wrong for man to sit in judgement."

"Sex trials turn me on and I can't control my erections."

"I know all cops tell lies. I was married to one."

I always told the jury panel that jury service is critical to the functioning of the criminal law; that it is the corner-stone of our democracy; and that for justice to be done, everyone must play their part. I explained that without intelligent, sensible people on a jury, wrong verdicts happen.

Jury Exemption Granted

The strangest application I have received to be excused from jury service was from a man who I later learned was a paranoid schizophrenic. His application shows many classic symptoms: mistrust, deluded and confused thinking, withdrawal from the world, suspicion, but with indicators of high intelligence and good education. The word usage, grammar and spelling in the document showed superior education.

Care must be taken to ensure that such applications are not the deliberate creation of some clever potential juror who simply wanted to create a fictional excuse not to attend jury service.

On reading this application, I believed this man was mentally disordered and not just cleverly trying to avoid jury duty. In any event, I was not prepared to take any chances. Having someone like that on the jury could be a nightmare for the other 11 jurors, even if he simply proved to be a sane conman!

Over the years, I have dealt with many accused and prisoners with psychotic and other mental disorders, mainly schizophrenia. This is a lifelong illness that can be reasonably successfully controlled with antipsychotic drugs which help to regulate the brain chemistry. One of the major problems, is that patients, feeling better as the result of their medication, decide they no longer need to continue taking it. They stop taking their medication, relapse back to serious illness, and often require further hospitalisation.

The reason they give up the drugs is that some have unpleasant side effects such as muscle spasms, drowsiness and blurred vision. Modern psychopharmacology is constantly enhancing and developing new medications, and many schizophrenics lead normal lives with regular and supervised use of antipsychotic drugs.

Here is an extract from the man's application to be excused.

> *For the past seven years, I have been subjected to constant psychic disturbances that are proving difficult to remove. It is the tormented spirit of an uncle who died 10 years ago. The*

spirit world has revealed to me that he was New Zealand's worst mass murderer, responsible for hundreds of civilian deaths in Italy in 1943 and a serial sex killing spree in five states of America from 1979 to 1991. Italy remains a military secret to this day. In America, he escaped without conviction.

A self-styled Satanist, he has committed acts of necrophilia and cannibalism, on occasion serving the cooked flesh of victims to his wife and daughters. This fiend has since formed contacts with aliens and demonic energies close to the physical world. They are interested in controlling our minds and I have been threatened many times.

Experiencing their persistently invasive nature, prolonged contact in any confined space such as a court or jury room would, in my opinion, result in possible contamination of fellow jurors, influencing of witnesses, and abduction of deceased crime victims now in spirit. My uncle has been described by spirit guides as the worst antichrist energy ever created. He has threatened to ruin my life by disturbing everyone I show an interest in.

I have been advised that someone with my sort of higher energy from the Christ mind should not be serving on a jury.

Hung Juries

After some excellent research into the dynamics of jury decision-making, and a thorough and erudite Law Commission Report on the topic in 2001, the law was changed in 2008 and judges can now take majority verdicts of 11-1. The Law Commission found that 13% of all High Court trials in 2000 resulted in hung juries. From 2008, until my retirement in 2013, I had several trials where the jury reached a majority verdict. The court may accept a majority verdict in a criminal trial if the jury, having retired to consider its verdict, has deliberated for at least 4 hours; and the jurors have not reached a unanimous verdict. The foreperson of the jury must state in open court that there is no probability of the jury reaching a unanimous verdict; and that the jury has reached a majority verdict. The judge must also consider that the jury has had a reasonable time for deliberation, having regard to the nature and complexity of the trial. Before that, the judge asks them to reach a unanimous verdict if they can.

Mixed Bag

I had an unusual jury day: one lady had a wooden leg, another a weak bladder; a third a noisy cellular phone.

Three Questions

Mr Dooley:[1]

> *Whin the case is all over, the jury'll pitch th' tistimony out iv the window, an' consider three questions: 'Did Lootgert look as though he'd kill his wife? Did his wife look as though she ought to be kilt? Isn't it time ve wint to supper?'*

Letting the Jury Know

I was a bit errant. The jury had just acquitted a criminal well known to me. He got off charges of robbery and injuring with intent. Before thanking the jury, I announced that his acquittal on the two charges would be noted but that I could not release him from custody, because at 2.15pm I was to sentence him on two other charges to which he had pleaded guilty when arraigned on Monday.

I explained that I needed time to consider the probation report on him. I also told the uneasy jurors that he was also facing sentence upon the two further assaults on his girlfriend, one further dangerous driving charge, and a charge of resisting a police constable.

The jury looked suitably aghast to hear that he was such a bad lad – with nine previous convictions for violence – and no doubt got the impression that I was not sympathetic with part of their verdict.

At 2.15pm I sentenced him to 9 months' imprisonment, with conditions as to alcohol and anger counselling. Some of the jurors from the morning jury watched. He stood, with solemn demeanour, with a copy of *The Good News Bible* conspicuously held in his hands. I thought this was either a cunning sentencing ploy (which can seriously backfire) or that he had experienced a sudden conversion to a more peaceful belief system, and a genuine change of heart. I asked him. He said he had found the Lord. I commended him and hoped his newfound Christian beliefs would in the future prevent him from wielding tomahawks and trying to run down people on the footpath. He nodded sagely in reply.

Challenged

Prospective jurors are often mortified when lawyers challenge them as potential jurors. Some find it a gross slur upon their character. They do not realise that they may

---

[1] Mr. Dooley was the Irish bartender, and observer of American life, created by journalist Finley Peter Dunn between 1893 and 1915, and reincarnated again between 1924 and 1926.

be challenged for no other reason than they look like Phillip, Duke of Edinburgh, Jack the Ripper, Albert Einstein or Mary Mary, Quite Contrary, or any appropriate genetic combination of two or more of these.

How do lawyers challenge a juror?

Looks too rich? A surly witch?
Because she's white? Looks too bright?
His skin is brown? From out of town?
Looks too dumb? Chewing gum?
Has tattoos? Smells of booze?
Wears a suit? Looks a brute?
Ring in nose? Funny clothes?
Too alert? Too high skirt?
High on drug? Looks a thug?

What other tests are surer?

The answer to my corny poetic query: Many.

We differ from courts in the USA, where considerable research, time and effort is exercised in assessing the likely attitudes of prospective jurors. We use a very much hit or miss value judgment based on nothing more than name, age, address, occupation and on the spot assessment of appearance and demeanour.

Off the Hook

These are the best ways to avoid jury duty. When the clerk calls your name, walk from the back of the court:

(1) Staggering drunk.
(2) With your hair dyed red, white & blue, preferably teased.
(3) With the words "Fuck Justice" printed on your sweatshirt.
(4) With the words "Stamp out Crime" lipsticked on your forehead.
(5) Drooling spittle off your chin.
(6) Wearing your grandfather's First World War campaign medals.
(7) With huge hearing aids in both ears.
(8) Quietly singing "God Defend New Zealand!"
(9) Lustily rendering "Onward Christian Soldiers!"
(10) Winking at the Judge, smiling, and saying "Judge Jeffries, I presume!"
(11) Shouting to the clerk, "Speak up, I can't hear you!"

Punishing the Jury

Up until the late 17th century, judges sometimes punished juries who reached a decision with which the judge disagreed. That changed with Bushel's Case[1], which involved jurors sitting on the case against William Penn[2] and William Mead. The two men, both Quakers, had been arrested in 1670 for illegally preaching a sermon, unlawful assembly and disturbing the peace, but four jurors, led by Edward Bushel refused to find them guilty.

Instead of dismissing the jury, the judge sent them back to reconsider their verdicts. Despite the judge demanding a guilty verdict, the jury this time unanimously found Penn guilty of preaching, but acquitted him on the more serious charges of unlawful assembly and disturbing the peace. It acquitted Mead of all charges.

The jury was then subsequently kept for three days without "meat, drink, fire and tobacco" to force them to reconsider and bring in a guilty verdict. When they refused to do so, the judge ended the trial. As punishment, the judge ordered the jurors be imprisoned until they paid a fine equal to a year's wages. Four jurors either refused or could not pay the fine, and stayed locked up for several months.

One of them, Edward Bushell, sought a writ of *habeas corpus*.[3] Chief Justice John Vaughan granted his application, and released the four men. He described the power to punish a jury "absurd" and forbade judges from doing this in the future.

General Belgrano

Another jury defied the British Government. In 1982, during the Falklands War, a British Royal Navy submarine sank an Argentine light cruiser, the General Belgrano. 323 sailors were killed. Three years later, a senior civil servant, Clive Ponting, leaked two government documents showing that the cruiser was outside an exclusion zone and was moving away from a Royal Navy taskforce when it was sunk. Ponting was charged with breaching section 2 of the Official Secrets Act 1911.

The judge directed the jury that Ponting had no defence in that it was not in the "public interest" for the documents to be released. The jury thought differently. Much to the chagrin of a red-faced Government, the jury acquitted Ponting and he walked free. The Thatcher government responded by passing legislation which removed the public-interest defence.

---

[1] 124 E.R. 1006

[2] He was imprisoned several times in the Tower of London for religious reasons. He later founded the American State of Pennsylvania.

[3] An ancient court order directing a prison warder to deliver the imprisoned individual to the court to show a valid reason for that person's detention.

Ponting's counsel at the trial, Graham Laughland, later a judge, called the cover-up "Under Watergate" and revealed that MI5 had been tapping both his and the phone of other defence lawyers.

"Good morning!" Laughland would greet the director of public prosecutions when the latter phoned him daily to talk about the trial, always adding "and good morning Sergeant Bloggs".

In cases like this, the jury, despite proof of an illegal act, may think the law is wrong and that the accused should not be punished.

Mindless

English is a strange tongue. It is easy to convey the wrong impression. A friend of mine was summing up to a jury:

> *Ladies and Gentlemen, you must be impartial and fair in your deliberations. You must decide the case only on the proper evidence you have heard in this court room. If you have heard or read anything outside this court, please put it from your minds, if you have any.*

Fining the Jurors

In late November 2003 at Rotorua I was to preside over a 5-day trial for manufacturing methamphetamine. Only 51 of the 123 prospective jurors answered their jury summonses. I was unable to proceed with the trial because we had insufficient people to ballot a jury. I exercised a rare power that I had never used before. I issued warrants to arrest 63 of the people who had failed to show up for jury service.

The lawyers and staff and press were astonished but amused at the novelty. The staff prepared the arrest warrants for all the noncompliant non-attenders and I signed them that afternoon. The police acted with alacrity and over the next few days some very sheepish citizens appeared before me. Two had a reasonable excuse. The rest I fined $200 plus costs.

The newspapers gave it a big headline and published their names. It got the message across. People must realise that jury duty is a cornerstone of our democratic society. While jury service can be a considerable burden, each case is of great importance. Every case is important to the parties involved, but a criminal case is particularly important because there are valuable interests at stake, such as the liberty of the persons involved, and often their honour, reputation and pride. Justice must be administered equally and fairly.

Oddities

All Dicks

The Bay of Plenty Times referred to me as Judge Richard Callander. I had some fun with the court reporter: Working with us was a newly-appointed visiting judge, Richard Watson, a delightful man who became greatly admired as a judge and parole board convenor. I seized the golden opportunity and said:

> *I notice the media these days like to refer to judges by their first names. It is a shame it sometimes get them wrong. My name was confused with those of my brethren in yesterday's paper. I was confused with Judge Richard Kearney and Judge Richard Watson. I was referred to as Judge Richard Callander. Does your newspaper think we are all Dicks?*

Further Reading

The following are from the shelves of Law Libraries, and to show I have not made them up, I have included the Publisher's name and year of publication:

Crime and Law by Adrienne P Swindells (London, Hart-Davis Educational, 1978)

Violence Against Wives by Emerson and Russell Dobash (Shepton Mallet: Open Books, 1980)

Causes of Crime by A Fink (Philadelphia, Pennsylvania, University of Pennsylvania Press, 1938).

Criminal Life: 'Reminiscences of 42 Years as a Police Officer' by Superintendent Bent (Manchester, John Heywood, 1891)

Punishment by Robin Banks (Harmondsworth: Penguin Books, 1972)

End Jot

Now that my judging days are over, I can reflect on the saga of human fallibility that these jottings demonstrate. Mistakes, not just of those who appeared before me over the decades, but also my own.

Some have queried my use of the word "geriatric" in the title of this book. They preferred "senior". But to me "geriatric" has a nicer, amusing and more realistic tone, the ring of old age and failing faculties.

Remember, not everyone gets to be a geriatric judge. You have to live long enough, keep breathing, drink quality alcohol, avoid salads, and when spousal supervision is absent, shun all pointless exercise. I knew I was a geriatric judge when the Court of Appeal Judges started looking immature, and most court officers and young lawyers hadn't been born when I first went on the bench.

Hearing aids are a give-away. At a social event I was chatting to a group of young lawyers when one said, "Judge, we are all very pleased you are now wearing hearing aids. Your decisions are now based on the evidence!"

"Never tease or speak heartlessly to an old judge." I replied "I might not hear as well, but I can still bite!" I replied.

I told them the delightful anecdote about Sir Winston Churchill[1] after he stood down as UK Prime Minister in 1955. He was alone, slumped in an armchair in the Members' Bar of the House of Commons. Some young Members of Parliament failed to see him, and their conversation went:

"It's very sad about old Winston. He's getting awfully forgetful" said one.

"Shame, isn't it?" said another. "He's really very doddery now, I gather."

"Not only that," added the third, "but I've heard that he's going a bit - you know – gaga."

"Yesh," growled a deep and famous voice from the nearby armchair, "an' they shay he'sh gettin' terribly deaf, as well!"

I attribute those many memorable years to the happy collegiality and support of fellow judges, the friendship of notable lawyers, the unstinting assistance of court registrars and officers, the good sense of police prosecutors, and above all the unwavering support and love of my wife Suzanne.

A career on the District Court is never boring or routine. There can be few other professions so interesting and full of surprises, sometimes distressing, sometimes amusing. As with general practitioners of medicine we deal with a broad parade of

---

[1] For several years I have greatly enjoyed membership of the Churchill Dining Society which meets several times a year to discuss and commemorate the extraordinary life of this remarkable leader.

humanity and are not restricted to a specialist focus, and there lies the fascination of our generalist role.

The Māori proverb says it well:

> *He aha te mea nui o te ao*
> *(What is the most important thing in the world?)*
> *He tangata, he tangata, he tangata*
> *(It is the people, it is the people, it is the people.)*

I have no regrets. I would download the song of my life and play it on 'repeat'.

And finally, in the words of Huckleberry Finn:

> *"And so there ain't nothing more to write about, and I am rotten glad of it because if I'd knowed what trouble it was to make a book, I wouldn't a tackled it; and I ain't a-goin' to no more."*

AUTHOR

Born at Palmerston North, New Zealand, 1940.

Schooled at College Street Primary, Palmerston North Normal Intermediate, Scots College Wellington, Palmerston North Boys High School, and the Thacher School, Ojai, California. Attended Victoria University of Wellington, graduating Bachelor of Arts (psychology) and Bachelor of Law.

Practiced as a lawyer in Palmerston North from 1963 to 1978 – a partner in the law firm of Fitzherbert Abraham & Co.

For 35 years, from 1978 to 2013, a Magistrate, District Court Judge, and Chief Justice of Western Samoa (1 year). Served as a convenor of the NZ Parole Board member for 14 years.

Awarded the NZ 1990 Commemoration Medal in 1990, and the Queen's Service Order (QSO) in 2013 for services to the judiciary.

Author of "*Court in the Act*". (Reeds Publishers) 1999. Contributor to "*Grumpy Old Men*", P. Little and D.D. Vinicombe, Auckland, Paul Little Books, 2013.

Married to Suzanne. Two children (Richard & Tessa), two step-children (Scott & Grant), 13 grandchildren, and 3 great grandchildren.

TABLE OF CONTENTS

Made in United States
Troutdale, OR
11/03/2026

56845398R00162